Scenes from the Bathhouse

SCENES FROM THE BATHHOUSE

and Other Stories of Communist Russia

by Mikhail Zoshchenko

TRANSLATED, WITH AN INTRODUCTION, BY SIDNEY MONAS

STORIES SELECTED BY MARC SLONIM

Ann Arbor Paperbacks / The University of Michigan Press

Second printing 1971
First edition as an Ann Arbor Paperback 1962
Copyright © by The University of Michigan 1961
All rights reserved
ISBN 0-472-06070-8
Library of Congress Catalog Card No. 61-13499
Published in the United States of America by
The University of Michigan Press and simultaneously
in Don Mills, Canada, by Longman Canada Limited
Manufactured in the United States of America

Mikhail Zoshchenko was born in 1895. His father was an artist, a nobleman, and a bit of a philanderer. His mother was a woman who demanded much and received little. Distressed by her son's behavior, she accused him of being like his father—"a solitary" and "a frozen heart." It wasn't exactly a happy family, but intellectually cultivated and financially comfortable.

He grew up in St. Petersburg, that "unreal city" of fogs and floods, the capital of a decadent empire, and the source of a great literary mythology that expressed the alienation of man from nature and from his own humanity. As a writer Zoshchenko remained fairly immune to the power of this myth. His positivist bent was too strong. He wrote as a detached observer of the street and the everyday, of manners rather than morals, of the commonplace, rather than of the phantasmagoria of Gogol and Bely, the writers of the myth. As a personality, however, he was a true alienated product of the "artificial" city and, like many great comedians, a morose, melancholic, estranged man, driven to humor and "play" as his only means of handling a gross and cacophonous world.

He was a strange, frail, sensitive, detached, proud, and rather difficult child. He read a great deal, especially in the biologic sciences, which caught his interest at an early age. He undoubtedly read Gogol and Leskov. His independent spirit made school uncomfortable for him, and he did not do well there. He found it difficult to forgive a schoolmaster who commented "Rubbish!" on one of his early compositions.

World War I broke out while Zoshchenko was still enrolled as a student at the University of St. Petersburg, and he hastened to volunteer. He was several times wounded, several times decorated, and promoted rapidly to the rank of major. He suffered not only the hardships of war and the responsibilities of command, but the vagaries of his own temperament—by no means a heroic one.

In the summer of 1916 he was gassed, and his health went to

pieces. Then, assigned by the Kerensky government to administer a military post office in Archangel at the time of the Allied occupation of that port, he rejected an opportunity he had there—proffered by an attractive Frenchwoman—of emigrating to Paris. Soon after that, he volunteered for the Red Army and saw action again in Lithuania, but his health forced him to retire within six months.

Zoshchenko's early melancholy persisted and drove him to take on a series of bizarre jobs. He worked as an instructor in poultry husbandry on an experimental collective farm; he was a detective, a professional gambler, a telephone operator for the border guard, and (for him, perhaps the most bizarre job of all) a clerk-typist. On the whole, he preferred nonclerical, nonintellectual work; no job, however, held him for long. In 1921 he was back in his native Petrograd, discovering his real and permanent profession—that of a writer.

In the early twenties Zoshchenko was associated with a group of young writers who called themselves the Serapion Brethren after the hermit Serapion as he is portrayed in a tale by E. T. A. Hoffmann, a writer they admired. These young men were what Trotsky called "fellow travelers." They were willing to go along with the Bolsheviks but were eager to maintain a certain independence of outlook and to avoid party discipline. In response to the enthusiasm of party literati for using the arts as effective propaganda, Victor Shklovsky, a talented critic and a Serapion Brother, posed a question: "Can you drive nails with a samovar?" He answered: "Yes, you can. But that is not what it is for."

The Serapion Brethren did not favor "art for art's sake." Their preoccupation with style was of a very different kind from that of the symbolists. They abhorred the mystique of inspiration and the cult of art. They were not religious. Symbolism tasted stale to them. The Brethren preferred to think of themselves as craftsmen rather than geniuses. They tried for a fresh language based on popular usage, on the vocabulary and syntax of the street and countryside. What they had over reality was not so much a firm grip as a light touch.

These men were vivid and original experimenters, and Russian literature of the twenties owes much to them. Their independence of spirit was not so deep, however, as to involve them in tragic consequences when the relative freedom of the twenties came to an end. They did not struggle too hard when independence had to be abandoned. Of the prose writers of the group, Zoshchenko alone continued to write in much the same vein in the thirties as he had in the twenties. He was still not a hero, but he had a certain Schweikian talent for personal survival and for survival as a writer.

Zoshchenko is a very funny writer: that much needs no arguing. He is funnier to Russians than he is to those who see his stories at a considerable distance from the situations they describe and from the language that is so peculiarly appropriate to them. Yet, he is as far from being a local folk-humorist as he is from being a conventional, "classical" satirist. If he is a satirist at all, it is in the more ancient, original sense of the term—a writer of satyr plays. His theme is not the corruption of morals, but brute energy and animal desire which burn through manners as through a cardboard grate.

The theme which runs through all of Zoshchenko's works is the fiery resistance nature offers to history. He himself is a detached observer, neither on one side nor the other. He has been burned by both.

Zoshchenko's technique is that of the *skaz,* the oral tale. The tale is supposed to have a moral, instructional point, to illustrate something; that is the excuse for telling and listening. But the point gets lost on the way: the storyteller is caught up in the story itself or simply succumbs to the delight of having an audience. It is himself he expresses, and not the moral. Either he loses it completely and arrives at a conclusion as unexpected for him as it is for his audience, or he tacks it on by *force majeure,* exposing either his own clay feet or the insubstantiality of all conclusions, or both. In Russian literature it was Leskov who first developed this technique, derived from popular storytelling. The narrator is himself a character, whom we come to understand through the words and expressions he uses and misuses, his repetitions, digressions, the things he chooses to talk about, and the things we know are there between the lines but which he is clearly incapable of expressing. The difference between the *skaz* and the ordinary "point-of-view" story or novel is, first of all, its oral quality—the sound of the spoken voice—and, secondly, the untutored, "primitive" nature of the narrator, his unself-consciousness. Among American writers, Ring Lardner uses this technique in a number of places—in his baseball stories, and most successfully in the story called "Haircut." However, Lardner was much more of a moralist than either Leskov or Zoshchenko. He used the technique to condemn the narrator or to induce the reader to feel sorry for him. Leskov and Zoshchenko do this to a far lesser degree. As in Lardner, the narrator inadvertently expresses his own *poshlost*—his vulgarity, his trashiness, the cheap fake of his pretensions—but this is less important than the sheer absurdity of the tricks nature plays with him. Leskov was capable of sustaining this kind of interest over considerable length. Zoshchenko, like most moderns, is shorter-winded, but the brevity of his stories is part of their effect.

They are composed with care, with attention to details of diction, inflection, and rhythm. This is by no means obvious, and, indeed, the effect would be lost if it were. The materials are so primitive that the reader would instantly resent any kind of obvious manipulation on Zoshchenko's part as grossly unfair. The effects of spontaneity and immediacy, of the candid photograph, the sketch made hastily on the spot exactly as observed, the tape recording, are all indispensable to Zoshchenko's art.

The situations that provide the material for his stories are the most common and ordinary details of everyday Soviet reality, familiar not only to the average Soviet citizen but even to the casual tourist: the housing shortage, the scarcity of consumers' goods and the inefficiency of consumers' services, bad roads, bureaucracy and red tape, the ferocious juxtapositions of backwardness and material progress. These things are not merely the background for the stories: they determine motives, they shape or obliterate intentions, they conceal, they expose, they frustrate, they assume a shape and a character of their own, and they are felt as a natural force almost as intractable and indifferent to human concern as the desert or the sea. They may be tricked or circumvented, but they cannot be made to care; moreover, they will inevitably leave their stamp on the trickers and circumventers. A person may resemble the desert; the desert is never like a man.

Personal problems and private griefs, fine feelings and an aesthetic sense, are reduced, against this desert, to the scale of absurdity. It isn't fidelity or infidelity in marriage that counts; it's the availability of an apartment. People will, of course, attempt to inflate their feelings in talk, but they are betrayed by the language they use. The desert is not only around them, it is in them.

Zoshchenko uses careless language carefully. His narrators are not illiterate peasants, but they are usually not far removed from that condition. Their talk is anything but folksy. It is a weird mixture of peasant idiom, misunderstood highfalutin phrases, rhetorical flourishes, explanatory asides that are anything but explanatory, repetitions, omissions, propaganda jargon absurdly adapted to homey usage, instructional pseudoscientific words, foreign phrases, and proverbial clichés joined to the latest party slogans. For his diction and syntax, even more than for the situations in which they occur, Zoshchenko was charged with "caricature." In his autobiography, however, Zoshchenko insists that he merely records the language of the streets, arranging and selecting, it is true, but not exaggerating.

The struggle between nature and history, backwardness and revolution, produces the kind of anomalous situation that Zoshchenko delights in, and he swoops like a hawk on those peculiarities of the Russian language and its usage which reflect that struggle. His verbal "soup," the words he chooses for his palette, are often themselves the product of the kind of situation he is writing about. Take the story "*Kochergà*": here, the action centers entirely on the peculiarities of this everyday word.

Kochergà means "a poker," and nothing could be more ordinary. However, its associations are with dark little houses heated by wood stoves around which bearded faces nod. It is out of place in the office building of a modern bureaucracy. Because of the shortage of space, a new state institution is housed in an old building that has no central heating and is kept warm by means of six wood stoves located in different parts of the building. The old stoker tends these, mumbling into his beard as he carries his *kochergà* from one to the other. When an employee who accidentally bumps into him has her hand burned by the poker, the old peasant shows himself surprisingly on the side of history and suggests to the manager of the establishment a rationalization of his work. If there were a poker by each stove, the risk of singeing employees could be avoided. All the manager has to do is order five more pokers from the warehouse, but here the manager comes to grief.

Although it is a perfectly common word, *kochergà* follows an archaic declension pattern and has grammatical peculiarities. In Russian, the number five takes the genitive plural of the noun—but what is the genitive plural of *kochergà?* Nobody knows. The manager is a bureaucrat; he cannot afford to consult other institutions, such as the Academy of Sciences; it wouldn't do for his dignity and career. He exhausts all intellectual resources within his own establishment. In desperation he even calls on the stoker—he may be a peasant but he *is* a specialist in stoves—"been around them all his life." The stoker responds, using, naturally, the diminutive form so dear to peasant speech. For dignity, that won't do either: the manager doesn't want to be taken for a peasant. Finally, he attempts to resolve his dilemma by calling in a member of his legal staff to draft an order which will obtain the "five pokers" without having to refer to them directly. The resulting document is a masterpiece, but it comes to nothing. There is a shortage; there *aren't* any pokers. The warehouse answers using the diminutive form.

Zoshchenko's longer stories, which he calls novelle, are literary parodies. They are what happens when *poshlost* claims for itself not the intelligence but the sentiment of genius. "Michel Siniagin" is a parody of the literary memoirs that appeared with such frequency both in Russia and abroad in the ten years or so following the Revolution, written by men of the symbolist generation who had met Tolstoi or seen Blok disappearing around the corner. "Love" is a parody of the gnomic wisdom-literature *à la* Rozanov, dear to the apocalyptic generation of the Russian intelligentsia. Zoshchenko never forgave the schoolmaster and the editors who wanted him to "write like a classic." He takes the pretension to style and the pretension to fine feeling into the world of the housing shortage. It bounces like an oversized lead balloon.

The lead balloon is one kind of literary parody Zoshchenko uses; there is another, which he uses much more subtly, which we might call the cork anchor. In the story called "An Amusing Adventure," Zoshchenko adapts the traditional form of bourgeois bedroom farce to his own abbreviated story form and to the "new class" of the Soviet overprivileged. It would be a mistake, however, to see this as a satire on "new class" morality. Zoshchenko does not seem to have anything against the privileged status of his protagonists, nor does he seem to have anything against their marital infidelity. True, he makes fun of their lies and deceptions; he doesn't like lies. But who does? The story is, in fact, completely lacking in moral bite. The point, if we must have a point beyond the *brio* of the story itself, is that nature is still with us, even in the socialist society; that having a bedroom at all is often more important than who sleeps in it; that rationality is a convention like marriage, and a pretty frail one; and that contrary to the usual ending of bourgeois farce, bedroom tangles do not lend themselves easily to rational solution, but only to further bedroom tangles—if one has a bedroom, that is.

In the story called *"Liaisons Dangereuses,"* the parody, this time of Choderlos de Laclos' great psychological novel, is even more subtle. In the French novel, the supremely intelligent and self-conscious hero has succeeded in mastering his animal nature and completely subordinating it to his will and intellect, which are committed to power—that is, to asserting his superiority over other human beings. His greatest "success" is his own self-destruction. Unlike the other works which Zoshchenko parodies, *"Liaisons Dangereuses"* is a model of brevity and lucidity of style. But Zoshchenko's very stupid hero manages to achieve the same result by the opposite means in much briefer compass!

It should be abundantly clear by now that Zoshchenko was not a typical satirist of the period of the New Economic Policy (the NEP, 1921-28) like Ilf and Petrov. That period was, nevertheless, peculiarly congenial to him. Not only was it a period of vigorous experimentation in all fields—especially the arts—during which his stories could pass as *"samo-kritika"* ("self-criticism," dear to the Bolsheviks, in which everything can be taken for a ride except the big boys on top and the policy they make), but the NEP itself created a rather obvious Zoshchenko-like world. It was a period during which a prominent Bolshevik (Bukharin) put on the mask of Guizot to urge the still uncollectivized Russian peasants to "enrich themselves." It was a period during which free enterprise was considered embarrassing but necessary, and during which the new socialist society suffered all the ills its leaders attributed to capitalism—unemployment, graft, exploitation—but during which it was still relatively free and uncoerced. The interaction of the old and the new, the ideal and the real, the brilliant and the backward, in the landscape of an underdeveloped and rather primitive economy, produced Zoshchenko types and Zoshchenko situations with a profusion that even the talented Ukrainian writer from Leningrad could not take full advantage of.

From the time of the Five-Year plans, Zoshchenko's life as a writer became increasingly hazardous. In 1946 he was singled out, along with Anna Akhmatova, for particularly violent attack by no less a party figure than Zhdanov, a pseudo critic, who called him a "pseudo writer." The story Zhdanov attacked most particularly and crudely was the curiously innocent little parable, "The Adventures of an Ape." From that time on, Zoshchenko published little—a few stories, a few articles. In the early days of the thaw, he wrote a few sketches on writing and writers which appeared in the humor magazine *Krokodil*—mildly courageous pieces, not uninteresting but undistinguished. In general, his stories after 1946, though not different in substance from his earlier work, lack the force and fun of the real Zoshchenko.

He died in 1958 at what, for him, was a fairly ripe old age. An edition of his collected stories appeared shortly after his death and was quickly sold out. He seems to have left behind no imitators (with the possible exception of K. himself) and no disciples, and his name no longer appears in print in the Soviet Union, even for attack.

For the nontotalitarian reader it is at first a little difficult to understand the violence of Zhdanov's obliterating speech. It is true that Zoshchenko makes bureaucrats look absurd, that he exposes the inefficiencies and incompatibilities of daily life in the Soviet Union, and that he is more than a little wistful about the goods famine. But these things are well within the pale of *samokritika*. One can find their equivalents in almost any issue of *Pravda* or *Krokodil*. What, then, was the real reason?

A "pseudo writer": an interesting expression. It is a little like calling Harry Truman a "pseudo politician." The point is that Zoshchenko was a real writer and nothing but a writer, and that in spite of a few deliberately disconcerting gestures to the contrary, he never tried to drive nails with a samovar. In a totalitarian society, that is reason enough to blast away. However, there were even better ones.

Reading one or a few stories of Zoshchenko is not the same as reading him in bulk. He is, obviously, a very funny writer. Nevertheless, the over-all effect of his work is anything but funny. He leaves one with the sense of a dreary, depressing, mournful, almost intolerable world. One might well exclaim, as Pushkin was supposed to on reading Gogol: "How sad is our Russia!" Moreover, Zoshchenko's "objective correlatives" are very much more obviously *there,* in the real world, than Gogol's were. It is not so much a question of his violation of this or that canon of socialist realism, of his remaining inside or outside the bounds of *samo-kritika,* as of the total effect of his work. Altogether, one can hardly claim that Zoshchenko's stories would bolster the mandatory optimism of a Soviet citizen.

There is a short preface appended to one of the hospital stories. In it Zoshchenko states that *Krokodil* had entrusted him with a number of letters to the editor complaining of treatment in Soviet hospitals and had commissioned him to write either a conventional article, in the *samo-kritika* vein, or a sketch. He claims that he decided, after deliberation, on the latter; but we cannot believe for a moment that he deliberated at all. Any or even all of the details might appear in a conventional Soviet article; however, the hospital we see is a Zoshchenko hospital, and surely he could have created no other. It is the essence of everything that is wrong with hospitals at their worst, where science (which Zoshchenko respects almost as Gogol respected religion) goes astray in the hands of a contemptuous, case-hardened bureaucracy.

Again, Zoshchenko has never created a single "positive hero" (a *must,* for Soviet writers)—one that Zhdanov could look on with approval. Few of the stories are without some human pathos, and some (like "The Crisis," one of his funniest) actually approach the humor of Charlie Chaplin; unlike Chaplin's films, however, Zoshchenko's "little fellows" rarely came out on top.

For the most part, his protagonists are fools, knaves, charlatans, fakes, poseurs, reeking of *poshlost*. There are some exceptions. Nazar Ilich Sinebriukhov (the hero of "Victoria Kazimirovna"), although vamped by a false ideal, has heroic traits. So does the protagonist of "My Professions." However, most of his people are victims—either of themselves, or of history, or of nature, or of all three.

Let us examine more closely what happens when Zoshchenko takes nature to the bathhouse. You can't do without a public bathhouse when there's an acute housing shortage. There is something elemental and at the same time microcosmic about this locale, and Zoshchenko returns to it obsessively. There are three bathhouse stories in this collection, written about twenty years apart. The first is by far the funniest and makes the most vivid impression, and the other two depend on one's having read the first for their effect. For one thing, all three stories take place in the *same* bathhouse. By taking a good look at the décor, by noting how the arrangements change, and by listening to the quality of the talk, one can learn something of what the Five-Year plans have done, and what they have not done.

The first story is Chaplinesque. The "little fellow" is frustrated by the crude and irrational arrangements at every turn. He needs tickets to get his clothes back. "But where is a naked man going to put tickets?" He can't get himself clean because the other bathers, scrubbing out their dirty laundry, keep splashing him. He is denied even the elementary pleasure of hearing the soap squeak as he washes himself. Frustration at every point.

In the second story, conditions have improved considerably. Manners are more civilized—but only on the surface. Clothes are stolen. The manager who barges in when the theft is reported turns out to be a woman who embarrasses everyone in the men's dressing room. The "little fellow" who had his clothes stolen turns out, after some administrative confusion, to have been a thief himself. The problems here are already a little more complex.

The third story is scarcely funny at all. It is a "symbolic" story, not the sort of thing Zoshchenko does best. It ends on a note of real gloom, which Zoshchenko's attempt to modify by rather mechanical means does little to attenuate. The bathhouse by this time is everything a public bathhouse should be. The bathers are decorous and civilized. The manager is still a woman, the same woman, but elderly now and with some respect for the dignity of her male customers. Yet, something is wrong, in a deeper and far more complicated way. There is a malady.

One of the attendants is a bright-eyed young lad from the country. What is he doing, working at a job like this? He has ambition but no imagination. One of the customers is a stuffy, unpleasant, moralistic papa, who keeps lecturing his snively little boy (his name, shades of Gogol, is Icarus!) on public behavior. Another is an even more unpleasant, and even sinister, buttinsky who can't wait to denounce someone to the police. The central figure is an elderly mechanic who has earned a Soviet fortune by working for years at bonus wages in the Far East, for a motive that has now become irrelevant, and who carries his wealth as though it were an albatross. He cannot spend it; he cannot give it away; he is not a miser and takes no joy in keeping it for its own sake. "It's only money." However, in this case it is symbolic money. The old mechanic has won out against nature, but in the winning he has had to make himself the kind of man for whom the victory is useless. He leaves the bathhouse in deep melancholy. Zoshchenko doesn't bring this one off too well. This bathhouse is almost bathos; but against the background of the two other stories it is not without a certain power.

The cumulative effect of Zoshchenko's stories is, as I have noted, a depressing one. His work is poor in positive figures and entirely lacking in heroes of the imperative never-never-land type that socialist realism requires. In this struggle with nature, there are moments of real pathos and occasional little victories, but no triumphs. If orthodox Soviet critics try to palm off Gogol's nightmare world as "the Russia of his time," they would like to pass off Zoshchenko's Russia as a misfit "pseudo writer's" nightmare, or still better, ignore it entirely.

One aspect of Zoshchenko's work is depressing in a different sense: his curious lack of development as a writer. The third bathhouse story, it is true, involves a far more complex situation than the first; but Zoshchenko's means are not up to it. His successful pieces, in spite of their enormous range of incidents and their variety of observed detail, have a curious sameness. Nor is this a function of their brevity alone. (One has only to compare an early Chekhov story with a later one to grasp what a writer's development means.) Nor is it the limitation of his talent. At least there are a few striking indications that this is not the case.

"Victoria Kazimirovna," one of his very early stories, written in 1917 and published in his first volume, is of a quite different dimension than the rest of his work. The gallows humor, the crude and yet complex cogitations of Nazar Il'ich Sinebriukhov, his peasant's way of looking out for himself, knowing his life isn't worth much but that he has no other, his infatuation with the strumpet-aristocrat, Victoria Kazimirovna—these have a depth and a resonance and a poignance that is lacking elsewhere: "Only I remembered then just how that crow had flown over me . . . Och, I pulled myself together." That crow is Sinebriukhov's vision of his own death. Isaac Babel might have been glad to have written this story.

There is also that moment in the brief sketch called "Confession"—that inexpressible moment of terror when *baba* Fekla realizes that the priest doesn't believe in God either. And there is the strange case of the autobiography, which deserves some special attention.

In 1943, during the war, when a Soviet victory over the Nazi invaders was in the air but still a long way off, Zoshchenko began to publish in serial form an intensely personal prose work called

Before the Sun Rises, subtitled "a novella." It was not a conventional autobiography but took the form of a Freudian self-analysis —*only* the form, for the "flashbacks" are anything but free associations. They are concentrated evocations of the utmost simplicity and most careful composition.

Zoshchenko begins with his young manhood and pushes further and further back to the dawn of his consciousness. Where conscious memory fails him, he begins to draw on his dreams, and on Freud and Pavlov for their meaning, to discover the forces that shaped his infancy and to answer the question he poses at the beginning: Why am I such a melancholy man? He never answers the question. Possibly he never intended to. At any rate, publication was discontinued after three issues, and Zoshchenko was violently attacked in the party journal *Bolshevik* for his concern with himself, for his "nasty" friends and relations, for his interest in sex, for mentioning Freud, for being Zoshchenko. One can never be certain about such things, but in my opinion this tirade suggests as good a reason as any for Zoshchenko's over-all lack of development as a writer. The only directions in which he might have been able to move were padlocked for him from the outside.

Some of the brief flashbacks are masterpieces. "Nerves" has, again, the Babelian touch. A number of others have a poignance and depth that set them altogether apart from the rest of Zoshchenko's work. Their humor and irony are altogether gentler and more complex—almost Chekhovian—than the humor of the stories. The portrait that emerges is of a detached, restless, haunted, gentle, and very intelligent man in a rough world. But is the man Zoshchenko?

One has an almost uncanny sense, as one reads, of the author outside himself—if it is, indeed, himself he is describing, for the work is properly "a novella" and not an autobiography at all. There is a sad and at the same time deliciously funny moment toward the end of the published fragment, in which Zoshchenko is finally aware that the obsessive dread that has haunted him all his life is connected with water. He goes through the many notebooks he has unwittingly accumulated, filled with objective but entirely useless information about water: the percentage of water in the human body, in the world at large, the depth of seas, and the havoc wrought by floods. Without meaning to imply that it has the same power or that the effect was arrived at by the same means, or that it is in any way a scene of comparable achievement, there is, nevertheless, something here that reminds me of Aristophanes' image, in Plato's *The Symposium*, of the sundered halves of the once-whole human self pursuing each other across the great waste of the world. And one might recall Socrates' seemingly casual remark, at the end of the banquet, that comedy and tragedy are one.

CONTENTS

I've never been in America and I don't mind telling you I don't know a thing about it.

When it comes to foreign powers, though, I know Poland. And I can damn well expose it.

I spent three years on Polish soil in the German war . . . And, no! I don't care for Polacks.

There's every kind of slyness in their nature, I know.

Take a woman.

A woman of theirs will kiss your hand.

Only when you get to her hut, it's: "Nothing doing, *pan.*"

And she goes and wipes off your hand.

You just can't do this to a Russian man.

That peasant of theirs is absolutely a sly one. He's always going around clean, beard trim, saving up money.

Well I'll do a little clarifying of their nation for you. Take Upper Silesia . . .

Now, please, why should the Polack have Upper Silesia? Why this mockery of the German nation?

So live as a separate power if you want, all right, have your own monetary unity, but why such an impossible demand?

No, I don't like the Polacks.

So it's like this: I met this Polish miss, and she was the kind could make me sympathize for Poland, better, I think, if one doesn't visit this people.

Well, I just made a mistake.

I don't mind telling you, such a wonder came over me, I was in such a fog, that this charming beauty, no matter what she'd say, I'd up and do it.

Let's say I wouldn't agree to murder a man, my hand would shake. And there I murdered one, and another one, too. Murdered an old, old miller, and even if not by hand but only by way of a little personal slyness of my own.

And I myself, sad to think, approached this Polack girl frivolously, just like a bridegroom, even trimmed my beard and kissed her vulgar hand . . .

There was a Polish village called Krevo.

On one end there was a little hill, and the Germans had dug in. On the other, opposite end, a little hill, and we had dug in. And this Polish village was left lying there in the ravine between the trenches.

The Polish inhabitants, certainly, had been told to clear out, but there were some who just couldn't stand the idea of leaving their goods behind, so they stayed.

And how they managed to exist there—it's fearsome to ponder. The shells whistle and whistle over them, but they don't mind. They're Polacks. They live in their own way.

We came as their guests.

You might say we were on reconnaissance, but on our way we would absolutely wind up in a Polish hut.

More and more we would wind up at the miller's.

There existed just such an old, old miller.

His old woman would always say—he has, she would say, some money. Call it capital. But he just won't say where.

Seems he promised to tell before his death, but meanwhile for some reason he's afraid, and he hides it.

And this is exactly right about the miller—he hid his little pile.

He told me all about it once, in a heart-to-heart talk.

He said before he died he wanted to get some full pleasure out of family life.

Let them, he says, spoil me a little. Because, just tell them where the little pile is, they'll strip it like bark off a lime tree and throw it away on their lovers, even though they're my own blood kin.

I understood this miller and even felt sympathy for him. Only I wondered how he could get his full pleasure out of family life, because he has this disease, and I noticed his nails were blue.

But they catered to the old man.

The old man grouches and plays the fox, and they keep their eyes fixed on him and they look and they tremble before him, and they're scared he won't tell them about the money.

This miller had a family. His wife was getting on. And he had a stepdaughter, that charming beauty, the Miss Victoria Kazimirovna.

I was just telling you that sophisticated story about his excellency the old prince, and of course I wouldn't tell you anything that wasn't true, and I was telling you about those damn picky whores and how they were beating me with an instrument, only at that time there was not yet the beautiful Polack Victoria Kazimirovna . . . And could not yet be. She was another time and in another business.

And this is what I, forgive me, a poor peasant, went through.

There was this Victoria Kazimirovna, daughter of the old, old miller.

And it was to her we came as guests.

And how did it all turn out?

From the very first days you might say there were kind of relationships between us.

I remember once we arrived at the miller's . . .

We're sitting around giggling, and Victoria Kazimirovna picks me out of the bunch and plays up to me. You know how, sometimes with her shoulder, sometimes with her foot.

Feh, you, I break out in admiration, you're something I like! It was a charming occasion.

I was still on my guard then, and when I left her I kept my trap shut.

Only a bit later she starts taking me by the hand, and admiring me all over the place.

She says: I, Mr. Sinebriukhov, could even love you. (That's just the way she said it.) And I already have a something in my breast, even though you are not a handsome youth.

Only, she says, I have a little favor to ask of you. Save me, she says, for God's sake. I want to leave home and go to Minsk or some such Polish city somewhere around there, because —you can see for yourself—I'm wasting away here for the chickens to laugh at. My father, the old, old miller, has capital, so it is necessary to discover where he keeps it. It is necessary for me to live on money. I, she says, wouldn't do anything bad to my father, but if it isn't today, it's tomorrow he will die of quinsy and I fear he will not tell about his capital.

Here I started getting surprised. But she just sobs it all out, looks into my eyes, and goes on admiring.

Ah, she says, Nazar Il'ich, Mr. Sinebriukhov, you are the most cultivated and charming man here and somehow you will manage it.

And this is how I came to ponder such cunning: because I could see her beauty going to waste for nothing.

I'll tell the old man, think I, the old, old miller, that everyone from the village Krevo is being evacuated . . . He will undoubtedly dig for his goods . . . And then we'll be there to propose he should share up.

The next day I go to their place. My own beard is trimmed, you know, and I put on a clean shirt, and there I am just like a bridegroom on parade . . .

Now, Victorichka, I say, it'll all be taken care of.

I go up to the miller.

That's the way it is, says I; now, says I, Rear Company is going to give you an order tomorrow to clear out all inhabitants from the village Krevo on account of military activities.

Och, how he gets to trembling then, my miller, how he tosses about on his bed.

And him, as he was in his underdrawers—he bolted for the door and spilled not a word to anyone.

He went out the door, and I followed very quietlike.

It was practically night. Moon. Why, you could see every blade of grass. And he's moving along, noticeable as can be, all in white, like some kind of skeleton, and I go hopping along after him behind the shed.

And some damn German, I remember, started to shoot. All right. He's moving along.

He went just a little way and gave a yelp.

He gives a yelp and grabs quick at his chest.

I look, and blood is flowing across the white.

Nu, I am thinking, trouble—a bullet.

He was turning around, I see, back; his hands dropped and he went home.

Well, I just stare—there was something awful about the way he moved. He's not bending his legs, they're stiff, and the step is terrible heavy.

I was running to him, I'm afraid myself, I grab and grab him by the hand, but his hand is growing cold and I see there's no breath in him—deceased.

And with an invisible power he climbed to his home, the ages closed for him, and as he knocks on the floor, so the floor rumbles —earth calls unto herself the deceased.

Then there was shrieking in the house, wailing in front of the corpse, and with the step of death he approached the bed, and here he was mowed down.

And such a panic went up in the hut, we sit and it's awful to hear our own breathing.

And that's how the miller died because of me, and that's how his pile vanished—amen for eternity—his capital.

Then Victoria Kazimirovna was much stricken with grief.

She is weeping and weeping, that whole week she is weeping—her tears will not dry.

And when I approach her, she drives me away and doesn't want to see me.

Only a week passed, I remember, and I am there. No tears, I see, and she even comes up to me lovingly.

What in the world, she says, did you do, Nazar Il'ich? You, she says, are to blame for everything, now you get us out of it.

Fetch me, though it be from the sea's bottom, a little capital, otherwise you are the number one criminal for me and I will go, I know where, to the transport. Ensign Lapushkin asked me to be his sweetheart, and he even promised me a nice gold watch with a bracelet.

Oh, bitterly I shook my head, and tell me, where was I supposed to dig up this capital, but she threw a little knitted shawl around her shoulders and bowed to me nice and low.

I'm going, she says, he is expecting me, Ensign Lapushkin is waiting for me. So please, farewell, Nazar Il'ich, Mr. Sinebriukhov.

Stop, I say, stop, Victoria Kazimorovna. Give me some time, I say, this has got to be thought through.

What is there, she says, for him to think about? Go fetch it, though it be from the sea's bottom, only carry out my request.

And then an idea dawned on me.

In wartime, think I, anything goes. Maybe the Germans will attack, and I could burn through a few pockets if it came to that.

And soon came just such a chance.

In our trenches we had a cannon . . . Och, God help me remember—Hotchkiss is the title.

Hotchkiss naval cannon.

A thin little muzzle it had, and kind of silly to see a shell in it, an insignificant shell at that. But anyhow, it didn't shoot too badly.

It would shoot and do its best to blow up as much as it could. Naval Lieutenant Winch was commander over it. Not a bad guy, the lieutenant's all right. He wouldn't beat you up, he'd just put you in front of a firing squad.

And we were very fond of that little cannon and always set it up in our own trench.

Here, let's say, is the machine gun, and here is a small clump of pines—and the cannon.

She annoyed Germany quite a bit, knocked off a hunk of the Polish church along the cupola, because there was a German observer there.

She also struck among their machine guns.

And right off she never gave the Germans any rest.

That's how the chance came about.

The Germans at nighttime stole off with her most important part—the breechblock. And at the same time they carried off the machine guns.

And how this happened—it's amazing to ponder.

It was quiet. I absolutely went off to Victoria Kazimirovna. The guard was drowsing by the cannon, and the second guard, imagine scum like that, went over to the platoon on duty. They were playing cards there.

Well, O.K. He went.

Only he's playing cards, and he keeps winning, the son of a bitch, and he doesn't take any interest to look what was happening.

And it happened: the Germans dusted off the breechblock from the cannon.

Only, toward morning, the second guard went up to the cannon and he sees: the first guard is lying there absolutely dead, and all-around robbery.

Och, then there was a to-do!

Naval Lieutenant Winch leaps on me like a tiger, he stands the whole platoon at attention, and he orders each man to hold a card in his teeth, but to the second guard, *three* cards like a fan.

Toward evening, his excellency the general rides over, and he's all stirred up.

He's all right, he's a good general.

As soon as he looked at the platoon, his anger left him. Thirty men standing as one, holding cards in their teeth.

The general smiled.

Step out, he says, chosen eagles, fly on the Germans, destroy the foreign enemy.

So stepped out, as I remember, five men, and me with them.

The general, his excellency, is admiring us.

Fly eagles, he says, by night, cut the German wire, seek out even just one German machine gun, and if it should come to pass —the cannon's breechblock.

All ri-i-i-ight.

And toward night we went.

I played along. I needed to.

In the first place I had my own little plan, and then I'm not one of those who wants to live forever.

I, you know, was once chosen for luck. Yes.

In the year sixteen, as I remember, a kind of dark fellow came around. People said he was a Romanian peasant. He came around with birds. He had a cage across his chest. And in the cage was not a parrot, a parrot is green, but some such one of them tropical birds. So she, the scum, a regular scholar that bird, dipped her beak in the cards and picked out each man's luck.

As for me, I remember, the planet Cancer predicted I'd live to ninety.

And a lot more was predicted that I've forgotten, but just as it was predicted, it will come out.

So then I remembered the prediction and just strolled right along.

We approached the German barbed wire.

Dark shadow. Still no moon.

We cut the loop very quietly, we let ourselves down into the trenches, in among the Germans, we went maybe fifty steps— there's a machine gun.

We dropped the German sentry to the ground and strangled him then and there.

It seemed very unpleasant to me, a bit awful in general, you know, this nightmare.

All ri-i-i-ight.

We dismounted the machine gun, decided who should take the stand, who the ammunition boxes, and on me, as I remember, they palmed off, their mother should have it so, the heaviest part, the body of the machine gun.

And this was so damn heavy, it was altogether dropping, not at all light, and step by step they were disappearing from me, and I'm dragging my tail after them, I'm in trouble.

I'd have to crawl up, then I look—the communications passage —I'm there.

And suddenly from around the corner steps an awfully healthy-looking German and his rifle's at the ready.

I threw the machine gun down at my feet and also slipped off my rifle.

Only I have a feeling the German wants to shoot, his head is on the stock.

Someone else might have got scared, someone else might very well have got scared. But it's nothing to me. I stand, and I don't even shake.

If I just turn my back, or give the breech a flip, there, absolutely, I'm finished.

So we stand face to cozy face. And in all, there's five steps between us.

We look each other in the eye and wait, who will run away.

And all of a sudden, the German starts to shake, he makes like to turn back.

So then I shot him.

And right away I remembered my little plan.

I crawled up to him, frisked through his pockets—it's unpleasant. Well, never mind, I forced myself. I took out a pigskin wallet, I took out a watch in a case (the Germans always carry a watch in a case), I heaved the machine gun up on my shoulder, and on I went.

I reached the wire—no loophole.

Any chance of finding it in the dark?

I started to push my way through the barbed wire—it was tough.

Maybe an hour or more I was shoving along, my back was broke, my arms were all torn.

Well anyway I just shoved through.

Then I rested peacefully, crawled into the grass, started to bandage up my arms, they're bleeding so.

And I completely forgot, God damn me, I'm still on the German side and it's getting light already.

I wanted to run. The Germans were raising a stink. It seems they found there was a mess on their side, they opened fire on the Russians, and if I was crawling along, they'd see me and kill me.

But this place here, I see, is wide open, and further on there isn't even any grass. And there's three hundred steps to the huts.

Well, think I, Rear Company just stay where you are. Lucky for you, Nazar Il'ich, Mr. Sinebriukhov, the grass hides you.

All ri-i-i-ight. So I lie still.

But maybe the Germans were feeling terribly insulted, anyway they are taking aim and shooting away at anything they see.

Around noon they leave off shooting. But I notice as soon as anyone sticks his head out up on our Russian side, they take aim.

Well that means they are absolutely on their toes and I have to stay put till dark.

All ri-i-i-ight.

I lie an hour . . . and I lie two. I interest myself in the wallet . . . Not much money, but at least it's all foreign . . . I am admiring the watch.

But the sun beat straight down on my head, and my spirit drooped. And thirst.

Then I started to think about Victoria Kazimirovna. Only, when I look up, I see there's a crow about to drop down on me.

I'm lying there alive. But maybe he thinks I'm carrion. And he's dropping down.

I try to shoo him away quietly.

Sssssh, I say, beat it, get the hell out.

I am waving my hand, but maybe he doesn't believe me. He sits himself right on me.

There's a scummy bird for you. Sits himself right on my chest. No way to pull him off. My arms are torn, I can't bend them, and he's at me hard with his beak and wings.

I swat at him. He shoves off and sits down again nearby. And then he moves back toward me, and he's even hissing. The snake, he smells the blood on my arms.

Well, think I, you've had it, Nazar Il'ich, Mr. Sinebriukhov. A bullet never touched you, but here's this garbagey bird, God forgive, ruins a man for no reason. Now the Germans would absolutely catch on as to what was going on just outside the barbed wire.

And what was going on? A crow was eating a man alive.

So we were at each other a long time like this. I'm getting ready to really let him have one, only I've got to be careful not to move so the Germans will see me, and, I tell you, I'm about ready to cry. My arms are torn, my blood is flowing, and here he's still nibbling.

Then I got to feeling so damn mad at him and he was just coming at me when I spring on him.

Kysh, I say, *you scabby rubbish!*

I cried out and the Germans absolutely heard it right away.

I jumped up. I run, my rifle beats against my legs, and the machine gun just lies there where I left it.

Then the Germans gave a yell and started shooting at me. But I don't hit the dirt—I just run.

And how I got to the first huts, I don't mind telling you, I don't know.

I just plain got there. I look, my shoulder's bleeding, I'm wounded.

Then behind the huts step by step I made my way back to my own and just dropped down dead.

I came to myself in the regimental infirmary, as I remember, in the transport.

Well I just whisk through my pockets. The watch is there. But the pigskin wallet? Just as if it had never been.

Now either I had left it at the place where the crow stopped me from hiding it, or the medics had lifted it.

I wept most bitterly. I decided to drop every opportunity, and just get better.

But then I find out. There lives here at Ensign Lapushkin's, in the transport, the charming Polack Victoria Kazimirovna.

All ri-i-i-ight.

Maybe a week went by. They decorated me with a George. And in this manner I appear before the Ensign Lapushkin.

I go into the hut.

Greetings, I say, your highness. And greetings, please, charming Polack Victoria Kazimirovna.

Then I see they are both beginning to look a little embarrassed. He stands up and hides her.

What, he says, do you want? I've been seeing too much of you lately. You've been hanging around too much under the windows. Beat it, he says, you son of the barnyard, so much for you.

But I stick my chest out and I answer proudly like this.

You, I say, may outrank me, but the business here is among other things a civilian one, and I have a right to be discussing it, just like anyone else. Let her, I say, the charming Polack herself, make a choice between us.

How he starts yelling at me!

Damn you, he screams, you Tambov milksop! How dare you! Take off that George, he says, and I'll really hit you one.

No, says I, your highness. You can't touch me. I'm a combat soldier.

And at the same time I stand waiting by the door for what she, the charming Polack, will say.

Well she just keeps quiet, hiding behind Lapushkin's back.

I sighed bitterly. I spat on the floor with a glob of spit. And I went my own way.

Just as I'd gone out the door, I hear some footsteps clipping along.

I look. Victoria Kazimirovna is running. The little knitted shawl is fluttering from her shoulders.

She ran up to me, she dug into my arm with her scratchy claws, but for awhile she just couldn't get a word out.

So maybe a moment went by. She kisses my hand with her charming lips. And this is what she says.

I bow low to you, Nazar Il'ich, Mr. Sinebriukhov . . . Forgive me all such, for God's sake. It's just that our fates are different.

I wanted to fall down right there. I wanted to tell her a thing or two . . . Only I remembered then just how that crow had flown over me . . . Och, I pulled myself together.

No, says I, for you, charming Polack, there is no forgiveness in all eternity.

In the village Usacha the other day they were holding the re-election of a chairman.

City comrade Vedernikov, sent by the party cell to the village under its patronage, stood on the freshly planed boards of a platform and spoke to the meeting.

"The international situation, citizens, is clearer than clear. It is not fitting to linger on it. Let us pass therefore to the current moment of the day, to the selection of a chairman to replace Kostylev, Ivan. This parasite cannot be trusted with the fullness of state power, and therefore he is to be replaced . . ."

The chairman of the village poor, the peasant Bobrov, Mikhailo Vasil'evich, stood on the platform beside the city comrade. While he was very much ill at ease because the city words were but poorly accessible to the understanding of the peasants, he nevertheless condescended, out of sheer good will, to explain the obscurities of the speech.

"In a word," Bobrov said, "this parasite—may a cow gore him—Kostylev, Ivan Maksimych, cannot be trusted and therefore he is to be replaced . . ."

"And instead of the afore-mentioned Ivan Kostylev," continued the city orator, "it is proposed to select a *man,* because we don't care for speculators."

"And instead of the parasite," explained Bobrov, "damn his soul, this bootlegger, even if he's a relative of mine on my wife's side, it's proposed to remove and appoint."

"It is proposed," said the city comrade, "to set up a list of candidates."

Mikhailo Bobrov tore off his cap from an overflow of emotions and made a broad gesture proclaiming the immediate establishment of a list of candidates.

The group was silent.

"What about Bykin? or Eremei Ivanovich Sekin, eh?" someone asked timidly.

"All right," said the city comrade, "Bykin . . . Let's write it down."

"Now we'll write it down," explained Bobrov.

The crowd, which had been silent until that moment, began in a frightening manner to set up a tumult and to cry out names, demanding that their candidates be immediaely raised to the office of chairman.

"Bykin, Vasia! Eremei Ivanovich Sekin! Mikolaev! . . ."

The city comrade Vedernikov wrote these names down on his mandate.

"Brothers!" someone shrieked. "This is no election—Sekin and Mikolaev . . . We need to choose advanced-type comrades . . . Really solid all the way . . . Someone who'll know his way around in the city—that's the kind we need . . . Who'd know everything through and through . . ."

"Right!" they shrieked in the crowd. "Some advanced types we need . . . That's the way it's done around here."

"A correct tendency," said the city comrade. "Mark the names."

Then the group hit a snag.

"How about Leshka Konovalov?" someone said timidly. "He's the only one who's come from the city. He's—a metropolitan deal."

"Leshka!" they shrieked in the crowd. "Step out, Leshka. Tell the group."

Leshka Konovalov pushed his way through the crowd, came up on the platform, and, flattered by the general attention, bowed city style, holding his hand over his heart.

"Speak, Leshka!" they shrieked in the crowd.

"Well, now," said Leshka, a bit confused. "Me you can choose. Sekin or Mikolaev there—is that a choice? That's country stuff, bottom of the barrel. But I scratched around the city for about two years. Me you can choose . . ."

"Speak, Leshka! Report to the group!" the crowd shrieked once again.

"I can speak," said Leshka. "Why not speak, when I know it all. Unlike you all, I'm a cultured man. For two years I shook loose from the grayness of country life. In the second place, my tongue is very fluent—I can make speeches. Nowadays that isn't just a pound of steam."

"You're right, Leshka," they said in the crowd. "Without a tongue a man's a sheep. Only the tongue makes men."

"That's just it," Leshka confirmed. "Only the tongue leads to fortune. The tongue plus knowledge. Of course, one needs to know—the law code, statutes, decrees. All this I know. I spent maybe two years . . . The way it was, I'm sitting in my cell, and they come running up to you. Explain, Leshka, look here, what does this note added on to the decree mean."

"What cell was that?" they asked in the crowd. "What kind of cell are you jabbering about?"

"What cell?" said Leshka. "Why Cell Number 14. We were doing time in the Kresty . . ."

"Nu!" the group was surprised. "What for, wise guy, were you doing time in jail?"

Leshka was troubled and stared distractedly into the crowd.

"The merest trifle," Leshka said vaguely.

"Politics, or did you swipe something?"

Leshka Konovalov, grasping that he had botched his candidacy, spoke once again with a fluent tongue:

"Well, no, there was nothing special against me. There was just some discrepancy in the cashbox. Well, you know you can't swim in water and not get a little wet."

Leshka waved his hand and hastily slipped away into the crowd.

The city comrade Vedernikov who had spoken of the new tendencies to select comrades who were acquainted with city life recommended voting for Eremei Sekin. And concerning Leshka he said: "Such likes we have to chase under the slogan—weeds out of the field, get out!"

Mikhailo Bobrov, chairman of the poor element, explained the meaning of these words, and Eremei Sekin was unanimously elected on the first ballot.

Leshka Konovalov abstained. This bottom-of-the-barrel country element was not to his taste.

CONFESSION

In Passion Week, Grandma Fekla splurged—she bought a twenty-kopeck candle and placed it before the saint.

Fekla spent a long time eagerly fitting the candle closer to the image. And when it seemed right, she stepped back a little distance and, admiring the work of her hands, began to pray and to request all kinds of advantages and favors for herself in return for the twenty kopecks she had spent.

Fekla prayed for a long time, muttering all her petty little requests through her nose to herself; then, after she knocked her forehead on the dirty stone floor, took a deep breath, and groaned, she went to confession.

Confessions were heard at the altar behind the screen.

Grandma Fekla waited in line behind some really old woman indeed, and once again she began crossing herself and softly muttering. One wasn't detained for long behind the screen.

Those taking confession went in there and, in a minute, sighing and quietly clearing their throats, emerged, bowing to the saints.

"The priest is hurrying," Fekla thought. "And why should he hurry? There's no fire here. He is making confession undignified."

Fekla entered behind the screen, bowed low to the priest, and kissed his hand.

"What is your name?" the priest asked, blessing her.

"My name is Fekla."

"Well, tell us, Fekla," the priest said, "what are your sins? In what have you been a sinner? Do you spread idle gossip? Do you seldom seek refuge in God?"

"I am a sinner, father, of course," said Fekla bowing.

"May God forgive," said the priest covering Fekla with the confession shawl. "Do you believe in God? You do not doubt?"

"I believe in God," said Fekla. "That son of mine has come home, of course. He speaks out, he judges, in a word . . . But still, I believe."

"That is well, mother," said the priest. "Do not give yourself lightly to temptation. Now what, tell me, does that son say? How does he judge?"

"He judges," said Fekla. "These, he says, are trifles—this faith of theirs. No, he says, God does not exist, and you only search the sky and clouds . . ."

"There is a God," the priest said sternly. "Do not give yourself up to this . . . And what else, remember, did your son say?"

"Oh, he said different things."

"Different things!" the priest said angrily. "And from whence comes all that surrounds us? From whence are the planets, the stars and the moon, if there is no God? Your son never said any such thing. From whence, pray tell, is all that surrounds us? Is it just chemistry? Recall. Did he not speak of this? Pray tell, is it all chemistry, eh?"

"He didn't say," Fekla said, blinking her eyes.

"And maybe it's chemistry," the priest said thoughtfully. "Maybe that's the way it is, mother, and there's no God. Everything's chemistry . . ."

Grandma Fekla threw a frightened glance at the priest. But he put the confession shawl on her head and began to mutter the words of a prayer.

"Well, go now, go," the priest said gloomily. "Don't keep the believers waiting."

Fekla once again threw a frightened glance at the priest and went out sighing and modestly clearing her throat. Then she went up to her own saint, looked at the candle, trimmed the burnt wick, and left the church.

WHAT GOOD ARE RELATIVES?

For two days Timofei Vasil'evich had been looking for his nephew, Serega Vlasov. On the third day, just before leaving town, he found him. He met him in a trolley car.

Timofei Vasil'evich boarded the trolley, took out a coin, and was about to give it to the conductor; only he looked—who could it be? The conductor's face seemed very familiar. Timofei Vasil'evich stared—yes! That's who it was—Serega Vlasov, his very own self, working as a trolley conductor.

"Well!" exclaimed Timofei Vasil'evich. "Serega! Is it really you, my fine friend?"

The conductor seemed embarrassed, checked his roll of tickets without any apparent need to do so, and said: "Just a moment, uncle . . . let me give out the tickets."

"O.K.! Go right ahead," his uncle said happily. "I'll wait."

Timofei Vasil'evich smiled and began to explain to the passengers: "He's a blood relative of mine, Serega Vlasov. My brother Peter's son . . . I haven't seen him for seven years . . ."

Timofei Vasil'evich looked with joy on his nephew and shouted to him: "Serega, my fine friend, I've been looking for you two days. All over town. And look where you are! A conductor . . . And I went to your address. On Raznochin Street. Not here, they answer. He went away, left this place. Where, says I, did he go, answer me, says I. I'm his blood uncle. We don't know, says they . . . And there you are—a conductor, aren't you?"

"A conductor," the nephew answered cautiously.

The passengers began to stare with curiosity at the relative. The uncle laughed happily and looked lovingly at his nephew, but the nephew was obviously embarrassed and, feeling that he was after all on duty, did not know what to say to his uncle or how to behave in his presence.

"So," the uncle said again, "you're a conductor on the trolley line?"

"A conductor . . ."

"Say, isn't that a coincidence! And I, Serega, my fine friend, I was just looking into the trolley—and what's that? The face on that conductor looks very familiar. And it turned out to be you. Ah, there's luck for you! Well, I'm so glad. I'm so pleased, really . . ."

For a moment the conductor shifted from foot to foot, and then suddenly he said: "You've got to pay, uncle. To get a ticket . . . Are you going far?"

The uncle laughed happily and slapped him across the change purse.

"I would have paid! I swear to God! If I'd gotten on another car, or if I'd missed this one—O.K.—I would have paid. I would have paid my good money. Ah, there's luck for you! . . . I'm going to the railroad station, Serega, my fine friend."

"Two stops," said the conductor wearily, looking to the side.

"No, you don't mean it?" Timofei Vasil'evich seemed surprised. "You don't mean it? You're kidding?"

"You must pay, uncle," the conductor said softly. "Two stops. Because you can't travel for nothing and without a ticket."

Timofei Vasil'evich, offended, pressed his lips together and looked sternly at his nephew.

"Is this the way you treat your blood uncle? You rob your uncle?"

The conductor stared gloomily out of the window.

"That's piracy!" the uncle said angrily. "I haven't seen you, you son of a bitch, for seven years, and what do you do? You ask money for a trip. From your blood uncle? Don't you wave your hands at me. You may be my blood relative, but I'm not scared of your hands. Don't wave, you'll give the passengers a chill."

Timofei Vasil'evich turned the coin over in his hand and put it back in his pocket.

"What do you think of the likes of him, brothers?" Timofei Vasil'evich appealed to the public. "From his blood uncle he asks. Two stops, he says . . .Eh?"

"You must pay," said the nephew, almost in tears. "Please don't be angry, comrade uncle. Because this isn't my trolley. It's a state trolley. It belongs to the people."

"To the people," said the uncle, "that's not my business. You could show a little respect for your blood uncle. You could say, 'Uncle, put away your hard-earned ten kopecks. Travel free.' Your trolley wouldn't fall apart on account of that. I was riding in a train the other day . . . The conductor was no relation, but still he said: 'Please, Timofei Vasil'evich,' says he, 'why bring up such a thing . . . just sit . . .' And he took me along . . . And he's no relation . . . Just an old village friend. And you do this to your blood uncle . . . You'll get no money from me."

The conductor wiped his forehead with his hands and suddenly rang the bell.

"Get off, comrade uncle," said the nephew officially.

Seeing the matter was taking a serious turn, Timofei Vasil'evich wrung his hands, took out his ten-kopeck piece again, and then again put it back.

"No," he said, "I can't! Pay you, you snot, I can't. Better let me get off."

Timofei Vasil'evich arose solemnly and indignantly and made his way to the exit. Then he turned.

"Driving out your uncle . . . Your blood uncle," Timofei Vasil'evich said in a fury, "Why, you snot . . . I can have you shot for this."

Timofei Vasilevich threw a withering glance at his nephew and got off the trolley.

Grigorii Ivanovich inhaled noisily, wiped his chin with his sleeve, and began to tell the story: Brothers, I don't like women who wear hats. If a woman's wearing a hat, or if she's got silk stockings on her, or a little pug-dog in her arms, or if she's got a gold tooth, then to me she's an aristocrat, and not a woman at all but an empty space.

In my time, of course, I once courted an aristocrat like that. I went strolling with her and took her to the theater. It was in the theater, in fact, that it all came out. It was in the theater that she exposed her ideology in its full measure.

I met her in the courtyard at home. At a house meeting. I look, and there stands just such a big deal. Stockings on her, gold tooth.

"Where are you from, citizen?" I say. "What number?"

"I am," she says, "from number seven."

"Please," says I, "good luck to you."

And all at once I found I liked her terribly. I began to go see her often. To Apartment Number Seven. As it happened, I'd go in a kind of official capacity. Like this: "Anything wrong here, citizen, in the way of a broken pipe or toilet? Everything working?"

"Yes," she replies. "Everything's working."

And she wraps herself up in a woolen shawl and there's not a whisper more. Only with her eyes she's devouring away. And the tooth flashes in her mouth. I came to her for a month—she got used to it. She began to answer in more detail. Like, for example, "the pipe's working, thank you, Grigorii Ivanovich."

To get on, we began to take strolls along the streets. We'd go out on the street, and she'd ask me to take her by the arm. I was embarrassed, but I'd take her arm and tag along like a fish out of water. And what to say, I don't know, and in front of people I'm ashamed.

Well, and once she says to me: "Why," she says, "do you always take me out on the streets? My head's gotten all twisted. You could," she says, "if you're a man and a gentleman, take me to the theater, for example."

"Can do," says I.

And all at once on the following day the party cell distributed tickets for the opera. One ticket I received myself, and the other one I got from Vas'ka the locksmith, who gave his up to me.

I never looked at the tickets, but they were different. Mine was in the orchestra, but Vas'ka's was in the balcony.

Anyway, we got there. We took our seats in the theater. She took a seat on my ticket, and I on Vas'ka's. I was sitting in the last balcony and couldn't see a horse-radish. But if I leaned way out over the balcony rail I could see her. But not too well.

I was getting more and more bored, and went downstairs. I look—it's intermission. And she's coming out for intermission.

"Hello," says I.

"Hello."

"It's interesting," says I. "Is the pipe working here?"

"I don't know," she says.

And she goes to the buffet. I follow her. She walks along the buffet and looks at the counter. And on the counter there's a plate. On the plate some pastries.

And I'm such a goose, such an uncut bourgeois, I creep around her and offer: "If you would like," says I, "to eat one of those pastries, don't hesitate. I'll pay."

"*Merci*," she says.

And suddenly she maneuvers herself around to the plate with a vicious movement, grabs the one with whipped cream, and laps it up.

The money I had on me was damn little. At most enough for three pastries. She eats, and I go whisking nervously through my pockets. I look in my hand. How much do I have? About a pigeon's droppings' worth.

She ate the one with whipped cream and grabbed another. I let out with a quack. And then I keep quiet. Such a bourgeois kind of embarrassment took hold of me. Like this, a gentleman, and no money on him.

I walk around her like a rooster, and she giggles waiting for compliments.

I say: "Isn't it time to go back to our seats? Maybe they rang."

But she says: "No."

And takes a third.

"On an empty stomach—isn't that a lot? You might throw up."

And she: "No," she says, "I'm used to it."

And takes a fourth.

Then the blood runs to my head.

"Put it," says I, "back!"

And she got scared. She opened her mouth, and in her mouth the tooth flashed.

It seemed to me as though someone had touched a whip to my rear. It's all one, think I, there'll be no strolling with her now.

"Put it back," says I, "you damn bitch!"

She stepped back. And I say to the attendant: "How much for the three pastries we ate?"

The attendant takes it all indifferently—he takes his time.

"You owe me," says he, "for eating four pieces, so-and-so much."

"How," says I, "for four? When the fourth is still on the plate."

"No," says he, "though it's still on the plate, it was nibbled and it's been smutched by a finger."

"How," says I, "nibbled, if you please. It's your cockeyed fantasies."

But he still takes it indifferently—he wrings his hands in front of his mug.

Well, of course, people gathered around. Experts. Some say a nibble was taken, others—no.

And I emptied out my pockets—something, of course, spilled out on the floor and rolled away—the crowd laughs. But to me it's not funny. I am counting my change.

I counted the money—enough for four pieces and a little over. Dear mother, I'd picked a quarrel for nothing.

I paid. I turn to the lady: "Eat," says I. "It's paid for."

The lady doesn't move. She's embarrassed to eat it. And here some old joker butted in.

"Give it here," says he. "I'll eat it."

And he ate it, the scum. With my money.

We took our seats in the theater. We watched the opera. Then home.

And at home she says to me in that bourgeois tone of hers: "Enough swinery on your part. Those who don't have money shouldn't go out with ladies."

And I say: "Money isn't happiness. Pardon the information."

So I left her.

I don't like aristocrats.

I hear tell, citizens, they have some excellent bathhouses in America.

For example, a citizen just drives in, drops his linen in a special box, then off he'll go to wash himself. He won't even worry, they say, about loss or theft. He doesn't even need a ticket.

Well, let's suppose it's some other, nervous-type American, and he'll say to the attendant, "Goot-bye," so to speak, "keep an eye out."

And that's all there is to it.

This American will wash himself, come back, and they'll give him clean linen—washed and pressed. Foot-wrappings, no doubt, whiter than snow. Underdrawers mended and sewed. That's the life!

Well, we have bathhouses, too. But not as good. Though it's possible to wash yourself.

Only in ours, there's trouble with the tickets. Last Saturday I went to one of our bathhouses (after all, I can't go all the way to America), and they give me two tickets. One for my linen, the other for my hat and coat.

But where is a naked man going to put tickets? To say it straight—no place. No pockets. Look around—all stomach and legs. The only trouble's with the tickets. Can't tie them to your beard.

Well, I tied a ticket to each leg so as not to lose them both at once. I went into the bath.

The tickets are flapping about on my legs now. Annoying to walk like that. But you've got to walk. Because you've got to have a bucket. Without a bucket, how can you wash? That's the only trouble.

I look for a bucket. I see one citizen washing himself with three buckets. He is standing in one, washing his head in another, and holding the third with his left hand so no one would take it away.

I pulled at the third bucket; among other things, I wanted to take it for myself. But the citizen won't let go.

"What are you up to," says he, "stealing other people's buckets?" As I pull, he says, "I'll give you a bucket between the eyes, then you won't be so damn happy."

I say: "This isn't the tsarist regime," I say, "to go around hitting people with buckets. Egotism," I say, "sheer egotism. Other people," I say, "have to wash themselves too. You're not in a theater," I say.

But he turned his back and starts washing himself again.

"I can't just stand around," think I, "waiting his pleasure. He's likely to go on washing himself," think I, "for another three days."

I moved along.

After an hour I see some old joker gaping around, no hands on his bucket. Looking for soap or just dreaming, I don't know. I just lifted his bucket and made off with it.

So now there's a bucket, but no place to sit down. And to wash standing—what kind of washing is that? That's the only trouble.

All right. So I'm standing. I'm holding the bucket in my hand and I'm washing myself.

But all around me everyone's scrubbing clothes like mad. One is washing his trousers, another's rubbing his drawers, a third's wringing something out. You no sooner get yourself all washed up than you're dirty again. They're splattering me, the bastards. And such a noise from all the scrubbing—it takes all the joy out of washing. You can't even hear where the soap squeaks. That's the only trouble.

"To hell with them," I think. "I'll finish washing at home."

I go back to the locker room. I give them one ticket, they give me my linen. I look. Everything's mine, but the trousers aren't mine.

"Citizens," I say, "mine didn't have a hole here. Mine had a hole over there."

But the attendant says: "We aren't here," he says, "just to watch for your holes. You're not in a theater," he says.

All right. I put these pants on, and I'm about to go get my coat. They won't give me my coat. They want the ticket. I'd forgotten the ticket on my leg. I had to undress. I took off my pants. I look for the ticket. No ticket. There's the string tied around my leg, but no ticket. The ticket had been washed away.

I give the attendant the string. He doesn't want it.

"You don't get anything for a string," he says. "Anybody can cut off a bit of string," he says. "Wouldn't be enough coats to go around. Wait," he says, "till everyone leaves. We'll give you what's left over."

I say: "Look here, brother, suppose there's nothing left but crud? This isn't a theater," I say. "I'll identify it for you. One pocket," I say, "is torn, and there's no other. As for the buttons," I say, "the top one's there, the rest are not to be seen."

Anyhow, he gave it to me. But he wouldn't take the string.

I dressed, and went out on the street. Suddenly I remembered: I forgot my soap.

I went back again. They won't let me in, in my coat.

"Undress," they say.

I say, "Look, citizens. I can't undress for the third time. This isn't a theater," I say. "At least give me what the soap costs."

Nothing doing.

Nothing doing—all right. I went without the soap.

Of course, the reader who is accustomed to formalities might be curious to know: what kind of a bathhouse was this? Where was it located? What was the address?

What kind of a bathhouse? The usual kind. Where it costs ten kopecks to get in.

Anis'ia traveled thirty versts to get to the country hospital.

She set out at dawn and at noon she paused before the white single-storied house.

"Is the surgeon receiving?" she asked a peasant sitting on the porch.

"The surgeon?" the peasant asked with interest. "What, you sick?"

"Sick," Anis'ia answered.

"Me, too, my dear," the peasant said. "I ate too much grits . . . I'm number seven."

Anis'ia tied her horse to the post and went into the hospital.

The medical orderly, Ivan Kuz'mich, was receiving the patients. He was small, elderly, and terribly distinguished. Everyone in the area knew him, praised him and called him, without reason, the surgeon.

Anis'ia entered the room, approached him, bowed low, and sat down on the edge of a chair.

"Are you sick?" Ivan Kuz'mich asked.

"I'm sick," said Anis'ia. "That is, I'm sick through and through. Every bone pains and throbs. My heart is eating itself alive.

"What might it be from?" the medical orderly asked indifferently. "And since when?"

"Since fall, Ivan Kuz'mich. Since this last fall. In the fall I got sick. Since, you know, my husband Dimitrii Naumych arrived from the city, I've been sick. For example. I'm standing by the table rolling some mill cakes in flour. Dimitrii Naumych used to love these particular mill cakes. And where is he now, I think to myself, Dimitrii Naumych? He's a soviet deputy in the city . . ."

"Look, my dear woman," the medical orderly said, "don't overdo it. What are you sick from?"

"Well, I was just telling you," said Anis'ia, "I'm standing by the table rolling mill cakes. Suddenly Aunt Agaf'ia runs up like a ram and starts waving her hand. 'Go,' she shrieks, 'go quick, Anis'iushka. Your man just arrived from the city, and it looks like he's coming up the street with bag and stick.' My heart stopped. My knees knocked together. I'm standing there like a fool kneading the cakes . . . Then I threw down the cakes and ran into the yard. And in the yard the sun is shimmering. The air is light. And on my left near the shed a brown calf is standing scaring off flies with his tail. I looked at the calf—and the tears began to flow. Here, I think, Dimitrii Naumych will be so pleased with this particular brown calf."

"Please," the medical orderly said morosely, "stick to the point."

"But my dear Ivan Kuz'mich, I'm just telling you. Please don't get mad. I'm sticking to the point . . . I ran out the gate. I see, you know how it is, the church on the left, a goat's walking along, a rooster is scratching away with his foot, and on the right, I see, right on up the middle—there comes Dimitrii Naumych.

"I looked at him. My heart skipped a beat, I could feel a hiccup rising. Ah, I think, Holy Mother of God! Ah, I think, I feel a little faint! And he, he's walking along with a short, serious step. His beard is fluttering in the air. And he's wearing city clothes. And fancy shoes.

"As soon as I saw the fancy shoes it was as though something had been torn out of me. I think, oy, where do I come in, uncultured as I am, what kind of a wife do I make for him, a first-rate man and a soviet deputy.

"I stood like a fool at the post and my feet wouldn't move. I feel the post up and down with my fingers and I stand there.

"And he himself, Dimitrii Naumych, the soviet deputy, comes up to me slowly and says hello.

"He says, 'Hello, Anis'ia Vasil'evna. How many years has it been,' he says, 'how many winters, that we have not seen each other? . . .'

"I should have, fool that I am, taken the bag from Dimitrii Naumych, but I just look at his fancy shoes and don't move.

"I think, oy, it was a peasant who left me. Now he's wearing fancy shoes. He's been having talks with city folks, maybe even with Comsomol girls.

"And Dimitrii Naumych answers in a low voice: 'Och,' he says, 'look what you're like! Dark,' he says, 'ignorant, Anis'ia Vasil'evna. What,' he says, 'am I going to talk about with you? I,' he says, 'am an educated man and a soviet deputy. I,' he says, 'know maybe four rules of arithmetic. I know fractions,' he says.

'But you,' he says, 'look what you're like! Probably,' he says, 'you can't even sign your name on paper? Another man might very well throw you over, for your darkness and ignorance.'

"And I am standing at the post and getting words all mixed up: look here, Dimitrii Naumych, throw me over if you like, certainly, just as you like.

"But he takes me by the hand and answers: 'I was only joking, Anis'ia Vasil'evna. Stop thinking like that. I,' he says, 'am like this. Forget it . . .'

"Again my heart skipped a beat, I could feel a hiccup rising.

" 'Dimitrii Naumych,' I say, 'be at rest. I, too, certainly, can learn fractions and the four rules. Also to sign my name on paper. I,' I say, 'will not shame you, an educated man . . .' "

The medical orderly, Ivan Kuz'mich stood up from his chair and walked about the room.

"Well, well," he said, "that's enough, you're a long way off . . . What are you sick from?"

"What am I sick from? Why nothing, now, Ivan Kuz'mich. It seems to have gotten better now. I can't complain about my health. And Dimitrii Naumych himself said: 'I was just joking,' he said. That means he said all that just as a joke."

"Why, yes, he was joking," said the medical orderly. "Of course he was joking . . . Can I give you some pills?"

"I don't need any," said Anis'ia. "Thank you, Ivan Kuz'mich for your advice. I feel very much better now. Many, many thanks. Good-bye."

And Anis'ia, after leaving a bag of grain on the table, went to the door. Then she turned.

"Fractions, Ivan Kuz'mich . . . Where can I find out about these fractions? Should I go to the schoolteacher, or what?"

"To the schoolteacher," the medical orderly said, sighing. "Of course, to the schoolteacher. It isn't a medical matter."

Anis'ia bowed low and went out into the street.

POVERTY

Nowadays, brothers, what is the most fashionable word there is, eh?

Nowadays, the most fashionable word that can be is, of course, electrification.

I won't argue that it isn't a matter of immense importance to light up Soviet Russia with electricity. Nevertheless, even this matter has its shady side. I am not saying, comrades, that it costs a lot. It costs nothing more expensive than money. That's not what I'm talking about.

This is what I mean.

I lived, comrades, in a very large house. The whole house was using kerosene. Some had kerosene lamps with, some without a glass, and some had nothing—just a priest's candle flickering away. Real hardship!

And then they started installing electric lights. Soon after the Revolution.

The house delegate installed them first. Well, he installed and installed. He's a quiet man and doesn't let his tongue give him away. But still he walks a bit strangely, and he's always thoughtfully blowing his nose.

Nevertheless, he doesn't let his tongue give him away.

And then our dear little landlady, Elizaveta Ignat'evna Prokhorov, declares to us that she too wants to put in electric lights in our half-dark apartment.

"Everybody," she says, "is installing them. Even the delegate," she says, "has installed them. Why should we be more backward than other people? All the more so," she says, "since it's economical. Cheaper than kerosene."

You don't say! We too began to install.

We installed them, turned them on—my fathers! Muck and filth all around.

The way it was before, you'd go to work in the morning, come home in the evening, drink a bit of tea, and go to bed. And nothing of this kind was visible as long as you used kerosene.

But now when we turned on the lights, we see, here someone's old bedroom slipper lying around, there the wallpaper torn in shreds and hanging down, there a bedbug running away at a trot, trying to save himself from the light, here a rag of who-knows-what, there a gob of spit, here a cigar butt, there a flea hopping.

Holy fathers! You wanted to cry for help. Sad to look on such a spectacle.

Take the couch that stood in our room, for example. I used to think, it's all right, it's a couch. It's a good couch. I often sat on it evenings. And now I was burning electricity—holy fathers! What a couch! Everything's sticking out, hanging down, spilling out from inside. I can't sit down on such a couch—my soul cries out.

So, I think, I don't live very well, do I? Better get out of the house. I begin to develop a negative attitude. My work falls from my hands.

I see the landlady, Elizaveta Ignat'evna, is also going around mournfully, muttering to herself, fussing around in the kitchen.

"What," I ask, "is bothering you, landlady?"

She waves her hand.

"My dear man," she says, "I never thought I was living so badly."

I looked at her fixings—and it really wasn't what you'd call luxurious: in fact, her furniture was painful. And all around, disorder, strewings, litter, rubbish. And all this flooded with bright light and staring you in the eye.

I began coming home kind of depressed.

I come in, I turn on the light, stare at the bulb, and hop into the sack.

After giving it a good deal of thought, I got my pay. I bought some whitewash and started to work. I shook out the bed, killed off the bedbugs, painted over the woodwork, banged the couch back together, decorated, decontaminated—my spirit sings and rejoices.

In general, everything was going well, very well indeed.

But our landlady, Elizaveta Ignat'evna, took another course. She cut the installation wires in her room.

"My dear man," she says, "I don't want to live in the light. I don't want," she says, "my modest circumstances to be lit up for the bedbugs to laugh at."

I begged and argued with her—no good. She held her own.

"I don't want," she says, "to live with that light. I have no money to make repairs."

I tell her: "Why, I'll do the repairs for you myself for next to nothing."

She doesn't want that.

"With those bright lights of yours," she says, "I have to keep busy from morning to night with cleaning and washing. I'll manage," she says, "without the light, as I managed before."

The delegate also tried to convince her. And even quarreled with her. He called her an outmoded *petit bourgeois*. It didn't work. She refused.

Well, let her have it the way she wants. Personally, I live in the electric light and I am quite satisfied with it.

The way I look at it, the light scratches away all our litter and removes the rubbish.

* In an earlier variant of this story, the author left his hero as unreclaimed as the landlady.

Of course, losing an overshoe in a trolley car is not difficult. Especially if there's pushing from the side, and at the same time some bruiser steps on your heel from behind—there you are, without an overshoe.

Losing an overshoe is the simplest thing in the world.

My overshoe got lost in a hurry. You might say I didn't even get a chance to catch my breath.

I boarded the trolley—both overshoes, as I now recall, were where they should be.

But when I left the trolley—I look: one overshoe's there, not the other. My shoes, there. And my socks, I see, are there. And my underwear's where it should be. But no overshoe. One overshoe is missing.

And, of course, you can't run after a trolley car.

I took off the overshoe that remained, wrapped it in a newspaper, and went along. After work, I think, I'll do a little investigating. To keep from losing my property. Somewhere I'll dig it up.

After work I went to look. But first I took counsel with a friend of mine who was a motorman.

He straightaway gave me some hope.

"You say you lost it in the trolley. That was lucky," he says. "In another public place, I couldn't guarantee anything. But to lose something in a trolley—that's a sacred matter. Now there is a little office we have called Lost and Found. Go there and get it. It's a sacred matter!"

"Well," says I, "thanks." A load had been lifted from my shoulders. You see, that overshoe was practically new. This was only the third season I'd been wearing it.

The following day, I go to the room.

"Is it possible, brothers," I say, "to get my overshoe back. I lost it in the trolley."

"Possible," they say. "What kind of an overshoe?"

"Oh," I say, "the ordinary kind. Size number twelve."

"We have," they say, "twelve thousand number twelves. Describe its features."

"The features," I say, "are just the usual ones. The back, of course, is a bit torn. There's no lining on the inside. The lining wore out."

"We have," they say, "a little over a thousand overshoes like that. Aren't there any special marks?"

"Special marks," I say, "yes, there are. The toe looks as though it were cut clean off, but it's still hanging on. And the heel," I say, "is almost gone. The heel's worn out. But the sides," I say, "there's still nothing wrong with the sides."

"Be seated," they say, "right here. Now we'll go look."

And right away they bring out my overshoe.

Naturally, I was beside myself with joy. Really touched.

Here, I think, there's an outfit marvelously at work. And, I think, how many intelligent, responsible people have gone to so much bother about just one overshoe.

I say to them: "Thanks," I say, "you're friends for life. Give it right here. Now it's found. I thank you."

"No," they say, "respected comrade, we cannot give it to you. We," they say, "don't know: maybe it wasn't you who lost it."

"Of course it was me," I say. "I can give you my word of honor."

They say: "We believe you and fully sympathize, and it's quite probable it really was you who lost this overshoe. But we cannot give it up. Bring us some certification that you really did lose this overshoe. Let your house manager verify that fact, and then without any superfluous red tape we shall give back to you that which you legitimately lost."

"Brothers," I say, "sacred comrades, they just don't know about this fact at home. Maybe they wouldn't give me such a paper."

"They'll give," they say, "it's their business to give. What else are they for at your place?"

I cast one more glance at the overshoe and left.

The following day I approached the president of our house.

"Give me," I say, "a paper. My overshoe's going to pot."

"Did you really lose it?" he says. "Or are you just twisting things? Maybe you just want to lay hold of some extra consumers' goods?"

"God almighty!" I say. "I lost it."

He says: "Of course, I can't just go on your word. Now if you'd bring me some verification from the trolley park that you lost an overshoe—then I'd give you a paper. Otherwise I can't."

I say: "But they'll just send me to you."

He says: "Well, then, write me a declaration."

I say: "What should I write?"

He says: "Write the following: 'On this day an overshoe was lost . . .' And so on. You see, I'll add a note that you've lived here all along, until the matter's cleared up."

I wrote the declaration. The following day I received a formal verification.

With this verification I went to the Lost and Found. And there, just imagine, without any trouble and without any red tape they gave me back my overshoe.

It was only when I put on my overshoe that I began to feel thoroughly moved. "Here," I think, "real people are at work! Why, would they ever have spent so much time on my overshoe anywhere else? Why, they would have. just tossed it out of the trolley. But here a whole week hasn't made any difference—they gave it back."

The only trouble is that during this week while all the fuss was going on, I lost my first overshoe. All that time I was carrying it around in a package under my arm, and I don't remember where I left it. The main point is that it wasn't in a trolley. That's the awful part, that it wasn't in a trolley. Well, where to look for it?

For all that, I still have the other overshoe. I've put it on my bureau. If things ever get gloomy again, why, I'll just look at the overshoe and they'll seem brighter. *There,* I'll think, an office is marvelously at work.

I will keep this overshoe for remembrance. Let posterity admire it.

THE ECONOMY CAMPAIGN

How the economy campaign is making out in other cities, comrades, I don't know.

But here in the city of Borisov, this campaign has turned out quite profitably.

In the space of one short winter, in just one of our institutions, fifty feet of pine firewood was economized.

Is that bad?!

Ten years of such economy—that's five hundred feet right there. And in a hundred years you could easily economize three cords. In a thousand years you could just open up shop with firewood.

And what were the people thinking about before this? Why wasn't such a profitable campaign introduced earlier? Why, it's a shame!

Now, we started this particular campaign last fall.

Our manager is just like one of the boys. He consults with us about everything and talks to us as he would to his relatives. He even shoots cigarettes at us.

So then this manager comes up to us and announces: "Well, there you are boys, it's begun . . . Pull yourselves together. Economize on something over there . . ."

But how and on what to economize is not known. He hadn't been told, and couldn't think of anything right off, so he turned to us.

We began to talk it over, on what to economize. Maybe don't pay that gray devil, the bookkeeper, or something like that.

The manager says: "If you don't pay the bookkeeper, boys, that gray devil will wind up kicking up a fuss in the trade union. That won't do. We need to think of something else."

Here, thank you, our cleaning maid Niusha brings the woman problem to our attention.

"Since that's the way things are," she says, "then," she says, "it's possible, for example, not to heat the toilet. Why waste fuel for nothing there? It isn't a living room!"

"True," we say, "let the toilet stay cold. We would save maybe fifty feet. And if it gets a little chilly, that's not so bad. Maybe a nip of frost would keep the public from holding back. It might even lead to increased productivity."

So that's what we did. We stopped heating the toilet. We started underwriting economy.

Actually, we economized fifty feet. We were just starting to economize more when spring struck.

That was just too bad!

And if it hadn't been, we were thinking, for that damn spring, we might still have economized half a cubit.

Spring pulled a fast one on us. Even so, fifty feet, thank you, that's not just mud pies.

And if some kind of pipe there seems to have snapped from frost, this could be explained by the fact that this pipe had been installed back in the tsarist regime. In general, it is necessary to pull such pipes out by the roots.

Well, we managed very well without the pipe till fall. And in the fall some cheapish kind of pipe might have been installed. It isn't a living room.

True, our friend the plumber says: "You see," he says, "the very cheapest pipe is going to cost you more than what you saved on firewood."

That, if he's not lying, is the rub.

No, it seems this economy campaign needs to be carefully thought over. Otherwise, it turns itself away.

THE ACTOR

This is a true story. It happened in Astrakhan. An amateur actor told me about it.

Here it is as he told it.

Now you're asking me, citizens, if I was an actor? Well, I was. I played in the theater. I used to fiddle around with this art. But it was simply nonsense. There is nothing outstanding in it.

Certainly, if you think about it a little more deeply, there is much that is good in this art.

You go out on the stage, let's say, and the audience is watching. And in the audience there are friends, your wife's relatives, acquaintances from your house. You look—they are signaling down there in the orchestra—as much as to say, "Buck up, Vasia, don't be shy." And you, you see, signal back—as much as to say, "Stop worrying, citizens. We're all right. We're with it."

But if you think about it a little more deeply, there is nothing at all good in this profession. It just causes a lot of bad blood.

So once we put on the play, *Who Is To Blame?* Prerevolutionary. It's a very powerful play. In this play, in one act, bandits rob a merchant right in front of the audience. A very natural scene. The merchant, you see, is screaming and kicking out with his feet. But they rob him. A frightening play.

So we were putting on this play.

But just before the performance one of the cast who played the part of the merchant got drunk. And he was in such a state, the bum, we see he won't be able to play the part. And as he goes out on stage, he gives the footlights a kick with his foot, on purpose.

The director, Ivan Palych, says to me: "It won't do," he says, "to let him out in the second act. The son of a bitch, he'll smash all the footlights. Maybe," he says, "you could take his place? The audience is dumb—they won't catch on."

I say: "Citizens, I can't," I say, "go out on the stage. Don't ask. I just ate," I say, "two melons. No good will come of it."

But he says: "Help me out, brother. Just for one scene. Maybe this artiste here will sober up after that. Don't," he says, "tear down the work of cultural enlightenment."

In any case, they persuaded me. I went out on the stage.

And I went out while the play was going on, just as I am, in my own jacket and pants. All I did was stick on a false beard. And I went out. The audience may have been dumb, but they recognized me right away.

"Ah," they say, "Vasia's come out! Don't be shy," they say, "buck up . . ."

I say: "This is no time to be shy, citizens. Right now," I say, "is a critical moment. The artiste," I say, "has really tied one on, and he can't come out on the stage. He's blotto."

We started the scene.

In this scene I play the merchant. I scream, you see, and kick out at the bandits with my feet. And it seems to me as if one of these amateurs is really going through my pockets.

I huddled into my jacket. And I sidled off from the artistes.

I try to keep them off. I even hit them in the mug. God almighty!

"Keep away," I say, "you swine, I'm asking you like a gentleman."

But they creep up and creep up all around me, just as they're supposed to do in the play. They removed my wallet (eighteen chervontsi notes) and they are reaching for my watch.

I cry out in a voice not my own: "Help, citizens, they're robbing me for real."

And this produces a full dramatic effect.

The dumb audience goes wild and claps and cries out: "Attaboy, Vasia, attaboy. Let 'em have it, old boy. Hit the devils over the head!"

I cry out: "It won't help, brothers!"

And I lash out, right across their snouts.

I see one amateur is bleeding, but the others, the bastards, just got mad and pressed me closer.

"Brothers," I cry out, "what is all this? Why bring on all this suffering?"

Then the director speaks up from behind the scenes.

"Good man, Vasia," he says. "You're playing that part beautifully. Keep it up."

So I see that crying out won't help. Because no matter what I cried out, it would fit into the play.

So I got on my knees.

"Brothers," I say, "Director," I say, "Ivan Palych. I've had it!

Drop the curtain. They're filching my last penny," I say, "for real."

Then a number of theatrical specialists see that the words are not in the play, and they come out from behind the scenes. The prompter, too, thank you, climbs out of his box.

"Citizens," says he, "looks as if they really did pinch the merchant's wallet."

They dropped the curtain. They brought me some water in a ladle. We drank.

"Brothers," I say, "Director," I say, "Ivan Palych. What's it all about?" I say. "In the course of this here drama," I say, "someone lifted my wallet . . ."

Well, they conducted a search among the amateurs. But they didn't find the money. But someone found the empty wallet backstage behind the scenery.

The money vanished. As though it had been burned.

Art, you say? I know! I was an actor once myself!

The other day they dismissed from service the old postal specialist, Comrade Krylyshkin.

For thirty years this man received foreign telegrams and noted them down in a special book. For thirty years this man served according to his powers and capacities. So there you are! His enemies conspired against him, removed him from his accustomed place, and shook him from the service, because he didn't know foreign languages.

It's perfectly true, of course, that Comrade Krylyshkin didn't know these foreign languages. As far as languages are concerned, you know the saying, "he couldn't get them through his teeth." Be that as it may, the postal service and the foreigners did not suffer the least little drop because of this fact.

It happens that a certain telegram arrives with a foreign heading; without losing his grip in the least, Comrade Krylyshkin goes over to a certain desk, to a certain girl there, to a certain Vera Ivanovna.

"Vera Ivanovna," he says, "what is this anyway? I've gone," he says, "quite weak in the eyes. Be so kind," he says, "as to tell me what this jumble is."

Well, so she tells him: from London, for example.

He takes it and writes it down.

Or he brings the telegram to a certain intellectual-type worker.

"Well," says he, "handwriting has gone to pot nowadays. Chickens," he says, "can write better with their feet. So try and guess what's written down here. I bet you can't guess."

Well, they'd tell him: "from a certain place called Munich."

"Right," he'd say, "and I thought only specialists could figure it out."

Or another time, when there was a rush, Comrade Krylyshkin would turn directly to the public: "Pssst . . . young man, come over here to the window, take a look at this—what's this scratching on here? There's a sharp argument going on among us employees. Some say one thing, others something else."

For thirty years that hero of labor, Comrade Krylyshkin, sat at his post, and there you are, they fired him.

And it was a petty reason for which Peter Antonovich Krylyshkin flunked out. You could say it was an unlucky accident. He wrote down just a little bit inaccurately the name of a city from which a telegram had arrived. This telegram arrived from the city of Paris. And on it was written in French: "Paris." Peter Antonovich, from the purity of his heart, simply interpreted it in Russian script—from the city Rachis.

Afterwards, Peter Antonovich said: "I was licked, my dear fellow. The thing is, that name struck me as Russian through and through—Rachis. And that's how the old man got into trouble."

Nevertheless, they took Peter Antonovich Krylyshkin and they fired him.

And I feel very sorry for him! Well, where are you going to get an old-time specialist in foreign languages nowadays? Should have let him stay on!

Not long ago, citizens, they were hauling a load of bricks along the street. God almighty!

My heart, you know, fluttered with joy. Because, citizens, we are building. They're not hauling these bricks just for nothing. It means a little house is being built somewhere. It's been started—spit twice and keep the evil eye off!

Maybe in twenty years, maybe even less, each citizen will probably have a whole room to himself. And if the population doesn't make the mistake of increasing too rapidly, and if they let everyone have abortions, maybe even two rooms. And maybe even three per person. With bath.

That's how we're going to be living then, citizens! In one room, let's say, sleep, in another, entertain guests, in the third, something still different . . . Isn't that something! There'll be things to do in a free life like that!

Well, for the time being, it's a bit difficult on account of the space ration, which is limited in view of the critical situation.

I was living in Moscow, brothers. I just came back from there. I experienced this crisis at firsthand.

I arrived, you know, in Moscow. I'm walking along the streets with my things. That is, nowhere in particular. It isn't as though I had a place to stay—a place to put my things.

For two weeks, you know, I wandered around the streets with my things—I grew a beard and gradually lost my things. Well, so, you know, it's easier walking without my things. I'm looking for a place to stay.

Finally, there's a house where one guy on the staircase lets me in.

"For thirty rubles," he says, "I can set you up in the bathroom. A luxurious little apartment," he says . . . "Three toilets . . . Bath . . . In the bathroom," he says, "you can live all right. Even though," he says, "there's no window. There is a door. And water right at your fingertips. If you want," he says, "you can fill the bathtub full of water and dive under, even for the whole day."

I say: "Dear comrade, I am not a fish. I," I say, "don't need to dive. I'd just as soon," I say, "live on dry land. Take off a little," I say, "for the dampness."

He says: "I can't, comrade. I'd like to, but I can't. It doesn't depend entirely on me. It's a communal apartment. And our price on the bathroom has been very strictly set."

"Well," I say, "what can I do? O.K. Grab my thirty," I say, "and let me in right away. Three weeks," I say, "I'm pounding the pavements. I'm afraid," I say, "I might get tired."

Well, O.K. They let me in. I began to live.

But the bathroom really was luxurious. Everywhere, no matter which way you move—there's a marble bathtub, the water heater, and faucets. But there isn't much place to sit. Unless you sit on the side, and then if you slip, you fall straight down into the marble bathtub.

Then I built myself a plank of boards, and I'm living.

Within a month, among other things, I got married.

My wife, you know, was young and good-natured. She didn't have a room.

I thought that on account of this bathroom she'd refuse me, and I did not foresee any family happiness and comfort, but she didn't refuse at all. She only frowned a little, and she answers: "What of it," she says, "lots of nice people live in a bathroom. And if worse comes to worse," she says, "we can divide it off. In one place," she says, "we might make a boudoir, for example; and in another a dining room . . ."

"You can screen it off, citizen. But the tenants," I say, "the devils, won't let you. Even now they're saying: No remodeling."

Well, O.K. We take things as they are.

In less than a year a little boy is born to us.

We called him Volod'ka, and we go on living. We bathe him right here in the bathtub—and we live.

And, you know, it's even going pretty well. The boy, that is, is getting bathed daily and he doesn't even catch cold.

There's only one inconvenience—in the evenings the communal tenants pour into the bathroom to wash themselves.

At this time my whole family is pushed out into the corridor.

I even asked the tenants: "Citizens," I say, "bathe yourselves on Saturdays. You just can't," I say, "take a bath every day. When," I say, "are we supposed to live? Enter into our position."

But there are thirty-two of them, the bastards. And they're

all cursing. And in case I do anything, they threaten to smash me in the face.

So what is there to do—you can't do anything. We take things as they are.

After some time, my wife's mother from the province visits us in the bathroom. She settles down behind the water heater.

"I," she says, "have dreamt a long time of rocking my grandson. You," she says, "can't refuse me this pleasure."

"I'm not refusing you. Go ahead," I say, "rock. To heck with you. You can," I say, "fill up the bathtub and go diving with your grandson."

But I say to my wife: "Maybe, citizen, you have more relatives who are planning to visit us; if so, you better speak up right now, don't torment me."

She says: "Only a kid brother for the Christmas holidays . . ."

Since I hadn't expected any brother, I left Moscow. I am sending my family money by mail.

The stove I have works very badly. Sitting around it, my whole family is always stifling from the fumes. And that housing co-operative of devils refuses to make any repairs. They're economizing. On current expenses.

Recently they had a look at this stove of mine. They looked at the flues. They stuck their heads in inside.

"Nothing wrong," they say. "One can live."

"Comrades," I say, "it's downright shameful to utter words like that: one can live. We keep stifling from the fumes around your stove. Recently, even our kitten stifled from the fumes. Recently she even got sick at the bucket. But you are saying—one can live."

The housing co-operative of devils says: "In that case," they say, "we'll set up an experiment now and have a look whether your stove is really stifling. If we stifle now after turning it up—your luck—we'll repair it. If we don't stifle—we'll excuse ourselves for the heating."

We warmed up the stove. We deposited ourselves around it. We sit. We sniff.

Here, near the damper, the chairman was sitting; here, Secretary Griboedov; and here on my bed, the treasurer.

Naturally, the fumes soon began to spread through the room.

The chairman took a sniff, and he says: "Not a thing. Don't smell a thing. Warm air's coming out, nothing else."

The treasurer, that plague, says: "The air's quite excellent. And one can sniff it. From this, one doesn't get dizzy. In my apartment," he says, "the air stinks much worse, and yet I," he says, "don't go around whimpering for nothing. But here the air is quite smooth."

"Pardon me," I say, "what do you mean—smooth? Just look how the gas is streaming out."

The chairman says: "Call the kitten. If the kitten will sit still, that means there's not a horse-radish wrong. An animal is always distinterested in a case like this. It's not a man. You can trust it."

The kitten comes. Sits herself down on the bed. Sits calmly. And why does she sit calmly? It's a clear case—she's already gotten a bit used to it.

"Not a thing," says the chairman, "we're sorry."

Suddenly, the treasurer rocks on the bed and says: "You know, I've got to hurry. I've got business to attend to."

And he goes over to the window and breathes through the chink.

And he's turning green and actually swaying on his feet.

The chairman says: "We'll be going now."

I drew him away from the window.

"It's impossible," I say, "to get expert judgment that way."

He says: "As you like. I can leave the window. Your air is quite healthy to me. Natural air, good for the health. I cannot give you any repairs. The stove is normal."

But half an hour later, when this very chairman was lying on a stretcher and the stretcher was being carried to the first-aid ambulance, I spoke with him again.

I say: "Well, what now?"

"Why no," he says, "there will be no repairs. One can live." And so they did not repair it.

Well, what's to be done? I'm getting used to it. A man isn't a flea—he can get used to anything.

THE ELECTRICIAN

Brothers, I would never argue idly as to who's the most important man in the theater—the actor, the director, or maybe the stage carpenter. The facts will out. Facts always speak for themselves.

This affair took place in Saratov or in Simbirsk; in a word, someplace not far from Turkestan. In the municipal theater.

They played opera in this municipal theater. Besides the outstanding roles of the artists, there was in this theater, among others, the electrician—Ivan Kuzmich Miakishev.

When they took a picture of the whole theater in a group in the year twenty-three, they shoved this electrician somewhere to the side: technical personnel, they say. And in the center, on a chair with a back, they sat the tenor.

The electrician, Ivan Kuzmich Miakishev, said nothing about this boorishness, but in his heart he nourished a certain grievance. The more so since on the picture they had snapped him somewhat murkily, out of focus.

And here's what happened. This evening, for opening, they're playing *Ruslan and Lyudmila.* Music by Glinka. Conductor—Maestro Katzman. And at a quarter to eight two girls he knows come up to this electrician. Whether he had invited them beforehand or whether they just showed up is not known. So these two girl acquaintances show up, flirt intensely, and just ask to be seated in the main orchestra to see the show.

The electrician says: "Well, for God's sake, mesdames. I'll go get you a couple tickets right now. Sit down here in the box."

And he himself goes, of course, to the manager.

The manager says: "Today's a holiday. There's a whole slew of people. Every seat's taken. I can't."

The electrician says: "Ah, so," he says. "Well then, I refuse to play. I refuse, in a word, to light your production. Play without me. Then we'll see which of us is more important, who you can shove off to the side and who you set in the center."

And he went back to his box. He turned off the light in the

whole theater right up to the gallery, locked up the box with all his keys—and he just sits and flirts with his girlfriends.

Now, of course, everything is in a regular muddle. The manager's running around. The public is yelling. The man in the box office is whimpering, he's afraid somebody might run off with the money in the dark. But that beggar, the first opera tenor, accustomed to occupy the center, goes up to the director and says in his tenor voice: "I refuse to sing tenor in the dark. If it's dark," he says, "I leave. I," he says, "prize my voice more than that. Let the electrician sing himself."

The electrician says: "O.K., so he doesn't sing. Spit on him. Once he gets out in the center, he thinks all he has to do is start singing with one hand, another light goes on. He's a tenor, he thinks, so there are always lights for him. Now there are *no more tenors!*"

Here, of course, the electrician tangled with the tenor.

Suddenly the manager shows up and says: "Where are those two damn girls? Everything's gone to pot on their account. I'll seat them somewhere right now, may a fiend roast them!"

The electrician says: "Here they are, those damn girls! Only it's not because of them everything's gone to pot. Everything's gone to pot because of me. Now," he says, "I'll give you light. I don't begrudge energy on principle."

And that very moment he gave light.

"Begin," he says.

So they seat his girls in excellent seats and the show begins.

Now you can figure out for yourself who is more important in the complex theatrical mechanism.

Of course, if you examine the matter dispassionately, then a tenor is of immense value to a theater. Another opera cannot go on without him. But without an electrician, too, there is no life on the theatrical boards. So that each of the two represents a singular value.

And so there's no reason to put on airs: so to speak, look at me, I'm a tenor. There's no reason to avoid friendly relations; or to take a murky picture, not in focus.

THE RECEIPT

Not long ago a very curious thing occurred.

It's all the more interesting in that it happens to be a fact. There is nothing invented here, nothing in the way of pure fantasy. On the contrary, all is taken, so to speak, from life itself.

And it's all the more interesting that the affair has some love interest in it. For this reason many will regard it playfully, as a token of what at the given moment is happening on this fairly important and actual front.

So there you are, it was two years ago in the city of Saratov that such an event took place. A certain more or less unideological young man, Serezha Khrenov, who is really an employee, or, more likely, a sorter-receiver at a certain institution, began to keep company with a certain girl, with a certain working girl let's say. Or she began to keep company with him. As for how long it had been going on, there is by now no way of figuring it out. It is only known that they came to be seen together on the streets of Saratov.

They began to stroll along together and to go out. They even began to go around hand in hand. They began to utter some various loverly words. And so on. And like that. And et cetera.

But this young dandy of a sorter once remarks to his lady like this: "Look here," he says, "Citizen Anna Lytkina. Now," he says, "we go strolling with you, and we walk together, and absolutely," he says, "we cannot foresee what will come of all this. So," he says, "be so kind, give me a receipt: to wit, in the event that, and if, a child is produced, then you have no claims whatever on the designated person. And I," says he, "possessing a receipt like that, I will be," he says, "more affectionate with you. In the opposing instance, now, I," says he, "would sooner turn away from our love with you than subsequently suffer unrest because of our activities and pay money for the upkeep of posterity."

Either she was very much in love with him or this dandy had sunk her head in his own swamp of lack of ideology; in any case, she did not stand about vainly arguing with him, but took the paper and signed it for him. "To wit, and so forth, and in the instance of which, I have no claim whatsoever on him and I will demand no money from him."

She signed this paper for him, but naturally she said a few words to him while doing it.

"This," she says, "is rather strange on your part. I have never given such receipts to anyone before. And it's even," she says, "quite an insult to me that your love takes such odd forms. But," she says, "if you want to put it that way, then of course I'll sign your paper for you."

The sorter says: "So please be so kind. I," he says, "have been sizing up our country for the past ten years and I know what comes of this."

In a word, she signed the paper. And he, not being a fool, had the signature of her charming hand notarized in the housing administration, and he stored this precious document as close to his heart as possible.

To make it brief, within a year and a half they stood as sweethearts before the people's judge, and were in the process of reporting to him on their former feeling for each other, now extinguished.

She stood in her white knitted shawl and rocked an infant.

"Yes," says she, "I really did sign it in my stupidity, but then a child like this was born, and let the father do his bit too. The more so since I don't have any work right now."

But he, the former young father that is, stands cool as a cucumber and grins into his whiskers.

To wit, what is all this talk about? What's going on here anyway? What's coming off—I don't get it. When it's all so clear and obvious, and with all that, be so kind, *here* is the document.

He triumphantly flings open his jacket, grubs about in it a bit, and pulls out his cherished paper.

He pulls out his cherished paper and, smiling softly, puts it on the judge's table.

The people's judge examined this receipt, looked at the signature and at the seal, smiled, and this is what he says: "No doubt about it, the document is correct."

The sorter says: "Why, certainly, if you'll pardon me, of course it's correct! Why, there just isn't any doubt. Every rule," says he, "is observed, and nothing is violated."

The people's judge says: "The document, undoubtedly, is correct. But there happens to be an interpretation as follows: Soviet law is on the side of the child and once and for all defends his interests. And in this given instance the child cannot be held responsible by law nor can he be allowed to suffer just because his father accidentally turned out to be such a rather sly son of a bitch. And in force of that," says he, "your afore-mentioned receipt cuts no ice whatsoever, and its only value is as a souvenir. Here," says he, "take it back and store it in your breast as quick as you can."

To make it brief, it's been half a year now that the former father is paying money.

This book is a reminiscence of a certain man, as it were; of a little-known minor poet, with whom the author has come into contact during the course of a good many years.

The fate of this man, this author, has been an extremely striking one, and in view of this, the author has decided to write these, as it were, reminiscences of him, a kind of biographical novella, as it were, not for the edification of posterity, but simply for its own sake.

One needn't always be writing biographies and memoirs of remarkable and great men, of their exemplary lives and their great ideas and achievements. Someone has to respond to the experiences of other, let us say, more average people, who have not been, so to speak, inscribed in the velvet-bound book of life.

Because the lives of such people, in the author's opinion, are also sufficiently instructive and curious. Mistakes, blunders, sorrows, and joys are scarcely diminished in their measure because the man who experienced them, let's say, failed to paint on a canvas some charming chef-d'oeuvre—"Girl with Jug"—or never quickly mastered the piano keys, or, let's say, never discovered for the good and peace of mankind some superfluous comet or star in the firmament.

On the contrary, the lives of such ordinary people are even more comprehensible, even more worthy of astonishment than, let us say, some exceptional and extraordinary deeds and extravagances of an artist of genius, a pianist or a tuner. The lives of such simple people are even more interesting and even more accessible to the understanding.

The author does not wish to imply that you are now about to see anything of such exceptional interest, anything amazing in the way of experiences or passions. No, this will be a life modestly lived; described, moreover, a bit hastily, carelessly, and with many errors. Of course, the author tried as hard as he could, but for utter brilliance of description he lacked, as it were, that necessary calmness of spirit and love for petty detail and experience. Here there will not be that calm breath of a man overconfident and secure in his convictions, the breath of an author whose fate is protected and nourished by a golden age.

Here there will not be beauty of phrase, bold turns of speech, and exclamations over the greatness of nature.

Here there will be life simply and truthfully expounded. Moreover, the author's rather ticklish nature, his restlessness and his attention to other trifles, compels him from time to time to interrupt the flow of the narrative to resolve some topical problem or some doubt.

Concerning the book's chapter headings, the author is willing to concede that the headings are a bit dry and academic—they offer little to the mind or the heart. But the author keeps these headings for the time being. The author had wished to give this book some other title, for example: *In Life's Paws* or *Life Begins the Day after Tomorrow*. But he lacked the conviction and the gall to do this. Moreover, these chapter headings have probably already had some literary currency, and the author has been unable to find the necessary wit and inventiveness for writing new chapter headings.

September 1930

One Hundred Years from Now. Of Our Time. Of Adaptability. Of Duels. Of Stockings. Prologue to the History.

There, in the distant future, let us say within a hundred or perhaps even somewhat fewer years, when everything will have been decisively shaken down and established, when life will dazzle us all with its ineffable brilliance, some citizen or other, some such citizen with mustaches, in some such, as it were, short suede suit, or let us say in his silk evening pajamas, will take, let us imagine, our modest book, and will lie down with it on the couch. He will lie down on a morocco leather couch, or *there,* let us say, on a soft hassock or armchair, cushion his fragrant head on his clean, pure hands, and, meditating softly on things of beauty, will open the book.

"Interesting," he will say, eating a piece of candy, "how they lived at that time."

And his beautiful young wife—or, since it is the future, let us say the companion of his life—sits beside him wrapped in some kind of extraordinary peignoir.

"Andreus," she will say (or, since it is the future, "Theodore"), wrapping herself in her peignoir, "would you like," she will say, "to read some poetry? You'll just jangle your nerves," she will say, "staring at the night."

And she herself, perhaps, will take from the shelf some little volume in a gay satin binding—the verses of some well-known poet of that bygone time—and will begin to read:

> In my window swung the lily.
> I am all astew . . .
> O love, O love, O my Idylly,
> I will come to you . . .

This is how the author at the moment imagines such a water-color picture, so that his pen actually drops from his hand—and he simply has no wish to write.

Of course, the author does not assert that such little scenes will really be observed in the life of the future. No, once and for all, this is improbable. It is only a momentary fantasy. One can only half entertain it. Most likely, quite the opposite, most likely it will be a very, as it were, healthy, succulent generation.

These will be bronzed men of sunshine and health, who dress modestly but simply, without any special pretension to luxury or foppishness.

Moreover, perhaps they will never read such mangy lyric verses at all, or will read them only in exceptional circumstances, preferring to them our prosaic little books, which they will take in their hands with a complete spiritual tremor and with complete respect for their authors.

As the author is about to think of such real readers, however, difficulties again beset him, and again his pen drops from his hand.

Well, what does an author have to offer such excellent readers?

Sincerely acknowledging all the greatness of our time, nonetheless the author lacks powers sufficient to present a corresponding opus, one that fully depicts our epoch. Perhaps the author has corrupted his brain with his trivial everyday *petit bourgeois* occupations, with various personal sorrows and tasks, but he simply lacks the powers for an extensive opus of the kind that might have some interest for his future distinguished readers. No, surely it is better to close one's eyes to the future and not to think of the new generations that are growing. Surely it is better to write for the readers we know.

But here again, doubts appear and the pen drops from the hand. At the present time, when the sharpest, most necessary and even unavoidable theme is the collective farm, the shortage of scales or the construction of silos—it may be that it is simply untactful to write this way, just about the experiences of people who, essentially speaking, play no part at all in the complex mechanism of our days.

The reader may simply curse the author as a swine. "Eheh," he will say, "look what this one's writing about yet! *Experiences* he's describing, the plague. Look, now," he'll say, "what's the good, he starts piling up poems about flowers."

No, about flowers the author will not write. The author will write a novella, in his opinion even a wholly necessary novella, summing up, so to speak, the life of the past; a novella about a certain insignificant poet who lived in our time. Of course, the author foresees some cruel criticism in this sense on the part of young and frivolous critics who observe such literary facts superficially.

However, the author's conscience is clear. The author does not forget the other front either and does not shun writing about absenteeism, silage, or the liquidation of illiteracy. On the contrary even, such modest work suits him once and for all.

But along with this, the author feels an extreme urgency to write his reminiscences of this man as quickly as possible, for as time passes he will step beyond our ken, and overgrown with grass will be the path along which our modest hero passed, our acquaintance, and, we might as well say it, our relative, M. P. Siniagin.

For this last circumstance permitted the author to see his entire life, all the trifling details of his life and all its events as they unfolded in the last years. His entire personal life passed, as on a stage, before the author's eyes.

Here now, the one with the mustaches, the one in the short suede suit, if, God forbid, he squeaks through to that future century, will be slightly surprised and will sink brooding into his moroccan armchair.

"Lovekins," he will say, looking down his mustaches, "interesting," he will say. "the kind," he will say, "of a personal life they had."

"Andreus," she will say in a chesty voice, "don't bother me," she will say, "for God's sake, I'm reading poetry . . ."

But, as a matter of fact, reader, this kind of a man with mustaches in those peaceful times of his just won't be able to imagine our life correctly at all. He will probably think that we were squatting in mud huts, that we ate sparrows, and led some unthinkable kind of wild life, full of daily catastrophes and terrors.

True, one must say immediately, there were many who did not have the kind of personal life just mentioned—they dedicated all their powers and all their will to their ideas and to achieving their goal.

Well, there were also those who behaved less admirably, who *adapted* themselves and tried to bring themselves into step with the time in order to live comfortably and to eat a bit more fully.

And life took its normal course. They experienced love and jealousy, and the birth of children, and various great maternal emotions, and various other excellent emotions like that. And we went with our girls to the movies. And we rowed boats. And played the guitar. And ate waffles with whipped cream. And wore fashionable striped socks. And danced the fox trot to the household piano . . .

No, so-called personal life went on in a small way, as it always goes on in any other circumstances.

And the enthusiasts of such a life, as far as they were able, adapted and accommodated themselves.

Every epoch, so to speak, has its own psyche. And in every epoch thus far it has been singularly easy or, more likely, singularly difficult to live.

Take, for example, some assuredly disturbed century, let's say, the sixteenth. What we see there—well, it seems downright unthinkable. At that time, they went out and fought duels almost every day. They hurled visitors from towers. And thought nothing of it. It was all in the order of things.

Whereas for us, with our own psyche, it is downright frightening to imagine a life like theirs. For example, some feudal son of a bitch or other of theirs, some viscount or other, or some former *Graf* at that time, goes *strolling,* for example.

There he goes, strolling, and that means his sword is at his side: and, God preserve us, if someone should shoulder him a bit or cuss him out—right away, he has to fight. And it's taken for granted.

He goes for a stroll, and on his face there isn't even a trace of misery or panic. On the contrary, he walks along, and maybe he's even smiling or whistling. Well, he'll even kiss his wife carelessly when he says good-bye.

"Well, *ma chérie*," he'll say, "I'm gonna . . . take a little stroll." And she doesn't even flinch.

"Okay," she'll say. "Don't be late for dinner."

In our time, now, a woman would burst into tears and clasp his feet, begging him not to go out on the street, or would at least beg him to secure for her a life less calamitous. But then it was done simply and submissively. He took his good sword, felt the edge to see if it had been blunted by a previous skirmish, and went out to wander around until dinnertime, with almost every chance of a duel or encounter.

The author must say that if *he* had lived in that epoch, it would have taken quite a bit to smoke him out of the house. And he would have locked himself up all his life right down to our own time.

Yes, from our point of view, the life was unattractive. But they didn't even notice this then, and just lived, spitting away. And they even went calling on those who had towers.

So that, in this sense, man is quite magnificently constructed. Whatever life offers, he finds it charming. And those who can't, undoubtedly go off to the side so as not to be trampled underfoot. In this sense, life has very strict rules, and it isn't everyone who can lie across the path and have differences of opinion.

So now we come to the main point of our story, from which, actually, this book began. The author excuses himself if he has chattered superfluously, avoiding the issue. Surely these were all necessary moments and important problems, which demanded immediate resolution.

And as for the psyche, it is quite believable. It is fully confirmed by history.

So that now, with calm conscience, we pass on to our reminiscences of a man who lived at the beginning of the twentieth century.

In the course of his narration, the author will be forced to touch on many depressing matters, sad experiences, deprivations and needs.

But the author begs you not to draw hasty conclusions from this.

There are some crybabies who would be capable of ascribing all adversities merely to the Revolution, which took place at that time.

It's very strange, you know, but the matter here concerns not only the Revolution. It is true that the Revolution removed this man from his position. Yet one might say that a life like this would be possible and probable at all times. The author suspects that such reminiscences could actually be written about any other man who lived in another epoch.

The author begs you to note this circumstance.

You see, the author once had a roommate. A former teacher of drawing. He was a man cut off. He dragged out a miserable and unseemly existence. And this teacher always liked to say: "It wasn't," he'd say, "the Revolution that undermined me. Even if there *hadn't been* a revolution, I would have been cut off all the same; either I would have been caught stealing or I would have been shot in the war, or I would have been taken prisoner and given the business. I," he would say, "have known all along what I'm in for and what life has in store for me."

And these were golden words.

The author is not making a melodrama of all this. No, the author believes in the triumphant course of life; he is sufficiently *convinced* to be able to live with a song on his lips. Surely there are many people who think of this, and rack their brains trying to come to terms with man in this sense.

Of course, this is still, so to speak, the prologue to our history. The account still hasn't been settled. They say that people first began to wear stockings only two hundred years ago.

So that everything is in its place. A good life swims into our ken.

The Birth of Our Hero. His Youth. His Philosophical Bent. His Love for Beauty. Of Tender Souls. Of the Hermitage and a Remarkable Scythian Vase.

Michael Polikarpovich Siniagin was born in the year 1888 on the Pankovo estate in the province of Smolensk.

His mother was a noblewoman and his father a distinguished citizen.

But inasmuch as the author was ten years younger than M. P. Siniagin, he can say nothing of the tangle of his early years, until the year 1916.

But inasmuch as he was always—even at the age of forty— called Michel, it is apparent that he had a tender childhood, a good deal of attention, love, and affection. They called him Michel, and truly they could not have called him anything else. All other, *coarse* nicknames were little suited to his nature, to his delicate physique, and to his beautiful movements, so full of grace, dignity, and a sense of rhythm.

It seems that he finished the Gymnasium, and it seems that he studied another two or three years somewhere or other. His education was, in any case, most outstanding.

In the year 1916, the author, from the height of his eighteen years, being in the same city as he, involuntarily observed his life and was, so to speak, an eyewitness to many important and significant changes and events.

M. P. Siniagin was not at the front for the reason that he had suffered a hernia. And at the end of the European war, he loitered about the city in his civilian's mackintosh, with a flower in his buttonhole and a fine ivory-handled stick in his hand.

He walked along the streets, always rather doleful and languid, completely solitary, muttering to himself verses that he composed in abundance, possessing as he did a worthy talent, a taste, and a delicate sensibility for all that is beautiful and fine.

Pictures of the doleful and monotonous landscape around Pskov delighted him—birches, brooks, and the various little bugs that hovered over the flower beds.

He walked out of the city and, taking off his hat, followed the play of the birds and mosquitoes with a sensitive and understanding smile.

Or, tilting back his head, he gazed at the fat clouds as they scudded across the sky, and, then and there, composed appropriate rhythms and verses about them.

In those years there was still quite a number of highly educated and intelligent people with sensitive spiritual make-up and tender love for beauty and the depictive arts.

One must say directly that in our country there has always

been an exceptional stratum of intelligentsia, to which all Europe and even the whole world has listened attentively.

And, truly, these were very sensitive appraisers of art and the ballet, and the authors of many remarkable works, and the inspirers of many excellent deeds and of great accumulations of knowledge.

These were not, from the point of view of *our* understanding, specialists.

These were, simply, intellectual, exalted people. Many of them had tender spirits. And there were even some who wept simply at the sight of a superfluous flower in the flower bed or that of a little sparrow hopping on the dung heap.

The matter is of the past, but, of course, one must say, that in all this there was even a certain, a kind, as it were, of *abnormality*. And such a splendid blossoming undoubtedly could take place only at the expense of something else.

The author does not in any great measure possess the art of dialectic and is not acquainted with the various scientific theories and tendencies, so that he does not take it upon himself in this sense to seek out the reasons and the consequences. But one can, of course, reasoning roughly, dig something up.

If, let us suppose, there are three sons in a certain family. And if, let us suppose, one son is sent to school, fed with bread and butter and cocoa, bathed daily, and has his hair combed with brilliantine, but the other brothers are given nothing and all their requirements are curtailed, then the first son may quite easily make enormous strides both in his education and in his spiritual qualities. He may even begin to produce verses, and find himself moved by little sparrows, and talk on various exalted subjects.

Not long ago, now, the author was in the Hermitage. He observed the Scythian section. And there, there is a certain remarkable, solidly built vase. And they say that this vase of which I am speaking, if they do not lie, is more than two thousand years old. It's a very stylish gold vase. Of quite exceptionally delicate Scythian workmanship. It isn't known exactly for *what* the Scythians fashioned it. Maybe to drink milk out of, or to put flowers of the field in it so the Scythian king could smell them. It isn't known; the scholars have not clarified this point. But they found this vase in a burial mound.

And then suddenly on this vase I saw some pictures—Scythian peasants are sitting around. One average peasant is sitting there, another is picking his teeth with his fingers, a third is fixing himself a ball bat.

The author looked a little more closely—*holy fathers!* Well, they were exactly our prerevolutionary peasants. Well, let us say, of the year 1913. Even their clothes were the same. The same broad shirts, belts. Long, tangled beards.

The author was a bit beside himself even. What the devil! He looks in the catalogue. The vase is two thousand years old. But if you look at the pictures, it seems like a thousand and a half less. That means, either this is an outright swindle on the part of the scientific workers of the Hermitage, or such clothes and bats were handed down like that right up to our Revolution.

The author, of course, does not mean, by all these discussions, to reflect contemptuously on the former intelligentsia of which we were speaking. No, it was simply intended to explain here *how* and *why* and *on whom* the burden of conscience lies.

That stratum, one must acknowledge, was quite a good one, and there is nothing to be said against it.

As concerns M. P. Siniagin, the author naturally has no wish to compare him with those of whom we spoke. Nevertheless, this was also a man of a sufficiently intellectual and exalted level. He understood a good deal, loved beautiful trinkets, and always went into raptures over an artistic expression. He greatly loved such beautiful and excellent poets and prose writers as Fet, Blok, Nadson, and Esenin.

And in his own work, which was not distinguished by exceptional originality, he was under the powerful influence of these famous poets. And especially, of course, under the influence of that exceptional poet-genius of those years, A. A. Blok.

The Mother and Aunt of M. P. Siniagin. Their Past. The Purchase of an Estate. Life at Pskov. The Storm Clouds Gather. The Character and Inclinations of the Aunt of M. A. Ar—va. A Meeting with L. N. Tolstoi. The Poet's Verses. His Spiritual Make-up. Enthusiasm.

Michel Siniagin lived with his mama, Anna Arkadevna Siniagina, and with her sister, Maria Arkadevna, concerning whom there will be a special passage farther on, a special description and characterization on the grounds that this worthy lady, the widow of General Ar—v, plays a by no means unimportant part in our narrative.

And so, in the year 1917 the three of them were living together in Pskov as chance visitors, who happened to be in this small but famous town for reasons quite independent of their own wills.

At the time of the war, they arrived there in order to settle down with their sister and aunt, Maria Arkadevna, who by chance had acquired a small estate not far from Pskov.

On this estate, both the elderly ladies, after lives fairly stormy and gaily led, wished to pass the time in complete peace and quiet, close to nature.

This wickedly acquired property was thus appropriately called "The Lull."

And Michel, that sufficiently mournful young man, inclined to boundless melancholy and somewhat wearied by his poetic work and by the bustle of metropolitan life with its restaurants and chorus girls and jawing noise, also desired to live peacefully in silence for a certain time in order to collect his forces and once again plunge into all that is difficult.

Everything, however, turned out differently from what had been planned.

"The Lull" had been purchased only about two months before the Revolution, so that the family did not even manage to collect themselves there with their trunks and belongings. And these trunks, feather mattresses, divans, and beds were stored for the time being in the town apartment of acquaintances in Pskov. As things turned out, Michel himself and his aged mama and auntie were to live in this very apartment for several years more.

Distinguished by their free thought and having a certain, as it were, tendency toward, and love for, revolutions, neither of the elderly ladies lost their heads very much on the occasion of the revolutionary overturn and the seizure of estates from the landowners. Maria Arkadevna, the younger sister, however, having invested nearly sixty thousands of capital in this matter, nevertheless sighed once again, dropped a curtsy, and said *the devil knew what the hell was going on,* inasmuch as it was impossible to drive to the estate she had purchased with her own blood money.

Anna Arkadevna, Michel's mother, was a fairly inconspicuous

lady. She had not distinguished herself especially with anything in her life, excepting the birth of the poet.

She was a fairly quiet, elderly lady, who quarreled little and loved to sit by the samovar and drink coffee with cream.

As concerns Maria Arkadevna, however, she was a lady of quite a different stamp.

The author had not the pleasure of seeing her in her youth; it was well known, however, that she was an extremely endearing and sympathetic girl, full of life, fire, and temperament.

But in the years of which we speak, she was already an elderly lady who had lost her figure; she was more featureless than beautiful, but very active and energetic.

In this sense, they would speak of her former profession. In her youth she had been a ballerina and had worked in the *corps de ballet* of the Marinsky Theatre.

Hers had been even a certain degree of prominence, inasmuch as she had attracted the former Grand Duke Nikolai Nikolaevich. True, he soon left her, after having presented her with a certain special moleskin palatine, beads, and something or other else. But her career had been launched.

Both these elderly ladies were to play a fairly conspicuous part in the further life of Michel Siniagin, so let the reader not take it too closely to heart nor lose his temper because the author lingers on in his description of such, as it were, decrepit and faded heroines.

The poetic atmosphere that existed in the house, thanks to Michel, evoked something from our ladies too. And Maria Arkadevna was fond of saying that she would soon apply herself to writing her memoirs.

Her stormy life and her acquaintance with many famous people would make this worth while. She personally, as it were, had twice seen L. N. Tolstoi, Nadson, Koni, Pereverzev, and other noted people, and she wished to communicate to the world her impressions of them.

And so, before the Revolution had begun, this family arrived in Pskov and remained stuck there for three years. M. P. Siniagin said, every day, that he had not the slightest intention in the world of hanging around there, and that at the first opportunity he would depart for Moscow or Leningrad. The following events and transformations in his life, however, significantly postponed this departure.

And our Michel Siniagin continued his life under the skies of Pskov, occupying himself, for the time being, with his verses, and carrying on a temporary affair with a certain local girl, to whom in his ebullience he dedicated his poems.

Of course, these poems were not stamped with genius; they were not even very original; but their freshness of feeling and their naïve uncomplicated style made them remarkable in the common pot of the verses of that time.

The author does not remember these poems. Life, cares, and sorrows have driven from his memory the fine lines and poetic rhythms, but some fragments and separate strophes have been remembered on the strength of their authentic emotion.

> Petals and forget-me-nots
> Strewn behind the windowpane . . .

The author has not retained this entire poem called "Autumn" in his memory, but recalls that its ending was filled with public sorrow.

> Ah, tell me, tell me why
> And why in nature
> Things are so? And why
> Life holds no happiness at all . . .

Another of Michel's poems spoke of his love for nature and its turbulent elemental manifestations:

> *Storm*
>
> The storm has passed
> Through the window
> White rose branches
> Exude for me a wondrous smell.
> And still the grass is thick
> With transparent tears,
> And thunder thunders from afar
> Like a bell.

This poem was memorized by the whole family, and the old ladies, reciting it daily, repeated it to the author.

And when visitors arrived, Anna Arkadevna Siniagina dragged

them to Michel's room and there, pointing to the writing desk of Karelian birch, sighed and said with her eyes moist: "Here at this desk Michel has written his best things—'Storm,' 'Petals and Forget-me-nots,' and 'Ladies, Ladies . . .' "

"Mama," Michel would say, carried away, "cut it out, will you . . . Ah, come on now . . ."

The visitors would shake their heads and, neither quite approving nor quite in distress, would touch the desk with their fingers and say vaguely: "Mmm-so. Not bad."

Some mercantile spirits would even ask then and there how much the desk had cost and, with that, would switch the conversation to other tracks, less pleasing to Michel and his mother.

The poet devoted his attention to women; being, however, under the powerful influence of the noted poets of that time, he did not concentrate his emotions on any particular woman. He loved an unreal, some kind of unknown, woman, who was brilliant in her beauty and secretiveness.

A charming poem, "Ladies, Ladies, What Makes It Nice To Look at You," revealed this relationship very well. This poem ended thus:

> Therefore I am in love with an unknown lady.
> But when this unknown lady gets to know me,
> I lose desire to gaze at a known face,
> To give her a wedding ring I lose desire. . . .

Nevertheless, the poet did carry on an affair with a certain specific girl, and in this sense his poetic genius departed somewhat from his worldly needs.

Justice, however, requires us to note that Michel felt burdened by his earth-bound affair, finding it rather vulgar and petty. In the main he was afraid that he might somehow be snared, and somehow forced to marry, and that this might force him down to the level of ordinary, everyday activities.

Michel reckoned on a different, more exclusive fate. And as his future wife, he dreamed of some amazing lady in no way resembling the girls of Pskov.

He did not imagine in detail what his wife would be like, but thinking about it, he saw in his mind's eye some little dogs, some furs, some harness and carriages. She would emerge from the carriage, and a footman, bowing humbly, would open the gates.

The girl with whom he had an affair, however, was a some-what more ordinary girl. This was Simochka M., who was that year completing her course at the Pskov Gymnasium.

A Passion. Brief Happiness. Loving the Poet Passionately. The Widow M—va and Her Character. An Unexpected Visit. An Ugly Scene. The Engagement.

Maintaining a rather careless relationship with Simochka, Michel, no matter how much he may have been attracted to her, never for a moment allowed himself the thought that he might marry her.

This was a simple passion; it was not a serious, but rather a so to speak, *preparatory* kind of love, to which the heart need not be committed. Simochka was a charming, and even a won-derful girl, whose face was, however, unfortunately, broadly strewn with freckles.

But inasmuch as she had not entered deeply into Michel's life, he not only made no protest against this manifestation of nature, but actually found it quite charming and superfluous.

They both walked out into forest or field, and, there, recited poems aloud, or ran about arm in arm, like children, delighting in the sun and smell.

Nevertheless, one fine day Simochka began to feel herself be-coming a mother, concerning which she informed her friend. She loved his first maidenlike emotional reaction, and was even able to look at his face for a long time without tearing herself away.

She loved him with a touching passion, knowing very well that, as a provincial miss, she was no match for him.

The news imparted by Simochka profoundly stunned and even frightened Michel. He was not so much afraid of Simochka as he was of her mother, Mrs. M. . . , who was well known in the town, a very energetic, lively widow, burdened by a large family. She had somewhere around six daughters, for whom she searched out husbands fairly successfully and energetically, resorting with this in mind to every imaginable cunning, threats and even direct insults.

She was one of those quite dark-complexioned, rather pock-marked women. In spite of this, all her daughters were blonde and even almost white-haired, like their father probably, who had died two years ago of glanders.

At that time there were as yet no support payments and wedding exemptions, and Michel thought with terror of the possible circumstances.

He decidedly could not marry her. Not of *such* a wife had he dreamed, and not on *this* kind of provincial life had he reckoned.

All this seemed to him temporary, accidental, and transitory. And soon, another life would begin, full of glorious joys, delights, deeds, and beginnings.

And, glancing at his sweetheart, he thought that she could not, under those circumstances, be his wife—this white-haired girl with freckles. Moreover, he knew her elder sisters—all of them, having married, quickly faded and aged. And this, too, was not to the poet's taste.

By now he wanted to take off and go to Leningrad, but the following events detained him in Pskov.

The dark and pock-marked lady, the widow M., came to his apartment and demanded that he marry her daughter.

She came on a day and at an hour when there was no one in the apartment, and Michel, whether he liked it or not, was forced to take the whole blow on his own shoulders.

She approached him in his room and, at first even somewhat shyly and timidly, informed him of the purpose of her visit.

The modest, dreamy, delicate poet, at first, even politely tried to deny her, but all his words carried little conviction and did not penetrate into the consciousness of the energetic lady.

Soon the polite tone altered to a more energetic one. Gestures followed, and even ugly words and yelling. They both yelled at the same time, each trying to drown the other out and at the same time morally establish his will and energy.

The widow M. had sat down in an armchair, but, with the blood rushing to her head, she began to pace about the room with immense strides, moving, for greater persuasiveness, a chair, the bookcases, and even the heavy trunks. Michel, like a drowning man, tried to pull himself out of the deep water, and, not succeeding, shouted and even tried physically to push the widow into another room or into the hallway.

But this widow and loving mother suddenly and unexpectedly hopped up on the window sill and declared in a powerful voice that she would that instant leap from the window into Assembly Street and die like a dog if he did not agree to this marriage. And, having opened the window, she dangled on the sill, risking at every moment the plunge down.

Michel stood stunned, and, not knowing what to do, ran now to her, now to the table, then hurled himself clutching his head into the corridor to call for help.

By now people had begun to collect on the street below, pointing with their fingers and expressing the boldest proposals with regard to the lady who was yelling and leaping about on the window sill.

Anger, outrage, the fear of scandal, and terror fettered Michel, and he now stood, demoralized by this lady's extremely energetic character.

He stood at his desk and observed his visitor with terror. She yelled out stridently like a tradeswoman and demanded an answer.

Her feet slid along the window sill, and each incautious movement might well have caused her to plunge from the second floor.

It was miraculous August weather. The sun blazed from the blue sky. A sunbeam played on the wall from the open window. Everything was familiar and beautiful in its charming ordinariness, and only the screaming and yelling woman violated the normal course of things. All aflutter, and begging her to cease her outcries, Michel gave his agreement to marriage with Simochka.

Madame immediately and willingly, then, got down from the window, and in a calm voice begged him to excuse her for her perhaps rather noisy behavior, accounting for this in terms of her maternal emotions and sensations. She kissed Michel on the cheek, calling him her son and sobbing away out of the sincerity of her emotions.

Michel stood as one submerged in water, not knowing what to say or what to do or how to escape from calamity. He accompanied the widow to the entrance, and, having succumbed to her will, quite unexpectedly even for himself, kissed her hand, and, decisively confused, expressed the hope they would meet again soon, mumbling disconnected words that had little to do with the matter in hand.

The widow, silent, majestic, and beaming, left the house, first powdering herself up a bit and touching up the lines of her eyebrows, which had been knocked somewhat askew.

Nervous Shock. Literary Heritage. A Meeting. The Wedding. The Departure of Aunt Maria. A Mother's End. Birth of a Child. Michel's Departure.

On the evening of this ill-omened day, after the departure of his uninvited guest, Michel wrote his well-known poem, subsequently set to music: "O Pine Trees, Pine Trees, Answer Me . . ."

This calmed him somewhat. But his shock had been sufficiently serious and significant so that at night Michel felt, with his heart beating wildly, uncontrollable terror, nausea, and dizziness.

Thinking that he would die, the poet, with trembling hands, dressed only in his drawers, leapt out of bed, and, clutching his heart, awakened his mama and auntie, with grief and terror. The ladies had not yet been informed of what had happened. Explaining nothing, he began to babble of death, and insisted that he wanted to arrange for the final disposition of his manuscripts. Shaking, he approached the desk and began to pull out heaps of manuscripts, sorting and arranging them, pointing out which in his opinion ought to be published and which ought to be put away for the future.

Both these ladies, no longer young, torn from their nightly routine, in their petticoats, with their hair in disorder, wandered about the room in their grief, and, wringing their hands, tried to persuade Michel, and even attempted to propel him by force into his bed, deeming it necessary to lay a compress on his heart or paint his side with iodine and thus draw off the blood which was rushing to his head. But Michel, begging them not to trouble themselves about his essentially insignificant life, insisted that it would be better for them to remember what he was saying concerning the disposition of his literary heritage.

Having sorted the manuscripts, Michel, running about the room in his underwear, began to dictate to Aunt Maria a new variant of "Petals and Forget-me-nots," which he had not yet managed to put down on paper.

Weeping and choking with tears, Auntie Maria, by candlelight, stained the paper, mangling and confusing the strophes and rhythms.

Feverish work distracted Michel somewhat from his suffering. The beating of his heart continued, but less violently, and his dizziness changed to drowsiness and complete apathy. And

Michel, to everyone's surprise, fell softly asleep while lighting a cigarette in his armchair.

Covering him with a rug and making the sign of the cross over him, the old ladies withdrew, terrified by *such* a nervous organism and by the unbalanced psyche of a poet.

The following day Michel arose refreshed and bold. But the terror of the previous evening had not left him, and he informed his relatives of his traumatic experiences.

Drama and tears were in full swing when a little note arrived from Simochka, begging him for a meeting.

He went to this meeting, haughty and restrained, not thinking, however, because he *did* have a certain basic decency, of dodging or shirking his promises.

The girl, who was very much in love, begged him to forgive her mother's unworthy behavior, adding that she personally, though she dreamed of tying her life to his, would never have risked resorting to such impudent demands.

Michel said in a reserved tone that he would do as he had promised, but that he could give no guarantees concerning their future life together. He might live in Pskov for a year or two, but in the long run he would move as quickly as he could to Moscow or Leningrad where he intended to continue his career, or where in any case he would seek out a life appropriate to his needs.

While not insulting the girl with his words, Michel nevertheless gave her to understand the difference, if not in their positions, which had been rendered equal by the Revolution, then at least in the significance of their lives.

The enamored young lady agreed to everything, looked proudly at his face, and said that she did not in any way wish to tie his life down, that he was free to act as he judged best. Somewhat reassured in this sense, Michel himself even began to say that this marriage was a matter already decided, but that *when* it would take place, he still could not say.

They departed as formerly, more friends than enemies. And Michel made his way home with steady step, in spite of the fact that the wound in his spirit could not heal so quickly.

In exemplary fashion, Michel married Simochka M. within half a year, in the winter, in January.

The forthcoming wedding had an extreme effect on the health of Michel's mother. She began to complain of life's boredom and emptiness, and her eyes grew sickly, she pined away, and she almost never got up from the samovar. The conception of marriage was somewhat different in those days than it is now, and in the opinion of old women it was a singular and decisive step and fraught with mystery.

Auntie Maria was also in a state of shock. She was somehow actually offended by the turn things had taken, and, more and more often now, said that there was no place for her here and that she would travel to Leningrad in the immediate future, where she would apply herself to her memoirs and the description of her encounters.

Michel, somewhat embarrassed by it all, paced moodily about the rooms, saying that if he hadn't given his word, he would spit on it all and would leave in whatever direction his glance took him. But in any case he wanted to let them all know that this marriage would not tie him down: he was the master of his life, he would not abandon his plans, and, probably within half a year or a year, he would follow in the footsteps of his auntie.

The marriage ceremony was performed simply and modestly.

They registered in the commissariat, and afterwards in the church. On the day of transfiguration, a modest wedding was arranged. All the relatives on both sides walked in a reserved manner, as though each in his own way had been offended in his feelings. And only the widow M., powdered and painted and in a veil, sausaged her way along through the church and through Michel's apartment where the wedding supper was held.

The widow alone spoke for all at the table, proposed toasts and made speeches and scattered compliments at the old ladies, somehow supporting by this means the gay atmosphere and the proper tone of a wedding.

The young bride blushed for her mother—and for her pockmarked face and for her penetrating voice, which gave way before no other—and sat at her place, hanging her head.

Michel, however, failed to throw off his restraint for the entire evening; a gloomy depression oppressed him, and the notion that whatever they might say, they had caught him in a trap like any common son of a bitch. And that this extremely energetic woman had captured him because of his panic, since it hardly seems likely that she *really* would have leaped from the window.

And when supper was over, after congratulations and pleasantries, he asked the widow about it, smiling crookedly and inclining an ear toward her.

"Surely you would never have leaped from the window, Elena Borisovna," he said.

The widow soothed him as best she could, swearing solemn oaths that she undoubtedly would have leaped immediately if he had not given his agreement. But in the end, with his crooked little smiles working on her temper, she said angrily that she had *six daughters* and if she got into the habit of leaping out of windows for each one of them, there wouldn't be enough windows in the building.

Michel looked timidly at her nasty, outraged face, and, having become quite confused, stepped aside.

"It's all a lie, regular egoism and deception," muttered Michel, color rushing to his face as he remembered the details.

The evening nevertheless passed pleasantly and by no means failed to honor the guests, and ordinary life began, with conversations of departure, of a better life, and of the fact that it was impossible in that city in any way to arrange one's destiny pleasantly, bearing in mind the revolutionary threat which was indeed becoming more and more menacing.

That very spring, finally, having pulled herself together, Auntie Maria Arkadevna departed for Leningrad; and soon she sent them a desperate letter from there, in which she informed them that she had been robbed on the road, and her traveling bag with part of her valuables had been carried off.

The letter was disconnected and confused—apparently the shock had reacted strongly on this lady, who was, after all, no longer young.

Around this time, quietly and unexpectedly, Michel's mother ended her life, without managing even to say farewell to anyone or to make her last dispositions.

All this acted strongly on Michel, who became a kind of quiet, timid, and even timorous man. Tears were shed, but this event was soon followed by another.

Simochka gave birth to a rather puny, but sweet child, and the new feeling of paternity, never experienced before, seized Michel, at least to some extent.

However, this did not last long; once again, he began to speak of departure, and now more realistically and decisively.

And, in the fall, having received another letter from Auntie Maria, which he showed to no one, Michel rapidly began to pack, saying that he was leaving all his movable property to his wife and child, leaving it in their full possession.

As formerly, and perhaps even more, the young lady was in love with her spouse and heard his words with terror, but did not dare to detain him, saying that he was free to act as he wished.

She loved him as formerly, and come what might, and he should know that here in Pskov there was someone who remained true to him and ready to follow in his footsteps, whether to Leningrad or into exile. Fearing that she might insist on accompanying him to Leningrad, Michel tried to lead the conversation around to other themes, but the young lady, weeping, continued to speak of her love and self-sacrifice.

Yes, she was not a match for him, she had always known that, but if he would sometime grow old or lose his legs, if he would become blind sometime or get sent to Siberia—then he could call on her, and she would respond with joy to his invitation.

Yes, she might even wish him catastrophes and misfortune— that would make them more equal in life.

Tormenting himself with pity and cursing himself for lack of spirit and for conversations like that one, Michel began to hasten the preparations for his departure.

During this time of explanations and tears, Michel wrote a new poem, "No, Detain Me Not, Young Maid," and began rapidly and hastily packing his trunks.

It was not for long that he tasted family happiness, and one fine morning, having secured official permission for his departure, he set out for Leningrad with two small trunks and a straw basket.

[The author goes on to follow Michel Siniagin through the decline of his career in Leningrad, his return home and his death.]

Nowadays, bribes aren't taken. Formerly, it was impossible to move a step without either giving or taking.

But nowadays human nature has changed very much for the better.

Bribes really are not taken.

Lately, we've been dispatching goods from the freight station.

There we are, standing at the station, and this is the kind of picture we see, in the spirit of Raphael:

The office for receiving freight. A line, naturally. Decimal metric scales. The weigher behind them. The weigher, an employee of the highest and most noble type, spouts numbers rapidly, takes notes, applies the weights, pastes labels, and issues explanations.

Only his friendly, likeable voice is audible.

"Forty. A hundred and twenty. Fifty. Take it away. Take this. Step aside . . . Don't stand there, idiot, stand on *this* side."

Such a pleasant picture of labor and rapid tempos.

Only suddenly we notice that, for all the beauty of his work, the weigher is still very demanding about the rules. He watches the interests of his fellow citizens and the state *very* closely. Not to everyone, but to every third or fourth person, he refuses to accept their freight. The container is a bit loose—he won't take it. One has only to look and one sympathizes.

Those with the loose container, of course, they hem and haw and feel badly.

The weigher says: "Instead of feeling badly, reinforce your container. There's a man loafing somewhere around here with some nails. Let him reinforce it for you. Let him knock a couple of nails through somewhere or other and let him tie some wire around it. And then come on up here at the head of the line— I'll take it."

Really, truly, a man is standing behind the office. In his hands he holds nails and a hammer. He works by the sweat of his brow and reinforces weak containers for whoever wishes. And those who are refused, they look at him with a prayer and offer their friendship and money for doing this.

But then comes the turn of a certain citizen. He's a certain blond type, in glasses. He's not an intellectual, just nearsighted. It seems he has trachoma in his eyes. Then he puts on his glasses, so it was even worse to look at him. Maybe, though, he works at the optics plant and they issue glasses there for free.

Then he puts his six boxes on the decimal metric scales.

"Weak container. Won't go. Take it back."

The one with the glasses, as soon as he hears these words, his heart drops. But before his heart drops, he pounces on the weigher, so he was almost close enough to brush his teeth.

The one in the glasses yells: "What are you doing to me anyway! I," he says, "won't take my boxes away. I," he says, "take state boxes from the optics plant. Where am I to poke around with my boxes? Where will I find transportation? And from where will I get a hundred rubles to take them back? Answer, or I'll make a cutlet out of you!"

The weigher says: "How should I know?" And at the same time, makes a gesture with his hand at his side.

The other one, because of his nearsightedness and because his lenses had gotten a bit misty, takes this gesture for something else. He flushes, remembers something long forgotten, fishes in his pocket, and digs out five rubles' worth of money in single ruble notes. And he wants to give them to the weigher.

Then the weigher turns purple at the sight of this money.

He yells: "Is *this* how you get it? A *bribe* you want to give me, you four-eyed horse?"

Of course, the one in glasses grasps right away the complete shamefulness of his position.

"No," he says, "I just pulled out the money for this reason: I wanted you to hold it while I took the boxes off the scales."

He gets really mixed up, tries some out-and-out nonsense, is about to excuse himself, and it seems even consents that they should abuse him verbally.

The weigher says: "For shame! Bribes are not taken here. Take your six boxes off the scales—they literally chill my soul. But seeing as they're state boxes, take them to that there worker and he'll reinforce your weak containers. And as far as the money is concerned, you can thank your lucky stars I don't have time to tangle with you."

Nevertheless, he calls over still another employee and says to him in the tone of a man who has just undergone a grave insult: "Do you know, just now somebody wanted to give me a bribe. Remember such nonsense? I'm sorry I was in a hurry and didn't take the money to show. Now, it's hard to prove."

The other employee answers: "Yes, it's too bad. You should have done it to advance history. Let them not think *our* blossoms are out for pollinating as they were in the old days."

The one in the glasses, who had quite crumbled away, drags off with his boxes. They are reinforced for him, brought back in a Christian manner, and once again are being weighed on the scales.

Just then it begins to dawn on me that I also have a weak container.

And since it isn't yet my turn in line, I approach the worker and ask him in any case to reinforce my dubious container. He asks me for eight rubles.

I say: "You're kidding. *Eight rubles,*" I say, "for three nails!"

He says to me in an intimate tone: "It's true, I'd do it for you for three, but," he says, "put yourself in my delicate position— I have to share up with this crocodile."

Now I'm beginning to grasp the whole mechanism.

"In other words," I say, "you share up with the weigher?"

Now he gets a little embarrassed that he let the cat out of the bag, babbles a lot of nonsense and *non sequiturs,* mutters about his small salary and the high cost of living, gives me a big discount, and sets to work.

Then comes my turn in line.

Admiring the sturdy container, I put my box on the scales.

The weigher says: "Container a bit weak. Won't go."

I say: "What do you mean? I just now had it reinforced. That guy over there with the tongs reinforced it."

The weigher answered: "Ah, pardon me, pardon me! I'm sorry. Now your container is sturdy, but it *was* weak. That's eternally clear. Pardon me means pardon me."

He takes my box and writes the invoice.

I read the invoice, and there it says: "Weak container."

"What the hell," I say, "are you gizmoes up to? With an invoice like that," I say, "they'll undoubtedly tear the whole package apart along the way and pick it clean. And with *that* invoice, I can't collect the insurance. Now," I say, "I'm wise to this whole gizmo combination."

The weigher says: "Pardon me means pardon me, I'm sorry."

He crosses out the invoice—and I go home, meditating along the way on the complex psychic organization of my fellow citizens, on the reconstruction of character, on slyness, and on that reluctance with which my fellow citizens fulfill their appointed tasks.

Pardon me means pardon me.

In our time, we have written something about bathhouses. We warned of the dangers. That is, the problem of a naked man hanging onto his tickets, and so on.

Since then, a number of years have passed.

The problem touched on by us has called forth heated discussions in the bath and washhouse trust. As a result of this, special lockers have been installed in some bathhouses, where every passenger may store his clothes, whatever they might be. After this, the locker is locked with a key. And the passenger may hasten to wash himself, rejoiced in spirit. And he may tie this key around his neck. Or, in an extreme case, he need not let it out of his hands. And thus he may wash himself.

Speaking briefly, in spite of this, you still have the kind of events that unfolded in one of our Leningrad bathhouses.

A certain technician of ours wanted, after having washed himself, naturally, to get dressed. And suddenly he notes in terror that his entire wardrobe has been stolen. Only the thief, a kindly soul, has left him his vest, his cap, and his belt.

He sobbed right out, this technician. And he stands there beside his locker with nothing on—and right away he loses all perspective. He stands beside his locker wearing the suit in which his mother bore him, and makes despairing gestures with his hands. He is stunned.

But he is a technician. Not without education. And he simply cannot imagine how he will be able to go home now. He just sways on his feet.

But then he angrily puts on the vest and cap, takes the belt in his hands, and in what you might call an abstracted manner walks blankly along the corridor of the bathhouse.

Some of the public are saying: "Thieves are stealing something in this bathhouse every day."

Our technician, his head spinning, begins to speak with a kind of old-regime intonation, using words like "sirs." Most likely, due to his great agitation, he had lost certain qualities of his newer personality.

He says: "The main thing that interests me now, sirs, is how I'm going to get home."

One of the as-yet-unwashed says: "Call the manager over here. Got to give him something to think about."

The technician says in a weak voice: "Sirs, call the manager for me."

Then the bath attendant in one of the stalls runs out and soon appears with the manager. And at this point all those present suddenly note that this manager is a woman. The technician, having removed his cap, says pensively: "Sirs, what kind of a business is this anyway! This tops it! At this point we were all presuming to see a man, but suddenly, just imagine, a woman walks in. This," he says, "that in a man's bathhouse there are such managers—this simply," he says, "is a kind of Kursk anomaly."

And, having covered his manhood with his cap, he sits down on the divan exhausted.

The other men say: "That the manager is a woman—that really is a Kursk anomaly."

The manager says: "For you, perhaps, I am a Kursk anomaly. But where I am across the hall is the ladies' section. And there," she says, "I am far from being a Kursk anomaly."

Our technician, having wrapped himself more tightly in his jacket, says: "We did not mean to offend you, madame. That you should get on your high horse. It would be better," he says, "if we considered instead what I will be going home in now."

The manager says: "Naturally, before *me,* the managers here were men. And in this male half here they were very good at their job; but in the ladies' section—everybody was going off their rocker. These managers had been dropping around *too often* there. So now it's rare that a man is appointed to this job. More and more it goes to women. And as far as I'm concerned, I'll damn well come over here when I have to, or when anything's been taken, and it doesn't hurt me a bit. But if I'm always going to run up against insults here and everybody who takes a bath is going to be calling me a Kursk anomaly, then I warn each and every one of them that if he insults me while I'm doing my duty, I'll have him carted off to the police . . . Now what was it happened to you?"

The technician says: "Sirs, why is she getting on her high horse? To hell with her. I am at a loss to see how I will get home without pants, and *she* does not allow me to call her a Kursk anomaly. And she threatens to haul me off to the police. No, it would be better if the manager were a man. At least he'd be able to lend me a spare pair of pants. The fact is the manager's a woman—and that little fact will finish me off once and for all. I am now convinced, sirs, that it will be some days before I get out of this bathhouse—just look."

The bystanders say to the manager: "Listen, madame, maybe you have a husband here in the bathhouse. And maybe he has an extra pair of pants. Then let *him* have them to wear for awhile. Because people are getting awfully excited. And they don't grasp how he's going to make it home now."

The manager says: "In the ladies' section I have complete peace and quiet, but in this half, every day, things happen, like it was a volcano blowing up. No, sirs, I am refusing to be the manager here. My husband is working in Viatka. And no pants of his can be brought into the picture. What's more, this is the second time there's been a robbery here today. It's a good thing that the first time only little things were stolen. And *who* would supply me with pants again? Then this is the way it stands, sirs: if there is anyone who has any spare pants, let him have them, and I won't even look. I'm beginning to get a migraine from all these things going on."

The bath attendant says: "All right, I'll give my spare pants again. But of course it will be necessary to sew them up a bit because they are government issue. There's a lot of stealing around here and this month they've taken away my pants. First one takes them, then another. But these are my very own."

Here the bath attendant gives our technician chintz trousers, and one of the customers gives him a jacket and bedroom slippers. And soon, our friend, restraining himself from tears only with difficulty, is arraying himself in this museumlike costume. And in this absurd manner he emerges from the bathhouse, little conscious of anything.

Immediately after his exit someone yells: "Look, there's some sort of extra vest lying there and one sock."

Then they all crowd around these discovered objects.

One says: "Probably the thief dropped this. Take a good look at the vest, see if there's anything in the pockets. Lots of people keep documents in their vests."

They go through the pockets and immediately they find confirmation there. There is a pass in the name of Selifanov, an employee in the central tailoring shop.

Now that the thieves' tracks have been uncovered, everything is beginning to come clear.

Then the manager efficiently calls the police and within two hours investigators arrive at this Selifanov's place.

Selifanov is awfully surprised and says: "Why, sirs, you have gone out of your minds. I myself had my things stolen in the bathhouse today. And I even submitted a report about it. And as far as this vest of mine is concerned, undoubtedly the thief dropped it."

So everybody apologizes to Selifanov and they say to him: it's a misunderstanding.

But suddenly the manager of the tailoring shop where this Selifanov works says: "Yes, I am persuaded that you yourself came to grief in the bathhouse. But tell me: where did you get this piece of drape that's lying on the chest? This drape is from our shop. It's missing from our place. And you undoubtedly took it. It's a good thing I was curious and came along with the investigators."

Selifanov begins to stammer disconnected words, and soon he admits he stole this drape.

So right away, they arrest him. And with this, our bathhouse story comes to an end and other matters begin. We shall pass over them in silence, so as not to confuse two different themes.

In general, both our bathhouses and the people who wash themselves in them, it would seem, could brace themselves up a bit these days and look more efficient. It could be that some special thought should be given to bathhouses on this account, so people wouldn't be able to steal property in such places of responsibility.

But here, compared with other institutions, there is still considerable lagging to the rear.

And that is too bad.

A ROMANTIC TALE

A certain young poet, of fairly attractive and determined appearance, the author of a book called *Towards Life,* fell in love at a health resort with a certain miss who wasn't a bit foolish either.

She was not a poetess but she had always had an inclination for poetry, and it was because of this that our poet quite melted away on her account.

Moreover, to clinch it, she pleased him as a type. That is, her appearance corresponded to his ideals.

She was a blonde at a time when, as he put it, brunettes predominated in the south where they were—and these evoked no poetic emotions in him. All the more since he was a lyricist, and, as he put it, a singer of the revolutionary everyday. As a result of which, he fell in love with this miss to the point of losing his mind.

But normally—he's a poet. Has a world outlook. A passionate absent-minded nature. Writes verses. A lover of flowers and good food. And every kind of beauty is accessible to him. And he understands psychology. Knows women. And believes in their mission.

He met her on a southern seacoast, where he arrived in the month of September while he was on vacation. And she also arrived there in September on her vacation.

And there they had the unexpected fortune of meeting each other. They got acquainted there. And a passion for her arose in him. And she too was exceptionally attracted to him.

And they spent the whole month there as though in a fog.

On the one hand—the sea, nature, a careless life with all their needs provided; on the other hand—an understanding that could dispense with words: poetry, shared experiences, beauty.

That is, the days flashed by as in a dream, one better than the other.

But then time struck the hour of their separation. The time of departure approached.

She returned home to Leningrad and commenced the completion of her course in some unusual sciences they were teaching there. And he arrived home in Rostov or somewhere around there. And he continued writing his poetry.

But he could not continue writing there, since he remembered her person. He languished for her. And, being a lyricist, grew melancholy.

And so, having sat out a couple of weeks in his own southern city, he suddenly made a decision on the spur of the moment, and, saying nothing to anyone, pulled out in the direction of his miss in faraway Leningrad.

It was only at the last moment that he said to his wife: "I've fallen in love with someone else. We're going to separate. I'll send you money by mail."

And with these words he was off to Leningrad. With the greater speed since she had urged him to come. She had said to him: "Come as quickly as you can. I am living here entirely alone. All by myself. I am finishing a course in science. I am dependent on no one. And here we will be able to continue our passion for each other."

And now, recalling these tender words so full of profound significance, our poet hastened feverishly with increasing speed to meet her. And he was even surprised that he hadn't thought of going to her at once, since he had such splendid promptings.

Briefly speaking, he arrived at her place and soon held her in his embraces.

And they were both so happy that it is impossible to describe.

She asked him: "Is it for long?" And he answered her poetically: "Forever!"

But he could not stay long, inasmuch as she did not live alone in the dormitory.

Not without a certain disturbed feeling, he suddenly noticed four beds in her cozy room, at the sight of which his heart almost burst asunder in his breast.

She said: "I live here with three friends who are taking courses with me."

He said: "I can see that, and I'm a bit puzzled. You told me you were living alone, as a result of which I was so bold as to come. Seems you were bragging a bit."

She said: "I told you—'I live alone'—not in the sense of a room, but in the sense of emotion and marriage."

He said: "Ah, that's it. In that case it's a misunderstanding."

After which they embraced once again and were for a long time lost in admiration of one another.

He said: "Well, never mind. I'll live in a hotel for awhile. And there we'll see. Maybe you'll finish your education, or maybe I will write some valuable poems."

And she said: "That would be just fine."

He moved over to the Hermes Hotel and began to live with her there.

But he had already spent all his money and was really at a loss as to what he would do from then on. Moreover, to his misfortune, her birthday was only two days away at the time of his arrival. That is, one day she was to have a birthday. And our poet, not knowing much of life, was already quite sufficiently upset. But suddenly, on the second day after his arrival, providing no intermission, her birthday struck. And our poet was quite at the end of his wits because of the expenses this involved. On the first day he had bought her a sweet bun and had thought: it's only proper. But having learned of her birthday, he lost his head and bought her some beads. Imagine his surprise when she, having just been presented with the beads, said to top it off: "Today, on the occasion of my birthday and dressed in these beads, I'd very much enjoy going with you to some sort of restaurant."

And to this she added something about the poet Blok who in his time also enjoyed hanging out at restaurants and *cafés* for no particular reason.

And although he answered her evasively, "Well, Blok . . . ," nevertheless that evening he found himself accompanying her to a restaurant, where his sufferings reached their greatest intensity because of the dimension of the prices, of which in Rostov he had merely heard rumors.

No, he was not miserly, our poet, but he had been, so to speak, entirely cleaned out. Furthermore, being *petit bourgeois* at the core, he could not bring himself to tell her of his extreme position. Although he did remark that he was uneasy in hotels. But she, thinking he spoke of his nervous sensitivity, said: "One must take oneself in hand."

He did try to take himself in hand. And on her birthday he had tried to straddle his poetic muse so that he might dash off a few small poems with the objective, so to speak, of selling them to some journal or other.

But it didn't work. For a long time the muse wouldn't give, and when she gave, the poet was simply surprised at what he received from her. In any case, when he read the opus it became abundantly clear to him that there could be no question of an honorarium. What he got was truly unique, and the poet ascribed this in part to his haste and perturbation of spirit.

Then our young poet, after having reflected on the vicissitudes of fortune and on the fact that poetry was essentially a dark, dark business which in no way helped one to lead an easy life, went down to the free market and sold his overcoat.

And, lightly dressed, he accompanied his girl where she wanted to go.

After this, he counted on being able to live through a couple of days easily, and he tried not to think about anything and to enjoy himself fully, skimming the cream off a brilliant evening in the restaurant. And only after that, he decided, would he ponder his situation. And somehow get out of it. If worst came to worst, he thought of borrowing a certain amount from his miss.

But on the day after her birthday an early frost suddenly struck in Leningrad. And our poet, dressed in his light jacket, began to hop about on the street, saying that he had managed to temper himself at home in the south and that was why he walked around like that with almost nothing on.

In the course of things, he caught cold. And took to bed in his hotel, the Hermes. But there they expressed surprise at his impudence and said that he should pay for his room first and then he could get sick.

Nevertheless, seeing as he was a poet, they dealt with him humanely in the long run, and said they wouldn't touch him until he recovered. After words like that the poet quite weakened physically and for six days he did not rise from his bed, fearing all the while that they would charge even a recumbent occupant the same rate for the room.

His girl used to visit him and brought him something to eat, but what was to become of him was beyond comprehension. And perhaps he would not even recover.

The poet had thought that after he got better he might once again assault his muse with cannon fire. But she quite refused to let him compose anything sensible. And the poet lost heart to such an extent that he promised himself that in the event he managed to escape in one piece from the predicament he had created, he would straightaway find a job so that he would never in the future have to depend on pure art.

True, after the hotel manager had been visiting him in his room, the poet tried yet a third time to reach his inspiration, but except for three lines he could not squeeze anything out:

> At which time I gaze into the sky
> And I hear there chirring of propellers
> And someone floats down in . . .

But then the words "in a parachute" could not be forced into the measure of the line. And he could not bring himself to say "with parachute," since he didn't know aeronautical terminology. After this, the poet decisively succumbed to spleen and abandoned arms.

His dreams of borrowing something from his sweetheart also turned out to have been unrealistic. To his surprise, at the very moment he had decided to tell her about all this, she herself said something to him about it, but only on her own account and not on his. So that the poet, weakened as he was from his illness, did not at the moment even grasp the full asperity of his situation. She said there was still about a week to go before she received her allowance, and if he could swing it, he should lend her something, especially since she had bought his food while he was ill.

He said: "Certainly."

And after she left, he decided to liquidate his covert-cloth suit.

He sold the suit at the market, settled his affairs in part, and, dressed in shorts and a sweat shirt, he suddenly appeared one fine day at our office in the Leningrad Literary Fund, where he told us this tale of his.

And for this story we gave him a hundred rubles to buy a ticket to get back to his home town.

And he said to us: "This sum is enough for me to get home on. But I would like to stay here another week yet. I'd very much like to do that."

But we said to him: "You go now. And best of all settle yourself down to a job. And along with that, write some good poems sometimes. That would be the right way out for you."

He said: "Why, that's just what I'll do, if you like. And I agree

that young authors, besides their poetry, should have something
else to do for a livelihood. And that's what's being done. And it's
right that there should be a campaign to promote this."

And after having thanked us, he withdrew. And we at the Literary Fund thought in the words of the poet:

> O, how divine is the union,
> In which one has been born for the other.
> But people born for each other,
> Alas, join in a union quite rarely.

On this note our tale of the beginning poet comes to a close,
and another, even more unusual tale is about to begin.

A certain by no means bad-looking young person, a well-developed brunette, decided during the course of this year that she must without fail get rich.

That is, not that she wanted to acquire those fabled riches that once used to accumulate among millionaires and speculators in the lands of capital.

No, naturally, that wasn't what she wanted. That is, generally speaking, she had once wanted exactly that. Only she hadn't been able to grasp how to bring it off. And so, she decided to confine herself to the realm of the possible.

She wanted to have some kind of blue Ford car with, you know, a steady chauffeur. With a standard little *dacha*. A bank account. And naturally, a notable position for her husband so she could travel in the best circles and see everyone.

But her husband was an ordinary engineer. That is, he was a hydrologist. They have something to do with water. That being the case, he, naturally, was not going about projecting special kinds of pillars for which he might be rewarded with money and premiums as the creator of new ideas and perspectives.

Speaking briefly, he lived modestly on his seven hundred. And, being enthusiastic about his work, he was to a certain degree fully satisfied.

This sum did not satisfy his wife. And being an idle and empty woman, with a weakly developed world outlook, she dreamed of fabulous luxury and so forth.

And someone told her that in general, as things went, writers lived not at all badly. That some of them have typewriters, separate apartments, *dachas,* and sometimes, why, even automobiles. And let her search something out for herself among this layer of the population.

But Liza did not know where to look. And for this reason she latched onto the first author who came her way, not without a certain haste.

Just between us, though, this engineer of human souls, as luck would have it, seemed on occasion an insubstantial fellow. And to top it all off, he was addicted to alcohol. Thanks to which he expressed the wish, after a month was out, that she find a job somewhere. Inasmuch as he had little hope for her from himself, creating, as he did, weak books of little artistic worth which did not reflect in full measure the greatness of the epoch.

In general, he did not justify her hopes, and so she left this degenerate of hers, having lost in the process her faith in literature and in her own powers.

In any event, she returned to her husband. But although she returned, she had not lost her passionate hopes and only waited for something to happen to her as soon as possible.

And, lo and behold, at this point she made the acquaintance of a certain foreigner.

He was introduced to her in a restaurant. And she was told he was a tourist. And that he was living in a hotel, but that, not satisfied with this arrangement, he hoped to find a room in a private home for about two months. Did she by chance have one?

And although she had no such thing, nevertheless she rejoiced exceedingly and decided to send her saintly mother off somewhere for two months, if only that she might not miss this spoiled foreigner who could not live in noisy, uncomfortable hotels amidst ringing of bells and intrusive chambermaids.

Broadly speaking, she arranged a room for this tourist, this delicate aristocrat, in her apartment. And although her husband would not permit it, she stood her ground. And *he* moved over to their place, with his dazzling wardrobe, Eau de Cologne, photo apparatus, clothes hangers, and so forth.

And so Liza, believing that a crucial moment in her life had arrived, took up with this foreigner.

And *he* loved her exceptionally. And he made her a formal proposal. To this she agreed, and what's more, it even made her very happy, to such an extent that it's quite impossible to describe.

And then she threw over her husband at once. And began to live with *him* in her mother's room.

And although her foreigner spoke scarcely any Russian, and she, on the other hand, spoke only Russian, nevertheless this scarcely served as a barrier to their mutual international happiness.

In general she was happy and dreamed of Paris, London, the Mediterranean Sea, and so forth.

But within a month's time, the tourist, having learned to express himself more tolerably in Russian, once had a special talk with her in this language. And from this conversation it emerged that he was by no means planning to depart for Europe. On the contrary, he even wished to settle down here. And that because of the difficult circumstances of the depression, a certain enterprise had been forced to close down over there in Europe, and that he had even been left, as it were, without a job. For that reason he had arrived in the Soviet Union, hoping to find something here in the way of his specialty.

Paling visibly, she requested him to repeat these coarse Russian phrases of this and that. And he told her the same thing all over again, adding that he had great hopes of setting himself up here, inasmuch as he was a specialist in effervescent and mineral waters. And in the Soviet Union right now, *everyone* needs these. And if he managed to set himself up here, then within a year they could boldly take a trip to Paris, if that was what she still wanted.

Then she flared up and asked him, not without venom, why, given his position, simply that of the unemployed, he called himself a tourist, and why he didn't abandon his delicate habits, and why he didn't live in a cheap room but instead confused those around him with his appearance and behavior, permitting them in their ignorance to draw such conclusions.

Then he pointed out to her that he really had moved out of the hotel once and for all, and moved over to their place for the sake of economy, so to speak.

Then she wept and said that if this were so, everything she knew about the way the world was made had become confused in her weak brain. And that she had been of a completely different opinion concerning tourists. She had thought that they all, without exception, traveled for the sake of interest and curiosity, and not for the reason that *he* had come. She had never, you see, had anything to do with the unemployed. Of course, here in Russia, we don't even have any. And, lo and behold, *she* had found one. Why, she'd be better off marrying one of our clerks and at least receiving his hundred rubles a month.

And because she felt insulted and humiliated, she wept for three days. And ordered the tourist to move back to the hotel, inasmuch as her mother was living in the streets.

In general, she broke off with him, all the more so since her first husband had cut production costs in his job and had received a ten-thousand-ruble premium for this, as was announced in the newspapers.

Her husband, however, not yet knowing that she was going to return to him, had given away this money to a construction project. He was a great enthusiast and for the most part indifferent to money. So he just gave away this sum to the state.

When she returned and heard about this, she was so upset that her husband was afraid she might have a breakdown. And then, she, having calmed down somewhat, once again resolved in her heart to find something better.

And someone told her that that ill-fated writer with whom she had lived not long ago, and with whom she had not been happy, had unexpectedly struck it rich. He had given up writing his weak pieces and, suddenly and unexpectedly, had written a play, which, they say, for power, was not far beneath Boris Shakespeare or something of that sort. And that he was now, literally, splendidly at work.

She bewailed the fact that she had not anticipated this lucky streak, and wished once again to take up with this dramaturge. But he, it seemed, already had two families and was relatively happy.

Thanks to this acquaintanceship, she then began to move somewhat closer to the world of the theater, and here she found great possibilities. To top it all off, she became acquainted with a certain stage comedian, who, it was said, earned very, very large sums of money.

She had wanted to take up with this comedian at once, but at the last moment had become frightened of some kind of swindle or dirty trick on his part, as had been the case with the tourist, or something like that.

And she did not marry him, but decided that, if she could make it, she would become an artist herself.

And she began to study character dancing, so she could somehow go out on the stage and earn money like other people.

But as a result of her chronic unpleasantness with the tourist and the writer, her doctor discovered a neurosis of the heart and a nervous rash on her body. And so she had to learn how to sing.

And now she sings. And she's already begun to earn money regularly in closed concerts and in rest houses.

But she informed her husband that she would no longer live with him now. That, formerly, she had had old-fashioned views about money and matrimonial relations, but that now, since she was receiving up to a thousand rubles and more for her singing, she had fully re-educated herself and was even satisfied, and would do nothing to undermine the independence of women.

But her satisfaction lasted only so long as they did not tell her about her tourist. She was told that this foreigner of hers had found a very good place here in his rare specialty, that he received an excellent salary, that he had married a certain girl and had left with her for his native land in order to arrange his affairs and bring an automobile back here.

They told her that she really must have negotiated badly with him in Russian, since she had let such a splendid opportunity slip by.

This news, now, was really difficult for her to bear. She even lost her voice for awhile.

But within two weeks she had recovered, and now she is singing again, about as well as she can. But she still has the rash on her skin.

That's the kind of girls there are. And what can be done with them, if they want to make money in a way that isn't done among us.

As for the fact, after all this she became an artist—very good for her, but quite mediocre for the public.

And, naturally, in such cases it's always better to dance than to sing. And young persons should respect this ardent wish of the public.

AN AMUSING ADVENTURE

The wife of a certain employee, a fairly young and quite attractive lady, from a *petit bourgeois* family by birth, fell in love with a certain actor.

He was an artist of drama and comedy. And so, you see, she fell in love with him.

Either she had seen him on the stage, and he had subdued her with the splendor of his role, or, on the contrary, she had never seen him act, but he, perhaps, simply pleased her with his artistic mannerisms; the fact remains that she fell very much in love with him. And for a while she didn't even know what to do: to leave her husband and go live with the artist, or not leave her husband, but simply have an affair with the actor without attempting to build her life over again.

Seeing, however, that the dramatic actor didn't have very much —no position, and nothing very special—she decided not to leave her husband. All the more, since the artist himself was not exactly burning with the desire to marry her, being a man already burdened with a numerous family.

But since they loved one another, they managed to get together from time to time.

And he called her on the telephone and she ran down to watch him at rehearsals to see how smartly he performed in his role. As a result of all this, she fell even more strongly in love with him and dreamed of meeting him more often.

But since there really wasn't any place for them to meet, they, literally like Romeo and Juliet, began to meet on the street or in the movies, or ran off to a *café,* in order to be able to exchange some tender words.

But these brief encounters of theirs, naturally, satisfied them but little, and they were constantly grieving that life treated them shabbily, and that they didn't even have a place where they might speak of their mindless love.

She couldn't go to his place, naturally, because the artist was a family man.

And as far as his going to her place was concerned, she occasionally invited him when her husband was at work. But after having come a couple of times, he categorically refused to do so any more.

As a high-strung man, gifted moreover with an oversensitive, artistic imagination, he was simply afraid of being found at her place, thinking, well, wouldn't it be *something* if the husband walks in and starts big talk, with shooting and all that.

And under the pressure of such thoughts, the artist, when he was a guest at her place, so to speak, behaved abnormally and was generally half-dead with fear.

So she naturally stopped inviting him, seeing the man was in the throes of spiritual torment and out of this world entirely.

And so she says to him once: "Look here! If you want to see me, go to my friend's place your next free day."

The dramatic artist says: "Now *that's* what I call splendid! As you know, my profession demands fine nerves, and I," he says, "can't help feeling a bit tense at your place."

Her closest friend was named Sonechka. A very dear person, not uneducated. Seems she'd been in the ballet.

And our lady's husband fully approved of this friendship, saying that he could not hope for a better friend for his wife.

And so, our ballerina, after some ardent questioning, permitted her friend to use her place for conversations with the man she loved.

And so, on the morning of his day off, our artist dressed himself in the very best he had and hastened to his tryst.

One should say, however, that in the trolley a little episode occurred, a run-in with his neighbor. Well, generally speaking, some light insults were exchanged, a few yells and so forth. As a result of which, our artist, a man unable to restrain himself much more than he should, lost his temper a bit. And when his neighbor, after their exchange of insults, left the trolley, our artist, unable to hold himself back, spat at him. And was very glad that the trolley started up right away and his offended neighbor lost the opportunity of pursuing him as he wanted.

The mood of our artist was not spoiled, however, by this encounter. He met his soul mate and they went together to her friend's place, part of a communal apartment, a small but comfortable room, the key to which was now in their hands.

And so they went into the room, sat down on the divan so they might speak of their future life, but suddenly—someone knocked on the door. The young lady signaled the artist not to call out, but the artist remained silent even without her advice.

Suddenly a voice issued from behind the door: "Tell me, will she be back soon?"

Having heard the voice, our lady grew terribly pale and whispered to the actor that it was her husband's. And her husband must have seen them on the street and had followed them.

The dramatic artist, having heard of a similar pretty story, simply went into a state of shock and trembled all over and, holding his breath, stretched out on the divan, looking at his soul mate with profound melancholy.

But the voice behind the door says: "Then I'll write her a note. Tell her I was here."

And so, our lady's husband (and it really was he), after writing the note, slipped it under the door and left.

Our lady, very much surprised, instantly seized this note and began to read it. After which, she began to weep bitterly, to wail and throw herself on the divan.

The dramatic artist, brought back to consciousness somewhat by the sounds of his lady's voice, also read this note, not without surprise. It said: "Dear little Sonechka. By chance I got off early and hastened to you, but alas, you weren't in! I'll be back at three. A big kiss. Nicholas."

Our lady, through tears and weeping, says to the artist: "What could this mean? What do you think?"

The artist says: "Most likely your husband is having an affair with your friend. And he came here for no other reason than to relax a bit from his family life. Now your conscience should be at rest. Let me have your tender little hand."

And he was just about to lift her tender little hand to his rough lips, when a violent knock at the door is heard. And behind the door, the imperative voice of her friend: "Ah, open up right away! It's me. Was anyone here besides me?"

After hearing these words, our lady instantly burst into tears, and, having opened the door, gave her friend the little note, weeping all the while.

Having read the note, she was a little embarrassed, but said: "There's nothing surprising in all this. Since you know, I won't keep anything back. On the whole, I'd like you to leave instantly, since I'm expecting someone."

Our lady says: "What do you mean 'someone'? It's quite clear from the note that it's my husband you're expecting. A fine business—to leave at such a moment. Why, maybe I'd like to see how that rascal crosses the threshold of this hangout."

The young man, whose mood had been utterly spoiled by all these scrapes, wanted to leave, but our lady in the heat of her temper would not permit him.

She said: "My husband will show up at any moment, and then we will cut through this Gordian knot."

Hearing these words, so close to military terminology, the artist picked up his hat and began to say good-bye even more energetically and to leave. But at this point the friends began to exchange insults and to quarrel about whether he should go or not.

At first, both the friends wanted him to stay until the husband arrived, as material evidence. The first, in order to show her husband what kind of a bird this friend was, letting them use her room; the second, to show him what kind of a wife he had.

But after awhile they changed their minds. The friend suddenly did not wish to compromise herself, and the wife did not wish her husband to set eyes on her. Having talked this over, they ordered our artist to get out instantly.

The latter, quite content with the turn the argument had taken, had just begun to say good-bye when suddenly there was a knock on the door. And the husband's voice said: "Dear Sonia, it's me! Open up!"

At this point, a certain panic and confusion spread through the room.

The dramatic artist instantly suspended his breath and, falling into a fearful melancholy, wanted to stretch out on the divan so that he might create the role of a sick or dying man, but soon reflected that in this horizontal position he might be taken for someone lying frivolously on a divan, and so they might open fire on him all the more readily.

Impelled by this thought, he began to scurry about the room, knocking against everything with his feet and producing a terrible noise and clatter.

The husband behind the door was exceedingly surprised at the delay and clatter and began to pound on the door with increased energy, thinking something strange must be going on in the room.

Then the friend says to the artist: "This door here leads into my neighbor's room. I will now open it for you. Go through it. From there, you will find a door to the corridor and staircase. My best wishes!"

And she herself quickly opens the latch on the door and asks the artist to get out as quick as he can, all the more urgently that the husband, having heard all the noise in the room, was beginning to tear the door from its hinges in order to get in. Then our artist escaped the bullets, into the neighbor's room, and he would very much have liked to get into the corridor, when he suddenly noticed that the door to the corridor was locked on the outside, apparently with a padlock.

The artist would have rushed back to tell the ladies that he was in a critical position—the door was locked and he couldn't get out. But it was already too late.

The husband had been let into the room and a conversation had arisen there, into the midst of which the projection of the artist would have been most undesirable.

Then the artist, by no means a stolid man, felt himself instantly drained of strength because of the great number of events he had been through, and, feeling physical lassitude and dizziness, stretched out on the bed, assuming he was quite safe here.

So, you see, he stretches out on the bed and thinks various desperate thoughts—of this, that, and in particular of the foolishness of love's impulses. And suddenly he hears someone in the corridor turning a key in the lock. In a word, someone is standing by the door and would no doubt presently enter the room.

And suddenly the door is really opening, and on the threshold appears a man with a little basket of pastries and a bottle of wine.

Seeing the man lying on his bed, his mouth gapes in surprise, and, not getting it at all, he wants to slam the door behind him.

The artist begins to excuse himself and to chatter away in a confused fashion, and suddenly he notices with terror that the master of the room, the man who had just come in, was none other than the very man with whom he had swapped insults that morning and at whom he had spat from his seat in the trolley.

Unable to rely on his legs, our artist, like a child of tender years, once again stretches out on the bed, thinking that if worst came to worst it was after all only a dream which would soon pass away and then a splendid life would begin without any special unpleasantnesses or scrapes.

The man, whose surprise had given way to anger, had come in and says in a mournful voice: "What's going on here, gentlemen?

I'm expecting a visit from a friend at any moment, and here, just look, some kind of creep has stretched himself out in my room. How the hell did he get in? Through a locked door?"

The artist, seeing that his arms aren't being broken and no one is beating him up, says with some rise in spirit: "Ah, pardon me! I will leave this moment. I only lay down for half a second to take a little snooze . . . I didn't know this was your bed . . . So much has happened, I was feeling a bit dizzy . . ."

At this point the master of the room, whose surprise had again given way to anger, began to yell: "But this is really rude! Just look at him, he was lying with his feet up on my bed. Why, I wouldn't even let a friend of mine put his feet up there. There's something new for you! What a scoundrel!"

And he runs up to the artist, grabs him by the shoulders, and is literally pulling him off the bed—when suddenly he sees that the person of the artist is already known to him from the events of that morning.

At this point there follows a slight pause.

The master, beside himself, says: "Ah, so you've fallen into my hands, have you, fish face?!"

And he makes to grab him by the throat.

But just then there is a tender knock on the door. The master says: "Well, you can thank your lucky stars that the lady I've been expecting has arrived. Otherwise, I'd have made mincemeat out of you."

And taking the artist by the collar, he drags him to the doorway in order to heave him into the corridor like dirty laundry, to which object the artist fully consents and is even pleased.

But suddenly the door opens and on the threshold appears the quite attractive lady whom the master had been expecting and who had arrived, in a certain sense, as the savior of our ill-fated artist.

Our artist, however, on catching sight of this lady, simply staggered back from astonishment and even began to sway to and fro —inasmuch as the lady who had just come in was none other than his wife.

And speaking of coincidences, this was really something quite striking.

At this point, our artist, who had been extremely silent for the last two hours, suddenly began to spout and kick up a row, demanding explanations from his wife, and what did this mysterious visit mean.

His wife began to weep and wail and to say that this was her co-worker and that she really did visit him occasionally to drink a little tea and eat some pastries.

The embarrassed co-worker said that since they were even now, they might as well shake hands on it and the three of them sit down and have some tea. To this, the actor erupted with such violent abuse and such outcries that his wife went into a fit of hysterics. And her co-worker turned pugnacious again, remembering the humiliation of having been spat at.

And then all the neighbors ran in to see what was going on.

Among those who arrived was our lady with her husband and friend.

Having learned everything that happened, all six gathered in the room and took counsel as to what they should do next.

The ballerina spoke as follows to her friend: "It's very simple! I will marry Nicholas. The artist will marry you, and these two co-workers will also make a happy couple, working together as they do in one institution. That's the way we should do it."

The co-worker who had been visited by the artist's wife says: "Thanks, I'm sure! It seems she has a heap of kids, and I'm supposed to marry her. It's even supposed to be very simple."

The dramatic artist says: "I will thank you not to insult my wife. The more, since I have no intention of just giving her away to the firstcomer."

The artist's wife says: "Well, I wouldn't live with him anyway. Just look at the shape of his room! How could I live here with four kids?"

The co-worker says: "Why, I wouldn't let you in here with the children if you tried to ride in on a cannon ball. She's got a scoundrelly husband like that, and, to top it all off, she wants to take my room away. I see!—one of them's stretched out on my bed already."

Sonechka of the ballet says conciliatorily: "Let's work it this way, then. I will marry Nicholas, the artist and his wife will remain as they were, and we'll marry this stupid co-worker off to Nicholas' wife."

The co-worker says: "Thanks! Still no easier. Suppose I hitch up with her. Open your ear flaps wider. Why, I am seeing this shabby figure for the first time. How do I know, maybe she's a pickpocket?!"

The artist says: "You are requested not to insult our ladies. I consider that this is the right way out."

Our lady says: "Well, it's not, you know. I don't intend to leave our apartment for anyplace. We have three rooms and a bath. I'm not ready to go hopping off to any of these communal outfits."

Sonechka says:

"Because of three scoundrels, all our couples are breaking up—that's the way it would work fine. I with Nicholas, she with that one. And these as they are."

At this point an exchange of coarse abuse commenced among the ladies on account of this or that. After which, the men, bolstering their spirits, decided that everything should remain as it was before. On this they went their separate ways.

However, entirely as they were before, things did not go. Soon afterward, Sonechka married her neighbor, the co-worker of the artist's wife. And from time to time our artist came to visit her as a guest; she found him very attractive on account of his soft, defenseless character.

But our lady, disillusioned in the artist's domestic character, fell in love with a certain physiologist. As far as Nicholas is concerned, it seems he has no more romances now but buries himself entirely in his work. Nevertheless, he sometimes meets Sonechka, and on his day off he often takes little trips with her into the country.

The young woman of today does not like to hear diminutives. She doesn't like to hear about her "little mouth" or "little hands" or "little feet."

It makes her angry. And it can even, I think, produce an explosion.

A certain person put it to me this way: "What the devil does that mean, 'little feet.' I," she says, "take solid size nines, but you," she says, "have it all your own way. You're a scoundrel," she says, "and not a man. You," she says, "are ruining my life with your stupid sentimentality."

To put it frankly, I was quite taken aback at such words.

She says: "In the old days," she says, "spoiled ladies or countesses or such used to adore sentimentality like that in their boudoirs. But I," she says, "I spit on men like you."

"There you are," says I, "thank you. How," says I, "am I to interpret your words."

How, indeed, interpret her words, when she never called me once on the phone from that time on, and, when she met me in passing, never even said hello.

But it's true: the young women of today like something bold, heroic. They, I have noticed, are not pleased by anything run-of-the-mill. They would like a man to be a flyer, or, to stretch a point, at least an airplane mechanic. Then they blossom forth, and you can't recognize them.

But it would be interesting to ask them: What do you think, should every man be a flyer or an airplane mechanic?

Naturally, I'm not saying that the profession of airplane mechanic isn't, to a certain degree, an amazing one, or that it doesn't evoke various emotions in the beholder. Only, as I said before, it's impossible for *everybody* without exception to go flying around in the sky.

Some have to occupy more modest posts on the ground, in offices and so forth.

Then they also like cinema operators. Here, already it might be said that *nobody* knows why. The guy turns a little crank and thinks he's Napoleon.

Arctic explorers also evoke feminine admiration. Well, there's ice there. Snow. Northern lights. Just think!

Generally speaking, I've been married four times, and none of my wives *ever* exactly did a little dance for me. Well, the first two ran off with airplane mechanics. The third got together with a cinema operator. Well, as it is said, that's the way things go. But the fourth marriage really surprised me with its unexpectedness. And I, as the citizen who went through all this, feel obliged to warn other men against making similar marriages.

I was acquainted with a certain person. And decided to marry her. But I warned her honorably: "Keep in mind," says I, "I don't go fluttering around the sky. And for your pleasure," I say, "I can scarcely be expected to jump off the roof in a parachute just any old time. So that if you are enamored with the flying profession, then I, as it is said, have no further questions for you. And then we will withdraw the question of marriage."

She says: "Profession plays no part. And as far as flyers are concerned, I am indifferent to them. Only one thing matters to me, and that is that our union should be, up to a certain point, a free one. I do not approve of the stifling of personality. Before you came along," she says, "I was married for seven years, and my husband wouldn't even let me go to the theater with anyone. And I would like our marriage to be based on comradely circumstances. And if, for example, you happen to be attracted to someone, I will say nothing to you. And if I should meet someone who struck my fancy, you would not reproach me either. Then our marriage will have greater endurance, founded as it will be on the intelligent understanding of two loving hearts. And as far as my husband having some insignificant profession, why, that's all to the better. At least he'll know his place, and not demand the impossible from me."

I say to her: "I am getting married for the fourth time," I say. "As for intelligent understanding, I've had a lot of experience. One," says I, "doesn't like to hear diminutives. Another," says I, "runs off with a cinema operator. Now, you," says I, "propose something else to me. But," says I, "since you've taken my heart, let it be as you wish."

So, you see, naturally, we get married and live in various apartments. And everything goes well with us, and we are very close to each other. But, suddenly, within a week, she is attracted to a certain acquaintance of hers who has come back from the Arctic.

She says to me, according to our agreement: "If you wish, let us separate. But if you still have some feelings for me, then stick to our conditions. All the more so since my friend is leaving on an expedition again soon, and then you and I will make out together just like before."

So I, like a fool, am expecting him to leave in a couple months or so. And finally our neighbor-lady says: "You'll wait in vain You're through: she'll never come back to you."

But another month passes and suddenly my wife returns with these words: "I've left him for good, you see. The more so since he's gone off on one of his northern trips."

I say: "But now certain obstacles have arisen on my side. I," I say, "have been having an affair with our neighbor. But if you have any feelings left for me, then," says I, "I'm agreed to break off with her."

And so I began to break off with our neighbor. And just when I had broken off with her, I look: after a month of quiet domestic life, my wife has again run off, this time with a friend and fellow explorer of the guy who left for the Arctic. For some reason they left this polar gent behind. And she was attracted to him. And began to live with him.

So I, according to our conditions, am waiting a few months when suddenly I find out that she's about to have a child by him.

I say to her: "It's an interesting marriage we've got. These polar explorers," I say, "these airplane mechanics, and cinema operators are literally dragging me off my feet."

She says: "If you wish—wait till he no longer loves me or till the child grows up a bit. And then we will continue our conditions. But if you don't wish—do as you like. In general," she says, "you've been *devouring* me with your eternal whining, and you're never satisfied. I," she says, "don't depend on you. My *heart* advises me which contemporary men I should love and which I should hate. Not only," she says, "do you not wear the badge 'Ready for Labor and Defense!' but you just barely passed the first-aid course and for laughs. I'm not saying that you should be a Voroshilov sharpshooter or that you should go exploring somewhere in the north. It isn't these professions," she says, "that are dragging you off your feet. It's simply your unattractive character, so far removed from our contemporary life. There are no millionaires nowadays, and such likes can't cover up their wretchedness with capital. So it's necessary to improve your character if you want to earn a woman's love."

I say: "First, one doesn't like me to use diminutives; now, another bears another man's children. And to top it all, reads me lectures yet."

Suddenly she opens the door to the neighboring room and yells out diminutives: "Vanichka, this type here has started making scandals for us again. And although he's my husband, I wish you'd heave him to the devil. On his account," she says, "I feel I'm about to break out in hysterics."

And, suddenly, the friend of that guy who went off to the Arctic steps into the room. Real healthy-looking, tempered by the north wind. And to top it all, he's a parachutist, with a badge.

"Young man," says he, "why are you making trouble?"

I said good-bye to him and left with the intention of writing all this down so that other nonflying men might take warning against getting themselves into such an airtight hole, as it is said.

Personally, I'm against such free marriages. I'm in favor of a stronger kind of marriage based on mutual emotion. But where to find this emotion if I have never even seen a parachute? And have never lived in the far North?

I guess I'll just have to try and be a hero, so I can compare favorably to the rest of the population.

Once upon a time I am walking along the street, when, suddenly, I notice that women do not look at me.

Time was when you used to go out on a street like that, flashy as a beaver, as it is said, they'd look at you, send glances through the air, sympathetic smiles, chuckles, and grimaces.

But at this point, suddenly, I see—nothing of the kind!

Well, now, think I, that's too bad! After all, I think, a woman *does* play a certain role in personal life.

A certain bourgeois economist, or maybe he was a chemist, once expressed an original idea to the effect that not only our personal life, but whatever we do, is for women. And struggle, fame, wealth, honor, change of apartments, and the purchase of an overcoat, and so forth and so on—all this is done for the sake of a woman.

Well, no doubt he exaggerated it a bit, he was talking through his hat to amuse the *bourgeoisie*; but, as far as personal life is concerned, I am completely in agreement with this.

I agree that a woman plays a certain role in personal life.

After all, suppose, as it happens, you go to a movie; it's not so offensive to look at a bad picture. Well, you take a little hand in yours, you say a few silly words—all this embellishes contemporary art and the meagerness of personal life.

So now you can understand how I was feeling when I noticed, once upon a time, that women are not looking at me!

I think, what the devil? Why won't the old gals give me a glance? How come? What do they want?

So I go home, and right away I'm looking in the mirror. There, I see, standing out in bold relief, a shabby physiognomy. And a wan expression. And no color plays on the cheeks.

"Aha, now I get it!" says I to myself. "I've got to take better care of myself. I've got to put some oomph into my tired blood."

So I quickly go out and do some shopping.

I buy butter and sausage. I buy cocoa and so forth.

All this I eat; I drink and feed almost without stopping. And in a short time I get back that fresh, indefatigable look.

And in this aspect, I go flâneurizing down the boulevards. However, I am noticing, that just like before, the women do not look at me.

"Aha," I say to myself, "maybe I've developed a rotten walk? Maybe I haven't been getting enough exercise? Maybe I don't have enough muscles of the kind the ladies usually admire."

Then I buy a hanging trapeze. I buy a ring and weights and a special kind of bar.

I twist myself around all these rings and bits of apparatus like a regular son of a bitch. Every morning I chin myself on the bar. Free of charge, I chop wood for my neighbors.

Finally I sign up for a sports club. I row and punt. I go swimming till November. In doing this, I almost drowned once. I foolishly dove into a deep place, but without reaching bottom I was beginning to blow bubbles, not being able to swim very well.

For half a year, I pursue this thorny path. I submit my life to danger. Twice I clank my head, falling off the trapeze.

I bear all this in manly fashion and one fine day, tanned and taut as a spring, I go forth on the street, that I may intercept a by-now-almost-forgotten approving feminine smile.

But once again I fail to find this smile.

Then I begin to sleep with my window open. The fresh air invigorates me. The color begins to play in my cheeks. My face turns pink and red. And even assumes a kind of lilac shade.

With my lilac physiognomy I go, once, to the theater. And in the theater, like one possessed, I circle around the feminine audience, evoking jeers and catcalls and coarse remarks from the men, and even some pushes and shoves in the chest.

And as a result I see two or three pitiful smiles, such as I don't get many of.

There, in the theater, I go up to the big mirror and I stand admiring my tautened figure, the chest of which now measures thirty-five inches.

I flex my arms and take a stance, and I spread my legs, now this way, now that.

I am sincerely astonished at that fastidiousness on the part of women . . . What the devil do they want anyway?

I am admiring myself in this large mirror and suddenly I notice that I am not very well dressed. I will say directly—badly, and even improperly dressed. The trousers, too short, with bags at the knees, induce horror in me and even a shudder.

But I am literally dumfounded when I look at my lower extremities, a description of which would be out of place in creative literature.

"Ah, now I get it!" I say to myself. "That is what is ruining my personal life—I dress badly."

Depressed, I return home on halting legs, promising myself to change my habits of dress.

And so, in short order, I get myself a new wardrobe. Out of a lilac curtain, I get myself a jacket made in the latest fashion. I buy myself Oxford breeches, sewn out of two riding habits.

I walk in this outfit as in a globe of air, regretting such a fashion but wearing it to best advantage.

I buy myself an overcoat, with broad shoulders, at the market. And, once, on my day off, I go out on the Tver Boulevard.

I go out on the Tver Boulevard, and I step along like a performing camel. I walk here and there, I turn my shoulders, and I do little dance steps with my feet.

The women are looking at me askance with a mixed feeling of amazement and horror.

The men—they are looking less askance. They are making various remarks, the coarse and uncultivated remarks of people who do not understand the situation in its entirety.

Then and there I hear some phrases: "My God, what a scarecrow! Just look how that bastard has gotten himself up!"

They are heaping snickers, they are laughing at me.

I walk along the boulevard as through enemy troops, hoping for I don't know what.

And suddenly at the Pushkin Memorial I noticed a well-dressed lady who is looking at me with infinite tenderness and even flirting.

I smile in response and seat myself on the bench opposite.

A well-dressed lady with still some traces of faded beauty is looking at me steadily. Her eyes slide admiringly along my attractive figure and along my face, on which is written everything good.

I bow my head, shrug my shoulders, and, ideologically, I am admiring the harmonious philosophical system of that bourgeois economist concerning the value of women.

Then I turn to the lady again, whom I now notice is following my every movement with unblinking eyes.

Then I am beginning somehow to be a little afraid of those unblinking eyes. I don't even congratulate myself on my progress.

And already I feel like leaving. And already I feel like skirting the Memorial so as to sit down in a trolley and go somewhere where eyes are looking more in the direction of the outskirts and where there is no such unblinking public.

But, suddenly, this attractive lady approaches me and says: "Excuse me, honored sir . . . It's quite awkward for me," she says, "to talk about it, but you see, my husband had an overcoat, just like that one, stolen on him. Would you please be so kind as not to refuse to show me the lining."

Well now, naturally, I think, it would be awkward for her to begin an acquaintance without rhyme or reason.

I throw open my coat, and in the process I make the biggest, tightest chest I can.

Glancing at the lining, the lady lets out with a heart-rending shriek and begins to yell. Well, now, naturally, it's her overcoat! The stolen coat which this scoundrel (me, that is) is now wearing on his shoulders.

Her moans are shattering my eardrums. I am ready to sink through the earth, overcoat, new breeches, and all.

We go to the police station, where they draw up a statement of the case. They ask me questions, and I answer them honestly.

But when they ask me how old I am, I give the figure, and suddenly, on account of this almost three-digit number, I begin to tremble.

"Ah, there you have the reason they didn't look at me!" I tell myself. "I've simply grown old. And I wanted to blame the insufficiencies of my personal life on my wardrobe."

I give up the stolen overcoat which I had bought at the market, and, lightly dressed, with a disturbed spirit, I go out on the street.

"Well, okay, I'll make do!" I tell myself. "My personal life will consist of labor. I will work. I will help people. A woman isn't the only light in the window."

I begin to poke fun at the words of the bourgeois scholar.

"It's all lies!" I tell myself. "Idle fabrications! Typical Western nonsense!"

I laugh. I spit to the right and to the left. And I turn my eyes away from approaching women.

MY PROFESSIONS

I don't know how many different professions there are. An intellectual friend of mine told me that on our planet there were, in all, three hundred and ninety professions.

Well, undoubtedly he was exaggerating, but in all likelihood there really are about a hundred professions.

No, I have not tried all hundred, but *fifty* professions, now, I have really experienced.

So you have before you a man who has experienced in his own right fifty professions.

It's interesting, the things I've been.

No, I certainly have never been any kind of economist, chemist or pyrotechnician, sculptor, and so forth. No, I have never been an academician or professor of anatomy or algebra or French. I will not conceal from you the fact that there are many intellectual positions I have not occupied, that I have never looked into telescope tubes to see the different cosmic phenomena, planets and comets, nor have I ever trudged along the highway with a surveyor's instrument. I have never built bridges nor the edifices along them, in which embassies would be lodged. Nor have I burdened my brain by mathematically calculating the number of white corpuscles in the blood.

These professions—why, I wouldn't conceal it from you—I have not experienced. I never had the education that would have been needed for these, nor the necessary knowledge of foreign languages. The more so, since I was partly illiterate before the Revolution. I could read a little, but I was never so bold as to attempt to write.

I served in the tsarist army then, and I was a corporal.

After the February Revolution, now, the boys up and say to me: "We've got a real gem of a regimental doctor. Excuse us, a regular plague. Won't give anybody leave, in spite of the Revolution. It'd be a good thing to get rid of him. It wouldn't be a bad idea," they say, "if *you* took over this job. Especially," they say, "since all positions are elected now. And we could choose you."

I say: "Why not? Naturally, elect me. I," I say, "am a man who understands the manifestations of nature. I understand that since the Revolution they're wanting the boys should hurry on home and have a look-see at what's going on. Kerensky," I say, "that's an artist on the throne, he's been spinning a top to a victorious end. And the doctor is playing his pipe for him, not letting our brothers take a little leave. Elect *me* doctor—*I'll* give you leave, almost everybody."

So, soon after that, they change the regiment's commander, and a lot of line officers, and our Goddam medic. And they issue an order naming me in his place.

Naturally, the work seemed difficult and mostly confused.

You just barely listen to a sick man through your tube, and he's whimpering and asking to go home. And if you don't let him go, he's really got it in for the doctor and is almost at his throat.

It's really a very dumb profession and not without danger for human life.

And if you give a patient pills—he won't eat them, and he's right away heaving them in the doctor's face and demanding he write him out a discharge.

Well, for form's sake, you ask—what have you got? But the patient himself, naturally, isn't prepared to name his disease, and in this way he puts the doctor in a blind alley, because the doctor can't know all the diseases by heart and can't write in every passbook simply: typhoid fever or dysentery.

Others, of course, say: "Write whatever you want, only let me go. Because my heart aches to go have a look how things are getting on at home."

Well, you write down for him: soul fever; and, with this diet, you let him go.

But soon this muddleheaded profession is beginning to bore me. So I write myself a pass with the designation: soul fever of the first category.

I leave the front, and that means that this particular career of mine is over.

Afterwards fate tosses me here and there, like, if you'll pardon the comparison, a shell on the stormy sea.

I become a policeman. Then a locksmith, a shoemaker, a blacksmith. I am shoeing horses that kick, milking cows, training mad and vicious dogs. I am playing on the stage. I ring up the curtain. And so forth and so on and et cetera.

This year I'm at the front again in the Red Army defending the Revolution from its many enemies.

Again I get out of it clean. I occupy the position of instructor in rabbit and poultry breeding. I become a detective in the criminal investigation department. I become a chauffeur. And, from time to time, I write critical pieces and witty articles about the theater and literature.

So, you have before you a man who has had in his lifetime fifty and possibly even more professions.

There were certain professions I had that seemed strange and surprising. Before the Revolution, I had one such very strange profession.

I was in the Crimea then. And I was working on a certain estate. There were four hundred cows. A mass of goats, lots of chickens, and rams enough for the devil. All this created a basis for the development of agricultural activity.

And they take me on there as a loafer.

In a word, my job consists of tasting the quality of butter and cheese.

This butter and cheese was sent abroad on a steamboat. And it was necessary to taste it all so the world *bourgeoisie* wouldn't choke on goods of poor quality.

Naturally, if *you* had the chance to go around tasting butter or cheese, I bet you wouldn't refuse. But if, let's assume, you went around tasting these products from morning to night and every day and throughout the year, you'd start howling like a wolf, and the light would grow dark before your very eyes.

No, I'd never been trained as a specialist in this business. And I happened on that profession quite by chance.

I was twenty-three years old then. I just didn't give a damn, and everything was whoop-de-do. And I was just bumming along Crimean roads hoping I'd find work somewhere.

There I am, walking along the road, and I sniff—smells of a milk economy. At this point, all the more because I hadn't eaten for two days. So I up and went after that sweet smell. I think: I'll stand guard over some cow or other, I'll milk her a bit, and in this way I'll get a little strength back.

Behind the fence, I see, there's a shed. In all probability, I think, the cows are there. I hopped over the fence. I go up to the shed. I see—no cows there, but lots of cheeses lying around. I just wanted to pinch a hunk of cheese—and suddenly the foreman walks in.

"You," he says, "one of our workers?"

No, I wasn't especially embarrassed. I think—I'll make out all right. There's nobody around, and the fence isn't far away. So I answer with a certain amount of cheek: "No, I'm not a worker here. But I have hopes along those lines."

He says: "Would you mind explaining, then, why you picked up that cheese?"

I say, not without cheek: "Well, you know, I wanted to try this cheese. Seems to me it's a little sour to the taste. You don't know how to make it, and you should be careful."

I see the foreman has even gotten a bit upset because of my words. I notice he doesn't even grasp what it's all about.

He says: "How's that? What do you mean, sour? What are you anyway, a specialist in milk economy or what?"

I thought he was joking, playing cat-and-mouse games with me, to work his temper up and really let me have one. And I say: "You guessed it. In milk economy I am the first specialist of the city of Moscow. And I simply can't walk past these milk products without trying them."

Suddenly the foreman smiles, shakes both my hands, and says: *"Golubchik!"*

He says: *"Golubchik,* if you are a specialist, I'm willing to pay you an enormous salary, only be so kind as to start work soon. In a few days, a foreign boat is going to be arriving here, we've got to send off our freight; but to sort out our goods, we need someone to test them. And I've been given to understand that the foreign *bourgeoisie* will *choke* on inferior products, and then unpleasantness would be inevitable. And, as luck would have it, our one specialist has come down with cholera. And now he categorically refuses to test anything."

I said: "If you like. What needs to be done?"

He says: "Six hundred and twenty casks of butter have got to be tested, and a thousand cheeses."

My stomach was quivering with hunger and amazement, so I answered: "If you like. What's all this talk? Just bring me a loaf of bread, and I'll set to, right now, with the greatest pleasure. I," I say, "have long dreamed of finding myself a profession like this —going around testing here and there."

And I think in my heart: I'll eat my fill, then let them make a pancake out of me. And, God knows, they won't be able to—I'll take off on my own well-nourished legs.

"Well," I say, "bring the loaf here, I'm in a hurry to get to work. Once something catches ahold of me, I've got to be at it right away. Bring the bread, or I'll get bored without my profession to practice."

I see—the foreman is looking at me with distrust.

He says: "I'm beginning to doubt that you're the best specialist in milk economy in the world. They test milk products *without* bread, and without *anything,* otherwise there's no way of telling what kind it really is, or judging the taste."

Here I see that I've slipped, but I say: "Sure, I know that. And you're pretty thick-skinned if you don't get it. I don't want the bread to *eat,* but I need it to put it in contact with these two products, and then I can see how sour they are, and when I test them I won't make a mistake about how spoiled they are. This," I say, "is the latest method used abroad. I," I say, "am surprised at your ignorance and isolation from Europe."

At this point, they show me around, here and there, cere-moniously. They sign me up. They dress me in white overalls, and they say: "All right, let's go to the casks."

But my heart's in my heels from fear, and my feet are hardly moving.

So, we went to the casks, but at this point luck comes to my rescue, and the foreman is called away on some urgent task. I gave a sigh of relief. I say to the workers: "Help me out, brothers. I don't know the least little thing about this business. So tell me quick—what do you taste the butter with, your finger or some special kind of silver?"

So, the workers laugh at me, they die laughing; nevertheless, they tell me what I have to do, and, more important, what I have to say.

So, the foreman arrives; I've put blinders on him. I let slip various special phrases, I taste in the correct way. I see—the man has practically blossomed out because of my high qualifica-tions.

And so, toward evening, having fed my fill, I decided not to leave this well-nourished position. And so I stayed.

The profession seemed stupid and confused. One had to taste butter with such a special, long, thin spoon. Had to scoop the butter from the bottom of the cask and taste it. And if it's a little spoiled or lacking a little something, or there's an extra fly or something, or it's a little salty—it has to be junked, so as not to arouse displeasure among the world-wide *bourgeoisie*.

Well, all at once, naturally, I couldn't tell the difference—*all* the butter tasted pretty good to me. But after awhile I learned, and even started bawling out the foreman, who was thoroughly pleased that he had found me. And he even wrote the owner a letter, where he spun out a lot of stories about himself and asked for a raise or some kind of badge for excellent service.

So, you see, I was naturally quite pleased with my profession during those first days. As it was, when you'd had enough cheese, you could try the butter for awhile. Better, I think, if there never had been such a job on this planet.

Later I see—everything is not as it should be.

After two weeks, I began to suffer, and already to dream of parting with all this.

Because by day you are testing fats, and you don't lay eyes on anything. You'd like to eat something, but haven't the stomach for it. And inside you feel miserable, and life seems boring and confused.

And with all this, it was strictly forbidden to drink. Impossible to take any wine or vodka in your mouth. Because alcohol kills the taste, so you'd do a bad job and quality would go to pot.

Briefly speaking, after two weeks, I would lie down after work with my stomach up, and I would lie in the sun without moving, hoping it's hot rays would sweat out the superfluous fat, and I might once again feel like walking, strolling, eating borsch and cutlets, and so forth.

Now, I had a friend in those regions. A certain excellent Georgian. Name of Misha. A quite remarkable man, and a spiritual comrade. And he too was a degustator, a taster. Only in another line. He tested wines.

In the Crimea, there were wine cellars like that—belonging to a local government department. And that's where he was testing.

And his thoroughly confused profession was even worse than mine.

He wasn't even allowed to eat. From morning to night he tested wine, and it was only in the evening he had a right to eat anything.

I suffered from fats, and didn't feel like taking anything in my mouth. And I wasn't allowed to drink. And appetite I did not have.

But with him, just the opposite. He was bursting with wine. From early morning, he is slurping various Crimean wines and scarcely can walk—and it's reached a point where the light is no longer dear to him.

So, by and by, we'd meet in the evening—me, stuffed; him, drunk—and we'd see our friendship is coming to a dead end. Neither of us wants to talk about anything. He wants to eat; I, on the contrary, want to drink. Our common interests are few, and there's a vile taste in the mouth. So we sit like idiots and stare out into the steppe. But there's nothing in the steppe. And over our heads—heaven and the stars. But somewhere, maybe, life goes on, full of happiness and joy . . .

So, once, I say to him: "Misha," I say, "we've got to go. Even though I've got a contract till fall, I just won't make it. I am refusing to eat butter. It lowers my human dignity. I'm taking off, I'm going to swipe a cheese and let my fat-assed foreman see me do it."

He says: "It's not a good idea to leave before fall. No work to be found now. We've got to think up something more original. Give me time. I'll think of something. Hunger makes me very inventive."

And so, once, he says to me: "You know what, why don't we exchange professions for awhile. I'll test butter and you test wine. Let's work it like that for a week or two, and then we'll change back again. And then again. That way, we'll have a kind of balance. And the main thing is, we'll rest, since those bloody devils won't give us any vacation and just keep us feeding and drinking without stop."

I am quite delighted with these words, but I express some doubt as to whether our foremen will permit it.

He says: "I'll see if I can work it."

So he takes me by the hand and leads me to his foreman in the wine department.

"Here," he says, "this short, experienced gentleman can easily replace me for two weeks. My aunt has come to see me from Tiflis, and I'm interested in having a look at her. And he'll be testing for me and looking after our interests."

The foreman says: "Okay. Show him the kind of wines we have around here and what he has to do. And come back in two weeks.

And now we've got quite a business on our hands. Instead of table wines we've just sent a load of 'Alikote' off to Moscow. Sheer disorder."

So then I, for my part, take Misha by the hand and bring him to my fat-assed foreman.

"Here," I say, "this tall, experienced gentleman can easily replace me for two weeks. My aunt has come to see me from Tiflis, and I'm interested in having a look at her and having some chats with her about this and that."

The foreman says: "Okay. Show him what's what around here and come back in two weeks. We've got a mess on our hands just now. Instead of creamery butter, we've sent off sour cream to Persia. The Persians might be offended and won't want to eat it."

So we started on our new jobs.

I test wine. And Misha tests butter.

But here we get into a lot of nonsense and confusion.

On the very first day, Misha eats so much butter and cheese that he comes down with cramps. And I, after my first twenty swallows of unaccustomed drink, got so woozy that I had a run-in with Misha's foreman. And I wanted to heave him into a wine cask because he said bad words about my friend.

So the next day they gave me my hat and ordered me to pack off.

And they settled accounts with Misha and ordered him to pack off too.

So we meet, and we laugh. We think—spit on it. We rested a couple of days, and now we can once again take up our trade.

But here it turned out that both our foremen smelled a rat and discovered our little trick, and the kind of two weeks we had in mind, and the kind of aunt we had in Tiflis, and the kind of experience we had.

They both call us in. They yell at us terrible loud and order us to pack off.

No, we were not especially sorry. I took a cheese and Misha some wine. And, all the way, we went and sang songs. And later we got some other work.

Soon after that the war broke out. Then, the Revolution. And I lost track of my friend.

And it isn't long ago I find out that he's living in the Caucasus and has a good, remarkable, command position.

And I dream of going to see him. I dream of meeting him and talking to him and saying: "How about it, old boy!"

Och, he's likely to be glad to see me! Maybe he'll say the same to me: "How about it, old boy!" And he'll have them serve me up the best shashlik.

Then he and I will eat and reminisce together about what we were and what we've become.

1. Lo, when Lady Death approaches our pillow with inaudible football, exclaims "Aha!" and begins to make off with our treasured and heretofore charming life—in all likelihood we will then regret, above all else, the loss of a certain emotion, which at this point we must give up.

2. Of all the marvelous manifestations and sensations strewn about us by the lavish hand of nature, we will indubitably, or so I think, most regret being cut off from love.

And, speaking in the tongue of poetic metaphor, while it is taking leave of this world, our departed soul will be beating and clamoring and begging to go back, and abasing itself, saying it still hasn't seen everything there is to see, and that it would like to have just one more look at this phenomenon.

But this is nonsense. It has seen everything. And these are only empty excuses which, more than anything else, depict the extreme majesty of our emotions and desires.

3. Certainly, there are, in addition to this, various exceptional and worthy experiences and sensations, concerning which we would also, in all likelihood, heave bitter sighs of regret when it came time for leave-taking.

Without a doubt, we would regret not hearing the music of chamber and symphony orchestras, not going to sea in a steamer (for example), not going out to pick fragrant lilies of the valley in the forest. It would be most sad for us to leave our glorious work, and not to lie on the seashore with the aim of resting.

Yes, these are all glorious things, and we would certainly regret all of them when it came time for leave-taking. And maybe we would even weep. But concerning love, rather special and most bitter tears would be shed. And when we bid farewell to this emotion, in all likelihood, the whole world will fade before us in its majesty, and will seem to us empty, cold, and of but little interest.

As a certain poet once said:

> Love ornaments life,
> Love is nature's charm . . .
> I am inwardly convinced,
> All that replaces love is naught.

So, you see, the French poet Musset said that all is naught in comparison with this emotion. But, of course, he was in part mistaken. Of course, he was overdoing it.

4. It's all the more important not to forget that a Frenchman spoke these lines. That is, a man extremely emotional by nature and, forgive me, in all likelihood a skirt chaser, who, because of the extremely agitated state of his feelings, is really capable of blurting out God-knows-what in this area.

They, the French, at home there in Paris, as far as we have been told, go out on the boulevard in the evening, and, except for various beauties whom they honor with the title "little chicken," decisively, from the very beginning, they see nothing else. That's what *they* are in the way of lovers of feminine beauty and grace!

So that we have some foundation in lightly snuffing the amazing ardor of these poetic lines.

5. But just look at a Russian poet. And the Russian poet isn't so far from the ardent Gallic mind. Even more so. Not only about love itself, but even about being in love, we find in his works amazing lines like these:

> Ah, loving, thou art more strict than fate,
> More imperious than our father's ancient laws . . .
> Sweeter than sounds of martial trumpet.

From which it may be concluded that our most famous poet considered this emotion to be one of the highest things on earth. Something with which even the strictness of the criminal law or the commands of a father or a mother in those days could not be compared. In a word, he says that there really isn't anything that can be compared with this emotion. The poet even has a kind of reference here to a call to military service—that this, too, is, as it were, nothing in comparison. In general, it would seem as though the poet were holding something back in his mind here. Allegorically, he expressed something about a martial trumpet and then he became somber. In all likelihood, he had something to do with military service in his time. Therefore, perhaps he resorted to this allegory.

In this sense, it's much simpler to deal with prose. In prose, there cannot be such obscurities. There, everything is clear. And, moreover, one can also use prose to explain poetry, as you see.

6. Another Russian poet provides us with lines no less powerful.

One should say that the house in which this poet was born and in which he spent the best years of his childhood once burned down. And it is curious to note with what the poet solaced himself after the fire.

He tells about it as follows. He describes it in a poem. Here is what he writes:

> It seems that all the joys of childhood
> Burned with the ruined house,
> And I wanted to die,
> And I went down to the water,
> But a woman in a boat slipped by
> Who was a second reflection of the moon,
> And if she wishes,
> And if the moon permits,
> I will build myself a new house
> In her unknown heart.

And so forth, somewhat in the same vein.

7. That is, in other words, making a free translation from the pride of poetry to democratic prose, one can in part understand that the poet, beside himself with grief, had wanted to throw himself in the water, but at this most critical moment he suddenly saw an attractive woman rowing in a boat. And so he unexpectedly fell in love with her at first sight, and this love pushed into the background, so to speak, all his incredible sufferings, and, for the time being, even distracted him from his preoccupation with finding himself a new apartment. All the more, that the poet according to the poem, just wanted to move right over to this lady's place, so to speak. Or he wanted to perform some building operations in her house, if she, as he murkily puts it, wishes, and if the moon and the housing administration permit.

Well, as far as the moon is concerned, the poet dragged it in to strengthen somewhat the poetic impression. The moon, one can say, really has little to do with it. And as far as the housing administration is concerned, it certainly cannot grant permission, even if the lady herself wishes, since these lovers have not registered in the marriage bureau, and in general this would be a rather impermissible combination.

8. I don't know, perhaps it is that our coarse soldierly intellect, having been under fire by heavy artillery in two wars, is not entirely able to understand the most delicate and most tender poetic interlacements of sounds and feelings. But we are so bold as to believe that this interpretation is approximately correct, thanks to a certain significance that life has, and to our understanding of the essential needs of people, whose lives do not always proceed along the course of flowery poetry.

Briefly, the poet at this point speaks of love as of an elevated emotion, and there is a certain degree of frivolity in this, an elevated emotion which can provide a man with the most essential things, not excluding an apartment. This latter assertion we leave entirely to the conscience of the poet.

But, of course, this is not the opinion merely of three ardent poets.

All the others, too, strumming away, as it is said, even on the most jingly lyres, have sung love songs even more shocking and brazen than these.

9. I recall something or other from Apukhtin:

> My heart is resurrected, loving again,
> Tram-ta-ra-ram, tam-tam . . .
> Along with all that is dear and blessed in my soul . . .
> Tram-ta-ra-ram . . .

Withal, it was no boy of eighteen who wrote this. A solid uncle of forty-eight wrote it, quite improbably, a man fat and unhappy in his personal life. Nevertheless, he, too, as you see, considered all to have been dead and lifeless as long as love had not arisen in his heart.

Even mad lines like this come back to me:

> What is love? O love! O love!
> It is a sun in the blood, it is the blood in flames . . .

Something of this sort, devil take it . . . how does it go . . .

It is a heavenly canopy, discovered anew.
Death reigns over the world, and over death—love.

10. Here, even French poetry, if you will, falls a little behind —one can say that one finds no such mad onslaught there as one does in these lines. But it was a Russian poetess who wrote this. She lived at the beginning of our century and was, they say, fairly attractive. In any case, she had a great poetic temperament. In general, one can see that the little lady was trembling when she wrote those lines. The fact, one can say, is, of course, more a matter of biography than an example to poetry . . . Her poor husband, in all likelihood, had quite enough . . . In all likelihood, she was capricious. Plays the fool. In all likelihood, she drags out the day in bed with her puss unwashed. And she's all the time reading her own verses out loud. And the fool of a husband sits there. "Och," he exclaims, "amazing, poopsie, sheer genius!" And she says: "Really?"

Fools! And then they both up and died. She, it seems, from tuberculosis, and he, too, in all likelihood, infected with something or other.

11. At this point, without a doubt, there are many skeptics, scholars, and pedants whose hearts have turned pale in their lonely wanderings across the northern lands of science, who, reading these verses, will, if you like, shrug their shoulders and say: There you are, this is the rather unrestrained view of somewhat too ardent hearts, overfree in spirit and corrupt in world outlook.

And they would be surprised that such a view and such verses exist concerning this emotion, and words such as *they* never knew and of which they did not even permit themselves to think, that concerning this emotion something like that had sometime been said.

And maybe they're right, and it really is surprising it's that way, and there is such poetry among us, but not long ago we happened on a certain little book in prose. Its author was the singer, Feodor Ivanovitch Chaliapin.

And in this little book, with complete frankness, he acknowledges that everything he did in his life, he did in the main for love and for a woman. That's the kind of views there are concerning love among poetically constituted people.

12. And as far as people of sober judgment are concerned,

philosophers and various thinkers of that kind, whose minds have shed much light on the most secret and complex manifestations of life, as far as these people are concerned, they have entered but little concerning this emotion in the common account; but, at times, of course, they have reckoned with it; they have laughed at it, and again even pronounced aphorisms out of their life wisdom.

From the more melancholy pronouncements, we can, if you wish, quote you the words of Schopenhauer, one of the gloomiest philosophers the world has ever known.

This gloomy philosopher, whose wife undoubtedly betrayed him at every step, pronounced the following words concerning love: "Love—it is the blind will to life. It deceives man with the phantasms of individual happiness and makes him an instrument for its aims."

13. Of the more foolish ancient pronouncements, we can quote the following: "Love is, as it were, the harmony of heavenly sounds."

Of the more poetic: "Never strike a woman, even with a flower."

Of the more sober, but with some inclination to idealism: "Love arises from those qualities which the lover prizes the more the less he himself possesses them."

The not unknown philosopher Plato even proposed the following theorem: "The essence of love consists of the polar opposition of the greatest possible contrarities."*

Of the more just pronouncements, we can quote the words of our most brilliant poet and philosopher Pushkin:

> Time came for her to fall in love.
> A seed that's fallen to the ground
> Stirs thus at the fire of spring.
> For long, her heartbeat's languishing
> Had made a tightness in her breast.
> Her soul expected someone's coming.

---

* It is curious that Plato never departed from this view in later life. In his famous book, *The Ideal State,* Plato establishes the following premises: "Woman should 'bear children for the state' from the age of twenty up to the age of forty years. Man can 'create for the state' from thirty to fifty-five years. The strongest should cohabit with the strongest. The weakest with the weakest. The children of the former should be educated; of the latter—thrown away." If, let us assume, this fantastic law had been promulgated in life, then the world would not have known Napoleon, whose father was twenty-two and whose mother was eighteen, nor Pushkin whose father was twenty-seven.

14. But this is, so to speak, the philosophy and mechanics of love.

As far as more precise investigations in this area are concerned, why, we know very little about it. And perhaps it isn't even necessary to know about it. Or perhaps, for that matter, it isn't necessary to know anything. Since consciousness corrupts and darkens almost everything it touches.

As Dostoevski quite rightly said: "Too much consciousness, and even consciousness itself, is a disease." And another poet said: "Woe from wit." And we maintain that this phrase was spoken far from accidentally. In general, how love arises— whether from psychic images, or whether, more likely, there exists some sort of precise formula for it yet to be derived from an undiscovered property of electricity—we do not know and, decisively, we do not want to know.

And so, acknowledging that we know little of anything about love, but acknowledging at the same time that this tender emotion is something of no little importance and even something grandiose, we take into our hands, with a special trembling and fluttering of the heart, the heavy tomes of history.

We want to see more quickly the notable role that this emotion has played in the life of nations. We want to see the grandiose events that have taken place because of love, or the splendid deeds performed on that account by individual citizens. We know what we want to see. And therefore, in order to put the spirit at ease, we make ourselves as comfortable as possible in an armchair, and, smoking a fragrant cigar, we begin to turn the yellowing pages of history with a confident hand.

And this is what we see there.

15. At first we find at our fingertips a whole bunch, devil take them, of petty love matters and foolish, nonsensical little affairs from daily life—various engagements, proposals, and marriages, concluded by practical and sober minds.

Here we see a certain duke . . . Here's the kind of man he is . . . He marries the king's daughter, entertaining hopes for the throne.

Here is another certain grand personage; hoping to add a series of cities to his estates, he too makes a proposal to a certain available princess . . .

The Russian grand dukes . . . Here's the kind they are . . . From the epoch of the Tartar yoke . . ." Vied with one another," as the historian writes, "in striving to wed the daughter of the khan, with the object of winning his favor for themselves . . ."

Here's still another instance, just imagine, Chilperic I . . . the Frankish king . . . marries the daughter of the Spanish king . . . As history literally writes, "With the object of striking a blow against his enemy, Prince Sigebert."

16. Withal, concerning these love affairs on a commercial scale, the historians write, one can say, without any inspiration, in such a flabby official style, as though of the emptiest, most trifling objects. The historians do not even add any exclamations of their own, such as "Aye-yai!" or "There's a prince for you!" or "Fooh, how unattractive!" or even "Look, still one scoundrel more!"

No, the unimpassioned historians exclaim nothing of the sort. Although, to be sure, if one began to exclaim, no exclamations would suffice, inasmuch as we see, perusing the course of world history, a whole ocean of similar cases.

But we, if you please, will not enumerate these commercial transactions in detail. We want to touch on more interesting questions. Although even in this area, of course, there have been a number of striking cases and surprising ancedotes, worthy of the contemporary reader's attention.

17. Here, for example, is a very amusing fact. We found it pleasing because of the, so to speak, obviousness of the subject. It is very characteristic, this fact. It is taken from old Russian life. From the epoch of Ivan the Terrible.

At that time, a German duke arrived in Russia, a certain Holstein.

What he did in his native Germany is not known, and historians have found out only that he visited Russia with the purpose of marrying, for political reasons, the daughter of Ivan IV's male cousin.

And so he arrived. Most likely, all powdered up. In some kind of silk trousers. Bows. Ribbons. Sword at his side. A kind of red snout, with reddish mustaches. A drunkard, perhaps, a braggart and a fop.

Here he arrived in Russia, and inasmuch as he had already discussed the matter in writing, the wedding day was designated at once.

18. Well, there's hustle, in all likelihood, extravagance. Mamochka's running about. Cutting up chickens. They're taking the bride to the bathhouse. The bridegroom is sitting with the

priest. Guzzling vodka. In all likelihood, lying through his teeth. As follows, in Germany, now, we . . . As follows, we dukes, you know, and so on.

And at this point a fairly mournful incident occurs. The bride, alas, unexpectedly ups and dies. She's returning from the bathhouse, poor thing, catches a devil of a chill, and dies in the course of three days.

The bridegroom, naturally, suffers indescribable grief, wants to go back to Germany. And all distraught, he is already taking leave of his erstwhile relatives, when, suddenly, they say to him: "Comrade Duke! Don't go yet! We still have a girl who might please you. *Her* sister. It's true, she's a little older, and maybe a little less interesting, but she might in any case do for you. The more so since you've made such a trip from Germany. It would be a shame to go back empty-handed."

The duke says: "Naturally, she'll do. Why didn't you tell me till now? It's clear that she'll do. What's all this palaver! Okay, let's have a look at her."

And so, in spite of the mourning, the wedding soon was celebrated.

19. But perhaps, devil take it, such facts and deeds took place only among tsars and dukes?

Perhaps it was only in royal palaces that such coarse calculations and loveless marriages took place, under the compulsion of some kind, I don't know what, of diplomacy, because of chronic impecuniosity or the unimportant circumstances of the lives of tsars.

Perhaps among simple mortals it was quite the contrary: Love flowed forth naturally and gladdened and rejoiced the hearts of those around?

To this question, one must answer in the negative.

Certain categories of simple mortals never, as it were, got as far as love. The upper classes, as is well known, married off their loyal slaves whenever they felt like it.

Not long ago, we read that Russian landowners quite often married off their peasants in the following fashion: They lined up their peasants by height and matched them off accordingly: tall men with tall women, short ones with short ones. And they sent off a list drawn up that way to the priest for execution.

Here, one can say, there was no such thing as love.

And as far as various, if you'll pardon the expression, bureaucrats, speculators, bagmen and so forth are concerned, these gentlemen, too, thought least of all about love. Their marriages were arranged in the manner of commercial affairs. And without a dowry they were not accustomed to take a single step.

20. Well, and if one touches on the life of a higher altitude and takes various counts, barons, and merchants, then these gentlemen, for all their easy life, also regarded love in the same way.

Here is a charming historical tale that depicts for us just how things were in this crowd.

In France at the time of Louis XV (1720) a certain speculator had, through some dark maneuvers, squeezed out an enormous income for himself. He had achieved everything. And he had everything. But he still wanted to marry into one of the oldest aristocratic families—that was the fantasy that flashed across his mind. With all his wealth, knowing no such thing as an obstacle, he decided to marry off his daughter to an impoverished marquis, who bore the distinguished family name of d'Oiau.

But at that time his daughter was only three years old. And the marquis was thirty. For which reason, the impoverished marquis, the enormous dowry notwithstanding, had no intention whatsoever of waiting twelve years.

Elegantly unfolding his hands and flashing his golden lorgnette, he said, in all likelihood in a hoarse voice, to papa-speculator: "Listen, I'd be glad to be a relative of yours, and the sum you propose would quite set me on my feet again, but your bride is terribly little. Let her grow up for a few years—then, let's see, maybe I'll marry her."

21. But the ambitious papa wanted immediately to become the relative of a marquis. That is to say, he wanted to join up with the higher aristocracy. So, then and there, he concluded the following agreement with the marquis. Every month he would pay the marquis an immense allowance, until the bride became of age. The marquis binds himself to marry her within twelve years. But the betrothal would take place right away.

And so, for nine years, the marquis punctually received his allowance and gave himself up to all the pleasures of life. But in the tenth year, the young twelve-year-old bride fell ill with diphtheria and died.

You can imagine for yourselves the tears the papa-speculator shed! In the first place, naturally, he grieved madly for his daughter, but in the second place, he couldn't help thinking how much money he'd thrown away for nothing. And, naturally, there were no hopes of getting as much as a penny back from the gentleman-marquis.

And *he,* rubbing his hands, no doubt, said to the grieving papa: "Now look, as far as the money is concerned, naturally, you understand how it is yourself. Since the girl has kicked the bucket —it's my luck."

22. But there is still more! There have been even more amazing incidents on the love front.

Now, it's very strange, for example, to read how men—various Beau Brummell types, barons, distinguished knights, cavaliers, merchants, landowners, and tsars—have gotten married without ever seeing their brides. Withal, this was a fairly frequent phenomenon. And yet, to us contemporary readers, it seems to a certain degree surprising.

In those days they only paid attention to how affairs and finances shaped up and what the bride's property situation was like, who her papa was serving, or where he reigned—and that's all. Well, maybe a few of the more cautious bridegrooms would ask approximately what kind of a companion-for-life they were getting, did she have a humpback or something—and that's all.

They made their agreement and got married, so to speak, in the dark, with their eyes closed. And they saw the bride only at the last moment.

No, in our time—why, it's even difficult to imagine how such things could be among us! Among us there might be, it is true, some wailing, nervous shouts, refusals, brews, a fist fight, and devil knows what. But in those days, this is the kind of thing that went on.

23. Naturally, a number of shocking and unpleasant incidents occurred.

For example, from among world scandals, two are well known.

One is a well-known incident which is performed even in the theaters, as a monstrous tragedy and drama of royal life.

The Spaniard, Philip II, an old man of sixty, decided to marry off his son and heir, the famous Don Carlos. He decided to marry him off to the French princess, Isabella, which was advantageous and necessary on account of high policy. He himself had not seen this princess. He knew she was youngish and trying to get married, but just what she was like, he didn't know.

But when, after the betrothal, he saw her, he fell in love with her and married her himself, to the immense grief of his son, who also proved not indifferent to his charming bride. After which, as is well known, there took place the drama between father and son.

24. The second instance took place in Persia. The Persian king Cambyses (son of the famous Cyrus) made a proposal to the daughter of the Egyptian pharaoh, Amasis II (five hundred twenty-nine years before our era). Cambyses made this proposal without seeing the bride. In those days traveling and moving were quite a complicated business. And, for a trip to Egypt, it took several months.

Rumor had it that the Egyptian pharaoh's daughter was distinguished for her great beauty and charming airs.

And, there, the powerful Persian king, whose father had conquered almost the whole world, up and sent a proposal to the Egyptian king's daughter.

The pharaoh, who loved his only daughter very much, did not want to send her off into unknown lands. At the same time, he was afraid of offending the sovereign of the world with a refusal. So he up and chose the prettiest girl among his slaves and sent her to Persia instead of his own daughter. He sent her as his own daughter, you see, and gave her instructions accordingly.

History tells that Cambyses, having married her, loved her very much, but when the deception was accidentally discovered, he mercilessly had her executed, and, offended in his finest sentiments, went to war against Egypt.

This was, if you will, one of the most powerful love dramas, from which may be seen how love began in those days and how it ended.

25. Ah, we see that dramatic episode before us so vividly, and that tragic moment when the whole deception was uncovered!

There they sit, embracing one another, on a Persian ottoman.

On a lower bench, there are, just imagine, Oriental delicacies and drinks—Turkish delight, halvah, and all that. And a stout Persian with a huge fan in his hands chases the flies off the sweets.

The Persian king, Cambyses, having drunk up a glass of their equivalent of sherry-brandy, is exclaiming his admiration for his charming wife and muttering various soothing words in her ear: like this, "Ah, my sweet little Egyptian pigeon, you . . . How is it there in Egypt? . . . Papa-pharaoh spoiled you terribly, no doubt. But how could he help spoiling you, when you're such a sweet little thing, and I have loved you, my dear princess, from the first time I saw your royal approach," and so forth.

26. At this point maybe she was depending on her feminine charms, or else nobody knows what happened in her feminine heart, only she smiled a silvery smile and said, "Well, now, just look at that, what dumb luck: the pharaoh's daughter still in Egypt, and *he,* the Persian king Cambyses, fallen head over heels in love with *her,* who had nothing whatsoever in common with the pharaoh's daughter. He loved a simple slave girl. *That* is what love did to a man's heart."

At this point, one cannot imagine what happened next without trembling.

No doubt he shouted in a wild voice. Leaped from the divan in his drawers. The slipper fell off from one of his bare feet. His lips turned pale. His hands shake. His knees wobble. "What?!" shouted he, in Persian. "Repeat what you just said! Ministers! Arrest the hussy!"

At this point the ministers ran in, "Ah, ah! What is it? Calm down, your majesty! . . . Look—you dropped a slipper off your feet; remember your royal dignity."

But, naturally, it isn't so easy to calm down when one's vanity has borne such an immense affront.

27. And so, in the evening, after they had expeditiously chopped off the poor Egyptian girl's head, Cambyses no doubt sat long in council with his ministers.

Waving his hands about and all atremble, he paces nervously up and down the room.

"No, *who would have guessed* the Egyptian pharaoh was that kind of a bastard, eh?" he exclaims indignantly.

The ministers sigh deferentially, shake their heads and spread out their hands, glancing at one another venomously.

"What should I do now, gentlemen, after an insult like that? Should I go to war against that scoundrel, or what?"

"We can go to war, your majesty."

"Only, the dog, he's a long way off . . . Egypt . . . Africa . . . Takes almost a year to get there . . . Seems we'd have to go on camels . . ."

"It's nothing, your majesty. The army will get there."

"I *was* nice to her," said Cambyses, upset all over again. "I took her in as an Egyptian princess, I loved her passionately, and then it turns out that isn't what she is . . . How about it, gentlemen?

What am I, a dog or what, not good enough for his daughter? Sending a hussy like that . . . Eh?"

28. The minister of foreign affairs says, trying to keep from laughing: "The important thing is, your majesty, that it's a world scandal . . ."

"That's exactly it! . . . I'm telling you—it's a scandal. Aye, what in the world am I going to do?"

"The important thing is, your majesty, that it won't go down well in world history . . . That is, Persia . . . Cambyses . . . condemned a girl to death . . ."

"Aye, what are you unsettling me for, you son of a bitch! . . . Gather the army! . . . Go on campaign! . . . Conquer Egypt and send it to the devil's mother! . . ."

In all, Cambyses personally led the army against Egypt and in a short time conquered it. The very old and hapless Pharaoh Amasis, however, died about that time. And his nephew Psamtik, expecting nothing good would come of all this, put an end to himself.

As far as the ill-fated princess is concerned, we have unfortunately found no clues in history concerning her fate . . .

A certain acquaintance of ours, who is a professor of history and who lectures at the university, told me that Cambyses gave away this Egyptian girl, as it were, into the harem of one of his ministers. But to what extent this is true, we would not take it upon ourselves to assert. But, naturally, it's possible. In all, love had scattered like smoke. From which it is clear exactly how much a pound of this emotion was worth.

29. So what does it signify? Does it signify that the matter is, as it were, of no importance? *Where*, then, is that famous love glorified by poets and singers? *Where*, then, is that passion which has been sung in marvelous poems? Can it be that these nibbling poets, these rhythm sewers and lovers of every beauty and grace, have allowed such a disturbing exaggeration to slip by? So that, reading history, we find no such experiences?

No, certainly, paging through history, we do find some. But these are very few. We had wanted some kind of unique pearl to glitter from every page. But, as it is, once in a century we stumble on some kind of doubtful little love affair.

So here we have scraped together a few such love stories. But to do this we have read through, and definitely with diligence, all the history of various, if you'll excuse me, Ethiopians and

Chaldeans, and from the creation of the world right on up to our own time.

And we've only managed to scrape up what you now see before you. Here, for example, is a fairly powerful love, thanks to which one daughter ran over her own papa in a chariot.

Here's how it happened.

30. The Roman emperor, Servius Tullius, had a daughter. This daughter had a husband, a man of fairly doubtful reputation. But, nevertheless, the daughter loved him exceedingly.

And here, this gentleman was thinking of knocking this daughter's noble father, Servius Tullius, off the throne. Of course, he was an old man, this Servius Tullius, and he had led some unsuccessful wars against those, you can just imagine, Etruscans. Nevertheless, to go knocking him off was too bad. All the more so, since it wasn't necessary to kill him. This was already piggishness.

But this energetic son-in-law, after having taken counsel with the old man's daughter, decided to kill her papa anyway. And she, for love of this cannibal, agreed.

And so this energetic son-in-law, having bribed a hired murderer, pitilessly finishes off the noble old man with a dagger in the open square. And he drops, without a word. And the people shout: "And who, gentlemen, is going to be our emperor now?"

And, there, the daughter of this murdered father, instead of weeping and falling all over her papa's corpse in grief, comes dashing up in a chariot and, wishing to hail the new emperor— her husband—with a shout of joy, runs over the corpse of her only recently murdered father with the wheels.

The scene, though to a certain degree repulsive, nevertheless has power. And the love of this imperial daughter comes across rather strongly. For she must have been very much in love in order to run over the old man at such a moment.

She stands in the chariot. She gives a whoop. Her hair has come undone. Her puss goes all askew. "Hurrah!" she shouts to the new emperor. And she drives across all that has fallen.

But in the crowd they cry out: "Look, that shameless wench hasn't even hesitated, it seems, to run over her own papa."

No, but anyway, *this was love.* And in part, probably, the wish to rule in her own right. In all, it is *not* unknown.

31. But here is an even more powerful love for you. One which involved a certain historical lady in the sunset of her life.

The Russian empress, Catherine II, in her declining years, at the age of about fifty-eight, fell madly in love with a certain dashing young beau—Platon Zubov. He was twenty-one years old, and he really was a very attractive young man. Although, his brother Valerian was even more attractive. Both their portraits are in the Russian museum—so it's really true: the brother was of untold beauty.

But the old girl didn't see the brother till later, and so, not knowing what was what, instantly fell in love with Platon. And when she saw Valerian, she sighed and said: "Yes, this young man could please me, too. But since I've already fallen in love with Platon, so, if you please, I'll go on with it."

But Platon, seeing that Valerian made an irresistible impression on the old girl, sent this brother of his off to war. And in the war a cannon ball tore off the beau's leg. So that the old girl devoted herself to Platon entirely and bestowed various amazing favors upon him.

It would be interesting to know how their romance began. The handsome young man probably felt terribly inhibited at first and quailed when the elderly lady pressed down on him. Naturally you'd quail. In any case, this is a sacred person, so to speak, empress of all the Russians and so forth, and suddenly, devil take it, a coarse business like this!

32. Let us imagine this romance.

"So, embrace me, little fool," said the empress.

"God almighty, I just don't dare, your majesty," muttered the favorite. "I fear and honor, so to speak, the imperial dignity."

"Ah, forget it. Just call me Ekaterina Vasilievna." (Or whatever her patronymic was.)

And the boy, smiling unnaturally, respectfully touched the aging shoulders of the empress. But then he got used to it, and received for his love rather more than it was worth.

In all, by the time he was twenty-four, this beau was already general in chief, viceroy of the region of New Russia, and commander in chief of all the artillery.

The lady, no longer young, fell in love with him more and more with every passing year, and scarcely knew how and with what to keep him happy.

She permitted him to glance through all secret dispatches and reports from abroad. All ministers and generals, before dropping in on Catherine, had to pass through his hands.

The youth entertained ministers and courtiers, lying on a couch in his silk Bokhara dressing gown. Elderly generals, trembling respectfully, stood at attention before the young beauty.

The elderly empress, in love beyond measure, entrusted him with all the most responsible state tasks. Love literally blinded her.

33. But all along, the lad had some very mixed-up notions about life and politics. For example, his project for a New Russia is well known.

In this amazing project the following are proudly indicated as capitals of the first order: Petersburg, Astrakhan, Moscow, and Constantinople. Among cities of the second order are indicated, for some reason: Cracow, Taganrog, and Danzig. In this project, there is the following phrase: "The sovereign empress of so vast an empire should be likened to the sun, who, with his beneficent gaze, warms everything that his rays can reach."

In all, one can judge from this project alone, how much the old lady had begun to spit on affairs of state and the extent to which world politics had faded in comparison with her last love.

But this instance shows us an aging human being in all her pathetic beauty, rather than the happier qualities of love.

Here, however, is the story of a great love for you, one which took place when the forces were in full flower.

34. This story is also fairly well known, having been performed on theatrical stages. So we will not linger on it especially long. This, you know, is the one about how the Roman consul, Mark Antony, loved the Egyptian queen, Cleopatra. In all, let us try to recall this story, all the more since it is a touching story and at the same time extremely surprising. An ambitious man, having achieved for himself, just imagine, immense power, fell in love with a woman and threw it all decisively away. He even threw away his army with which he had set out on conquest. And he stuck forever in Egypt.

He gave Cleopatra Roman lands—true, conquered by him—Armenia, Syria, Chilicia and Phoenicia; and lifted her to the rank of "empress of emperors."

The Roman Senate, seeing the military commander's scandalous activities, hastily removed Antony from the position of first consul. But the love-bound Antony did not even wish to return home.

Then Rome declared war on Cleopatra. And the famous struggle between them began.

Antony, along with Cleopatra, marched out against the Roman army.

The Roman army approached Alexandria, and the Roman consul Octavian wrote Cleopatra a letter to the effect that she could still save her life and throne if she'd only sacrifice Antony.

35. The lady empress, seeing that her private affairs were of little importance, decided to sacrifice her ardent lover.

And while Antony was engaged in the struggle with Octavian, Cleopatra informed her lover by way of a servant that she had taken her own life. She knew Antony was so in love with her that he would not survive his grief. And that's really the way it was: When he learned of Cleopatra's end, Antony ran himself through with his sword.

As it turned out, though, the wound wasn't fatal. And Antony, when he found out that Cleopatra was still alive, had himself brought to her on a stretcher. And, in her embraces, he died, having forgiven her for her deception.

This surprising story really tells of a fairly great love which decisively eclipsed everything else.

And a little later, Cleopatra also put an end to herself.

For this reason: that Octavian was getting ready to send her off to Rome as a trophy. Cleopatra had wanted to attract this leader too, with her flirting, but nothing came of it, and then she, not wanting to survive her shame, poisoned herself. And thirty of her servant girls poisoned themselves along with her.

And for some reason we feel sorry for this beauty, to whom Octavian said: "Put away thy net, O queen—you won't catch *me* in it." But she was already forty years old, and she understood that her song had been sung.

36. But there is still one great love, in the course of which a man forgot his revolutionary conscience.

This refers to the husband of the well-known Mme. Tallien.

At the time of the French Revolution the chief secretary of the revolutionary council was sent to Bordeaux by Robespierre to arrest the aristocrats who had run off there.

And, lo and behold, in the prison there, he made the acquaintance of a young woman who had been arrested—Teresa Fontenet. He fell in love with her and let her out of the prison.

Robespierre, when he learned that Tallien had released a prisoner, ordered her arrested again.

Then, Tallien, having joined forces with the partisans of Danton, conducted such a struggle against Robespierre that in a short time he was able to overthrow him. And one of the motives for this struggle was undoubtedly his love for Teresa Fontenet.

Later, Tallien married her, but she soon threw him over and married some kind of prince.

But this still isn't all that history knows.

Even beyond this, there have taken place from time to time small events, at first glance little worthy of note, but nevertheless, one can say, events that are literally like the sunlight breaking through the thicket of the forest. This was great love.

37. * Take, for example, the wives of the Decembrists, brilliant society ladies who gave up everything and voluntarily, though no one had exiled them, followed their husbands to Siberia.

* The sick Radishchev had been sent off to exile. Not long before this, his wife had died. Then his wife's sister followed him into exile . . .

* The son of a rich landowner, the brilliant cavalry guard officer Ivashov, loved the governess Camilla, who worked in his family's house. His parents, naturally, refused to let him marry her. But within a year when Ivashov was sent to Siberia for twenty years in the affair of the Decembrists, the young governess voluntarily followed him.

* The passionately loved wife of the English poet, Robert Browning, died. Bewailing her terribly, the poet placed in her grave the dearest thing he owned—a notebook of his new sonnets.

True, later, when the poet fell in love again, he managed to get this notebook back, but this is not so important.

* Napoleon, in the heat of battle, in 1796, wrote to Joséphine: "Away from you the world is a desert in which I wander alone. You are the only thought of my whole life."

* Lassalle wrote to Elena Denniguez: "I have a giant's powers and I multiply them by a thousand in order to conquer you. No one in the world can take you away from me . . . I suffer a thousand times more than Prometheus on his rock."

38. Chernyshevski, in love with his own wife, wrote to Nekrasov: "It isn't for world problems that people drown themselves, shoot themselves, become drunkards. I have experienced it and

I know that the poetry of the heart has the same rights as the poetry of thought."

  * The city of Weinsberg was besieged by the enemy. The conquerors permitted the women to leave the city before destroying it. At the same time, they permitted each woman to carry off in her own hands that which was most precious to her. And so, several women carried their valiant husbands in their arms.

Naturally, this last event is more like a legend. From time to time history loves to invent for the sake of, so to speak, moral equilibrium, something sentimental like that.

39. From among these sentimental anecdotes, the following is amusing.

A certain knight, going off to battle, entrusted his wife to a friend of his. The friend fell in love with the wife. The wife fell in love with him. But the oath of loyalty, naturally, was inviolable.

And so, in order to preserve and prove this loyalty, they sleep in one bed, putting a double-edged sword between them.

Maybe they really did put this sword between them, and maybe they really did sleep in one bed—we will not deny this historical fact—but as far as the rest of the story is concerned, you must excuse us, we are dubious.

In all, with this sentimental nonsense, we bring to a close our historical tales.

This is what history tells of love.

In all, it tells very little of this emotion. That is to say, yes, this emotion, it would seem, really exists. History, that is to say, has had to deal with this emotion more than once. That is to say, such-and-such historical events and incidents have taken place on this soil. And such-and-such deeds and crimes have been committed.

But that all this was just something too grandiose for words, in the sense that our poets have sung of it in their tenor voices— well, in that degree, history scarcely knows it at all.

On the contrary, commercial spirits have almost entirely straddled this emotion. And it does not represent any kind of danger for the calm flow of history.

40. No, this emotion has not hindered people from proceeding along the road along which patiently and in good conscience they go anyway.

And the historians are right to be telling us in monotonous

voices about what happened and about how many lumps of soot a bridegroom received in return for this or that feeling of his.

Well, of course, we have been talking of past centuries. And perhaps things have changed a bit nowadays?

Unfortunately, we have never been abroad, and therefore we are not in a position to satisfy fully your legitimate curiosity.

But we are of the opinion that it isn't likely great changes occurred there.

In all likelihood, or so we think, some marquis or other, with his sonorous name, still shows up as the bridegroom of a three-year-old. And papa pays him a monthly allowance.

And, in all likelihood, some sort of aging person, having forgotten everything in the world, still supports some kind of dancing Zubov and lavishes her favors upon him.

Everything, one must assume, goes as it once went.

And as far as we are concerned, well, some substantial changes *have* come to pass here.

FIRST SPEECH ON PUSHKIN

It is with a feeling of pride, I would like to note, that in these days our house is not being braided into the tail end of events.

In the first place, we have acquired for six rubles fifty kopecks a single-volume edition of Pushkin for general use. In the second place, a plaster bust of the great poet has been placed in the office of the Tenant's Co-operative Association, which in its turn serves to remind those who don't pay their rent on time of their arrears.

In addition to this, we have hung an artistic portrait of Pushkin before the main entrance.

And finally, this meeting speaks for itself.

Certainly, perhaps it's little, but speaking frankly, our Co-op Association didn't expect there'd be such a bustle. We thought, well, as usual, they will note in the press: there you are, poet of genius, lived in the stern epoch of Nicholas I; well, on the stage, there they'd start some artistic reading excerpts, or they'd sing something from *Eugene Onegin*.

But what is happening in our days—frankly speaking, it obliges our Co-op to be careful and to re-examine its position in the realm of creative literature, so we won't be accused of not appreciating poems and so forth.

Still, you know, it is well that in the sense of the poets, as it is said, God has blessed our house. It is true we have one tenant, Tsaplin, who writes verses, but in addition he's a bookkeeper, and, to top it all off, he's such a lout, I don't mind saying, I'm not even sure whether I should be mentioning him on Pushkin's anniversary. The other day he comes into the Co-op and he's theatening: "I," he yells, "will bury you, you long-tailed devil, if you don't move my stove for me before Pushkin's anniversary. I," he says, "am stifling from the fumes because of that damn stove and I can't write poems." I say: "Even taking into account how delicate relationships with poets are, I can't have your stove moved for you in the time specified because our mechanic has taken off." So that's why he's yelling. Hauled off after me.

Praise be, that among our tenants there aren't still more cadres of writers and such like, you know. If there were, they'd be nagging about stoves like this Tsaplin.

Well, *so what* if he can write verses. In that case, I, too, and my seven-year-old nephew can bring some pretensions to bear on the Co-op. At my place, he writes too. And some of his verses aren't at all bad:

> We children like the time when the bird is in the cage;
> But we don't like those folk who against the Five-Year-Plan rage.

Seven years old he is, and look how he writes! But still that doesn't mean I want to compare him with Pushkin. Pushkin is one thing, and the stifling tenant Tsaplin is another. A scoundrel like that! You see, my wife is coming in, and he's after me. "I," he yells, "am going to stick your head into my stove right this moment." Well *what is this,* I ask you?! Here the Pushkin anniversary is approaching, and he's setting my nerves on edge like that.

Pushkin writes so that his every line is beyond perfection. For a tenant of genius like that, we would move his stove even in the fall. But here we're supposed to be moving it for this *Tsaplin*— at this, I am thunderstruck.

A hundred years have passed and still Pushkin's verses call forth our astonishment. But, if you'll excuse me, where will Tsaplin be a hundred years from now? Such a rascal! . . . Or if this Tsaplin had been alive a hundred years ago? I can imagine what he would have been like in those days and in what form he would have come down to the present!

Speaking frankly, I would have been a Dantès to this Tsaplin, and I'd have drilled him full of lead. My second would have said: "Shoot at him *once*." But I would have let go with all five bullets, because I don't like scoundrels.

Great poets of genius die before their time, but this scoundrel Tsaplin remains, and he's still around to wear out our nerves.

(VOICES: Talk about *Pushkin!*)

Why, it's Pushkin I'm talking about. Not Lermontov. As I was saying, Pushkin's poems evoke our astonishment. Every line is popular. Even those who have never read him know him. Personally, I'm very fond of those lyric lines of his from *Evgenii Onegin,* "What's the matter, Lensky, why don't you dance?" And from "The Queen of Spades"—"Oh, how I'd like to be a little branch. . . ."

(VOICES: That's an opera libretto. Those aren't lines by Push-kin.)

What do you mean those aren't lines by Pushkin? What are you trying to do, throw a monkey wrench in the works?

Now that I leaf through our one-volume edition, though . . . I can see that "The Queen of Spades" is prose. . . . Well, now, take these lines: "If all the dear maidens could fly like birds. . . ." If they aren't by Pushkin, then I just don't know what to think about this here holiday. And to make a long story short, I'm *not going* to move Tsaplin's stove. Pushkin is one thing. Tsaplin is another. Imagine. A clod like that!

SECOND SPEECH ON PUSHKIN

Of course, dear comrades, I am not a historian of literature. I permit myself to approach this great occasion, simply, as it is said, in a human sense.

Such a clean-breasted approach, I submit, brings the image of the great poet closer to us.

And, so, a hundred years separate us from him! Time really flies incredibly swiftly!

The German war, as is well known, began twenty-three years ago. That is, from the time it began to Pushkin's time was not a hundred years, but in all only seventy-seven.

And I was born, imagine, in 1879. That means I was even closer to the great poet. Not that I could see him, but, as it is said, there were but forty years in all between us.

My grandmother now, still more clearly, was born in 1836. That is, Pushkin could have seen her and even taken her up in his arms. He might have cooed over her and, what's more, she might have wept in his arms, not realizing who it was that was holding her.

Of course, it isn't likely that Pushkin cooed over her, all the more since she lived in Kaluga, and Pushkin, it seems, never lived there; but one can still permit oneself this rousing possibility, the more so, it seems, since he might very well have taken a trip to Kaluga to see some friends there.

My father, on the other hand, was born in 1850. But Pushkin by that time, alas, was no longer, or else he might even have cooed over my father.

But my great-grandmother now, he might really and truly have taken up in his arms. Just imagine, she was born in 1763, so that the great poet could easily have gone to her parents and demanded that they let him hold her and coo over her . . . Although, on the other hand, by 1837 she was, if you like, sixty years old and a little over, so that, frankly speaking, I don't really know how they went about it and how they managed to arrange things . . . It could be that it was she who cooed over him . . . But that which is for us covered by the darkness of the unknown, probably posed no difficulty for them, and they got along beautifully as far as who cooed over whom and who rocked whom is concerned. And if she really was an old woman of sixty at that time, then, of course, it's absurd even to think that someone was cooing over her. It means rather that she herself was doing the cooing over somebody.

And, perhaps, cradling him and singing him lyric songs, she, unaware of it herself, aroused poetic feelings in him and, perhaps, along with his famous nurse Arina Radionovna, inspired him in the composition of several different poems.

As far as Gogol and Turgenev are concerned, practically all of my relatives might have cooed over them, since still less time separated them from these. In general, I will say this: children—the ornament of our life, and a happy childhood—this, as it is said, is a great and by no means unimportant problem, which has been resolved in our days. Kindergartens, nurseries, waiting rooms for mothers and children in our railroad stations—these are worthy tokens of one and the same enterprise . . . Ah, yes, now what was I talking about? Och—about Pushkin. Well, now, I'll tell you—Pushkin . . . A century to commemorate. And, soon, you see, other glorious jubilees will take place—Turgenev, Lermontov, Tolstoi, Maikov, and so forth and so forth. Time will come for spiels on them, too.

Just among ourselves, one might even be in general a little bit surprised—I mean, that is, if this were some other type of occasion—why such an attitude to poets exists. Take singers, for example. I wouldn't say that our attitude is bad exactly, but they simply aren't regarded in the same way as poets. Yet they too, you might say, are talents. And they too catch hold of the spirit. And they touch our emotions. And so on . . .

Of course, I am not going to make an argument. Pushkin was a great genius and every line of his is of immense and well-known interest. Some people, for example, honor Pushkin even for his light verse. Personally, I wouldn't go that far. Light verse—why, it's, you might say, just light. It isn't heavy industry; I mean, a major work. Not that just anybody could write it. But, you might say, you'd look at it and you wouldn't find anything too, so to speak, original or artistic there. Decisively not. Just imagine, for example, a collection of such—I'd call them simple—words, not on a very high artistic level:

> There goes the servant-boy on a home-made sled,
> The imp has frozen his finger stiff . . .

(VOICE FROM THE AUDIENCE: That's *Evgenii Onegin*—it's *not* light verse!)

Really? But when I was a kid we learned it as a separate poem. Well, so much the better. I'm delighted. *Evgenii Onegin*—that is a really great epic . . . But of course every epic is entitled to its own distinctive artistic defects. All in all, I'd put it this way: for children, this is a very interesting poet. And maybe in his own time that's exactly what he was, even; just simply a children's poet. But maybe he has come down to us in a somewhat different aspect. All the more so, since our children—well, you know how it is—they're grown up. Child's verses don't satisfy them any more. You know what I mean:

> The steam engine goes chuk-chuk-chuk
> And the wheels go tuk-tuk-tuk,
> State Publishing House, hip-hurrah!
> Give a hand to the author—hah!

You know, once we had to learn a light, foolish poem of Push-kin's by heart in class. Not the one about the broom, not the one about the little bird. No. Let's see . . . it was the one about the twig. As if a twig was growing along by itself, and the poet says to it, in a very artistic way:

> "Tell me, twig of Palestine . . ."

(VOICE FROM THE AUDIENCE: That's from Lermontov . . .)
Really? You know, I often get them mixed up . . . Pushkin and Lermontov—for me they are, as it were, a single whole. And that's why I don't make distinctions as to which was which . . .
(NOISE IN THE HALL. VOICES: You better talk about Pushkin's work!)
Comrades, that's just what I'm coming to. Pushkin's work evokes our astonishment. He used to get paid for his verses by the line in chervontsi. Moreover, they kept reprinting him constantly. And *he*—in spite of this, *he* just wrote and wrote and wrote. No kidding.
Of course, life at court got in his way quite a bit and kept him from writing poems. Now parties, now balls, now something else.

As the poet said himself:

> From whence this noise, these unrestrained cries?
> Timbrell and drums are calling someone somewhere.

Timbrell! That's what a man comes to . . .

We shall not, of course, linger on the facts of the poet's biography. These are well known to all. His personal life, though, you might say, on the one hand, a seven-room apartment, a coach; but on the other hand, the tsar himself, Nicholas the Stick, life at court, the lyceum, Dante's, and so forth. And just among ourselves, Tamara, of course, betrayed him . . .

(NOISE IN THE HALL. CRIES: Natalia! *Not* Tamara!)

Really? Och, yes, Natalia. Tamara—that was Lermontov's. That's what I'm saying. But Nicholas the Stick didn't, of course, write verses himself. And of course he couldn't help getting all hot and bothered because he envied the poet . . .

(NOISE IN THE HALL. DISTINCT EXCLAMATIONS RISING TO YELLS. SOME RISE: Enough! Away with the speaker!)

So I was just about to finish, comrades . . .

Pushkin's influence on us is immense. This was a great poet of genius. And it is appropriate for us to regret that he is not now living among us. We would carry him in our arms and we would arrange a fabulous life for the poet, if, of course, we knew that from him would emerge Pushkin. As it happens, we contemporaries are hoping for our own, we arrange an excellent life for them, give automobiles and apartments, and then it turns out that this one isn't Pushkin, nor that one either. You can't, as it is said, get blood from a stone . . . In general, it's a dark profession, God alone knows what they're up to. Somehow singers give more pleasure. They sing, and right away it's obvious what kind of voice they have.

And so, concluding my speech on the poet of genius, I would like to remark that, after the refreshments, there will be an artistic concert.

(LOUD APPLAUSE. ALL RISE AND MOVE TO THE BUFFET.)

I've decided to write a little pamphlet about those buildings which are now being raised for our habitation.

In any case, people spend a large part of their life at home. And even if it were for this reason alone, it would be permissible to focus society's attention on such a problem of no little importance.

I will tell briefly of that house in which I, as it is said, have the good fortune to live.

The house in which I now live is a very solid contemporary house of recent construction.

In the architectural sense, it is a very attractive building. It was built enthusiastically and not without spirit.

Every apartment has a balcony. The windows are wide. And the sun pours in a mighty flow, without difficulty, into the tiny comfortable little apartments. Everywhere there are bathtubs, dustbins. The staircase is quite appealing, but, unfortunately, a little narrow. So that pianos have had to be lifted up through the windows, a fact which has, in its turn, undoubtedly led to a slight lowering of the level of musical culture.

A composer of ours who had taken an apartment on the fifth floor suffered unspeakably when the object of his creative endeavor was stretched on the tightrope.

And really it was somehow unnatural. The more so since there was an awful lot of yelling when they began to put his musical instrument on the block. A groan went up, especially when they began to shove it through the window from outside. I tell you, *that* was a musical moment.

But the process ended successfully, which in any case does honor to the architect who was conscious of the fact that small windows would be a deathblow to composers.

One way or another, the piano was successfully installed in the dwelling. And the composer at once began to pound on it, so that the tenants on the fourth floor ran off at a gallop to complain to the house manager, since it seems that the sound carried rather amazingly well.

No, these fourth-floor tenants were unmusical people. You might think the sounds of a piano would hearten them. They were listening to music! Now I, for example, can distinctly hear the kitten sneeze in my neighbor's room. And I don't go running around complaining about these sounds. Because I understand very well why it sneezes. It's because our window frames are askew, the doors are crooked, there's a draft from all the cracks in the parquet floor. So the animal has caught a cold, and it's sneezing.

Toward spring, when the weather gets a little warmer, it will stop sneezing.

But these are trifles, nonsense. Not on these apartment-house bagatelles was the main attention of the architect concentrated. One must assume that his main task was to shape a building as beautiful as possible.

Well, in an artistic sense, too, our house is miraculously shaped. There are various stucco moldings: garlands, little circles. And somehow this soothes the gaze.

Under the garlands, the heads of horses are molded. And it's attractive to look at them, again and again.

To top it all off, beginning at the third floor and extending upward, two columns stand, for some reason, and, as the saying goes, to eat they don't ask.

Properly speaking, these two columns, as it were, might have no reason for being there. Because in any case the function of columns is to support something somewhere. But these columns, in a way, as it were, are not even supporting anything. And if you go into it at all, it turns out that the house is even supporting *them*. But even that is to the good, that the house is *supporting* them. In any case, the art of antiquity does not collapse.

And, if it did, such a mass of brick would collapse *with* it, that I thank you for Greek architecture.

But it's already the third year now that everything is going splendidly, and this is yet another indication of how staunchly the Hellenic art is maintained among us.

Our courtyard has considerable originality of structure. It, too, if you will, is on an ancient model. But there's already something of a Roman feeling here. In part it recalls the Roman baths or the small inner courtyards of Pompeii for domestic needs.

The small measure of the courtyard did not, however, hinder the architect in his striving to endow it with something extraordinary. In the middle of the yard, there is a large fountain. There is a pond of sorts, and, in the center, a plaster feminine figure with a jug. And on this it is fairly entertaining to look when you tiptoe lightly out the door in the evening.

No, in an artistic sense, our architect mobilized all his forces to the maximum. He might even have tried a little less. If you stop to think, the people who decorate these houses are bringing to them a new way of life.

Generally, if you're speaking about architecture, it's a big minus when, while they're putting up modern buildings, our architects are for some reason thinking about ancient Greece. It's a good thing it's not Egypt yet!

No, I repeat, I am not against columns that are supporting something there. But somehow it goes against my grain when it's the other way round.

An inhabitant of the village F., a certain comrade Lebedev, was thinking of having his child baptized.

Before this time, he had somehow been against religion. He didn't go to church. He had nothing to do with church activities. And even to the contrary—having advanced views, he had even belonged at one time to the atheists' club.

But in this season a daughter was born unto him. And so he was thinking of having her baptized.

Closer to the truth, it was his wife, that mother of little spirit, who put him up to this. And it wasn't even his wife, as much as her shortsighted parents, who set the tone for the whole thing. Inasmuch as they began to nag: "Och, you see, it's not nice if you don't baptize her, you see, suddenly she'll grow up, or, on the contrary, she will die and she'll be unbaptized and what then?"

Well, the frivolous conversations of politically backward people.

But Lebedev surprisingly did not want to baptize his daughter. Nevertheless, when they went at him, his spirit shook. And since the man had inner conflicts, he gave his consent. He put it this way to them: "Okay. Baptize her. Only I don't want there should be such a fuss about this problem. I am absolutely free to dispose of my own world outlook. If I want, I baptize; if I don't want, I don't baptize. But such conversations are being started here: talk, talk, talk. You see, I've baptized a dog's nose, turned back, you see, to the services of the church. You see, they'll say, it's not for nothing his father worked in bygone days for a house owner as senior gatekeeper."

At this, his wife said to him that if he himself weren't dragging around so about this matter of baptizing his daughter, then there'd be no fuss at all about this problem.

And so, the parents arranged things with the priest, for him to baptize their daughter. And for a five-ruble note that worthy one took upon himself to do this and designated a day and an hour for them.

And, meanwhile, the parents registered their child in the Registration Bureau under the name of Rose, received a certificate, and on the appointed day appeared in church for the baptism.

On that particular day they were baptizing another child there. And our friends, waiting their turn, stood and watched how it was done.

And Lebedev, being himself of an antireligious orientation and having, so to speak, a critical view of all that pertained to the church, simply could not remain silent. And all the time he kept needling the priest with his biting remarks.

No matter what the priest does, Lebedev snickers mockingly, and says to him, practically at his elbow: "Well, that's laying it on a bit thick," he says . . . or, "Well, what will they think of next? . . ." Or, glancing at the priest's reddish foliage, he suddenly says: "There wasn't a single redhead among the saints . . . But this one's got red hair."

This latter remark evoked laughter among the relatives. So that the priest even interrupted the baptism for a moment and scowled angrily at everyone.

And when he took up the Lebedev infant, Lebedev partly lost his sense of measure and openly began to chisel away at the priest with his mocking remarks.

And he even said: "Now, look, whiskers, see to it my kid doesn't catch cold, thanks to your baptism. I'll scorch your temple for you if she does."

The priest's hands were even trembling when he heard this.

He said to Lebedev: "Listen, I don't understand you. If you came here to bait me, I'm surprised at you. Have you considered within you what you are doing? At the very moment when I'm holding your daughter in my arms, instead of purifying prayer, anger against you rises in my spirit and bad language, and what kind of a send-off will I give your daughter into life? Why, maybe now her whole life will wither, or maybe she will be struck deaf and dumb."

Lebedev says: "Well, if you go corrupting my daughter on me, I'll tear your hide off you, just keep that in mind."

The priest says: "You know what? Better wrap your whelp up in the blanket and get out of the temple. And I'll give you back your five-spot and we'll part on good terms. Better that, than I should be hearing such squalor."

Here his relatives began to check Lebedev: "You see, really, button your lip; you see, you should wait till you get out of the temple before you let yourself go; you see, don't lead the priest on, or he'll drop your daughter on the floor, if that's what you want. Look, his hands are shaking and his knees are bending."

And so, although inner conflicts tore at Lebedev, he restrained himself and did not answer the priest in kind. He only said to him: "Well, okay, okay. I won't any more. Get on with the baptism, longhair."

At this point the priest began to pronounce the words of the ceremony. Then he turned to Lebedev and said: "What name shall I pronounce? What did you call your daughter?"

Lebedev says: "We called her Rose."

The priest says: "So that's it!—Ah, how much trouble you've given me with your visit. It isn't enough that you baited me. Now it's explained to me that you've given your infant a name like that. Rose—why, that's a Jewish name. And I refuse to baptize her with a name like that. Wrap her up in the blanket and take yourself out of the temple."

Lebedev, who'd lost all control of himself, says: "Now that's better yet. First he threatens the child with withering, then he ups and refuses to baptize her. But this name is from the word 'rose'—that means it's a plant, a flower. It's another thing, for example, Rosalie Semenovna—she's the cashier from the co-operative. There I won't argue: it's a Jewish name. But *here* you can't refuse to baptize my child that way."

The priest says: "Wrap your child in the blanket. I won't baptize her at all. Among the saints I don't find any such name."

The relatives say to the priest: "Listen, we've registered her in the Registration Bureau under that name. What in the name of God are you making trouble about?"

Lebedev says: "I told you so. There's a priest for you. He goes against the Registration Bureau. And now it's clear to all what kind of a lousy political world outlook he has."

The priest, seeing that the relatives won't leave and won't take the child away, began to disrobe himself. He took off his brocaded gown. And here they all saw that he's now going around in trousers and high boots. And in this sacrilegious mode he goes up to the images and snuffs the candles. And he wants to spill the water out of the font.

But in the temple, among others, there was a certain person who had just arrived. This person had been in the neighborhood on business for the co-operative. And now it so happened that, just for something to do, he wandered into the church, just to see what was going on and how things were there these days.

And now this person took to speech, and he says: "I'm against these ceremonies, understand, and I'm even surprised at the darkness of the local inhabitants, but since the child's already wrapped up and his parents are burning with the desire to christen her, then you just have to go through with it, no matter what. And in order to get you out of the position you're in, I would suggest calling your child by a double name. For example, you call her Rose; why not just add Marie. So instead you'll have Rose-Marie. And there's even an operetta by that name, which indicates that it exists in Europe."

The priest says: "Among the saints I don't find any double names. And I'm even surprised that you're trying to lead me astray with this. If you like, I will call her Marie. But Rose—I wouldn't even think of pronouncing it."

Lebedev says: "Well, devil take him. Let him call her Marie then. We'll adjust it later."

The priest put on his robe again and rapidly, in the course of five minutes, went through the whole church operation.

Lebedev conversed with the visiting person and thanked him for seeing to it that the priest's activities did not go unremarked. So that everything blew over quite pleasantly.

But Lebedev's hopes that there might not be a fuss around this problem turned out to be unjustified. As you see, this story even broke into print. And not in vain. Don't go to churches if your world outlook tells you no. But if it should be you've already entered the temple—behave yourself, and don't bait the priest with stupid remarks.

THE STORY OF MY ILLNESS

In the spring of '38, the magazine *Krokodil* suggested I write an article on certain defects of our regional hospitals.

By way of material they presented me with a couple dozen letters from readers which had been received by that journal and by the staffs of the Moscow newspapers.

The task of writing this article could be carried out in two ways: either write the usual journalistic article, listing the names and addresses of the guilty administrators, or—a comic sketch.

I chose the second way. Before the reader is an imaginary regional hospital, where, in the context of caricature, the authentic defects enumerated in the readers' letters are strewn.

Such a way of carrying out the task will achieve its goal in no less a degree than a concrete list of names and addresses. Further investigation has shown that many of the defects depicted in our comic sketch have been opportunely corrected.

Some of the shortcomings of the hospitals have, however, remained to this day.

Frankly speaking, I prefer to be ill at home.

Oh, I wouldn't say that it isn't brighter in the hospital and more cultivated. And perhaps they do watch the calories of your diet more closely. But you know how the saying goes: "Be it ever so humble, there's no place like home."

But they took me to the hospital with typhoid fever. The people at home thought that in this way they'd lighten my unbelievable sufferings.

Only they did not achieve their goal, inasmuch as I got stuck into some kind of special hospital, where everything did not entirely please me.

In any case, they carted off the sick man, they are writing his name down in a book, when suddenly he reads a sign on the wall: "Corpses Distributed from 3 to 4."

I don't know how other patients felt about it, but I jumped right back on my feet when I read that sign. The important thing is: I have a high temperature, and, in all, it may be that life is just barely managing to keep itself warm in my organism, and maybe it's hanging by a hair—and suddenly I happen to read a sign like that.

I said to the man who was registering me: "Why," I say, "comrade orderly, do you go around hanging up such vulgar signs? In any case," I say, "patients don't find it attractive to read such things."

The orderly, or intern or whatever he was, was surprised to hear me speak to him like that, and he says: "Look: a patient, he can hardly walk, his fever's so high, steam is practically coming out of his mouth, and still," he says, "he's going around making criticisms. If," he says, "you get better, then you'll have a chance to criticize. And if not, we'll distribute you from three to four, as the sign says, and then you'll know what it's all about."

I wanted to lash out at this orderly, but inasmuch as I had a high temperature, 103.8, I didn't pick a fight with him. I only said to him: "As you please, you enema pipe, I'll get better, so you'll answer to me for your loutishness. Is it proper," I say, "for a patient to hear such speeches? This," I say, "morally undermines their strength."

The orderly was surprised that a patient who was so sick has it out with him so freely, and at once he changed the subject. And at this moment a nurse came running up.

"Come along, patient," she says, "to the washtub."

These words also made me flinch.

"It would be better," I say, "if you didn't call it a washtub, but a bath. This," I say, "is *prettier,* and makes the patient feel better. And I," I say, "am not a horse that they should be washing me up."

The sister of mercy says: "Why should a patient," she says, "notice all these trifling details? It's likely," she says, "that you won't get better if your nose pricks up at everything."

At this point, she led me to the bath and ordered me to undress . . .

And so I began to undress, and suddenly I see in the bath under the water some kind of head is emerging. And suddenly I see that there is, as it were, an elderly woman sitting in the bath, in all likelihood one of the patients.

I say to the nurse: "Where have you taken me, you dogs, to

the ladies' bath? Someone is already swimming around here," I say.

The nurse says: "Why, there's a sick old woman sitting here. Don't pay any attention to her. She has a high temperature and doesn't react to anything. So don't you worry, and just go ahead and undress. And in time we'll haul the old woman out of the bath and fill it up with fresh water for you."

I say: "The old woman doesn't react, but maybe *I* still react. And it's pretty unpleasant for me to watch somebody splashing around in the bath like that."

Suddenly, the intern shows up again.

"I am seeing such a squeamish patient for the first time," he says. "*This* doesn't please him and *that* isn't good enough for him. A dying old woman is splashing around a bit, and *he's* expressing pretensions. And her temperature's maybe 104 degrees, and she's in no position to take anything into account; everything she sees, she sees as through a sieve. And in any case she wouldn't bear the sight of you in this world for a superfluous five minutes. No," he says, "I much prefer patients who come to us unconscious. Then at least everything is to their taste, they are satisfied with everything, and they don't go around presenting us with scientific reproaches."

At this point, the splashing old woman raises her voice: "Take me," she says, "out of the water. Or," she says, "I'll get out myself and steam all of you up."

At this point they carted off the old woman and ordered me to get undressed.

And while I was undressing, they swiftly let in hot water and ordered me to get in.

And knowing my character, they no longer tried to argue with me but kept saying "yes, yes, yes" to everything. Only after bathing they gave me an immense nightgown, not at all my size. I thought they were deliberately trying to palm this outfit off on me, but then I saw that this was a normal occurrence with them. The little patients as a rule were in large nightshirts, and the big ones in little nightshirts.

And my outfit even seemed a little better than the others. On my nightshirt the "Patient" stamp was on the sleeve and didn't spoil the over-all appearance, but on some patients the stamp was on the back, and on others on the chest, and this was morally degrading to human self-respect.

But, inasmuch as my temperature was going steadily up, I didn't stop to argue about these things.

But they put me in a small ward, where about thirty patients of various kinds were lying. Some, from the look of them, were very ill. But some, on the contrary, were getting better. Some were whistling. Others were playing chess. Still others wandered about the wards and were reading the charts at the head of the beds.

I raised a shout so the chief doctor would come, but, instead, this very same intern showed up again. But I was in a weakened condition. At the sight of him, I finally lost consciousness.

I think, in all likelihood, it was about three days before I came to.

The nurse says to me: "Well," she says, "you certainly have nine lives. You," she says, "have been through all kinds of experiences. We even put you near an open window accidentally, and then you started to get better unexpectedly. And now," she says, "if you don't catch anything from your neighbors," she says, "we can sincerely congratulate you on your recovery."

Nevertheless, my organism was not subjected to any other illnesses, and it was only just before I left that I came down with a children's disease—whooping cough.

The nurse says: "You must have gotten this infection from the neighboring wing. That's our children's section. And in all likelihood you incautiously ate off the same tray that a child with whooping cough had been eating off. That's why you came down with it."

All in all, the organism mended itself, and once again I began to get better. But when the matter got as far as signing out, then and there, you might say, I began to suffer and I took ill once again, this time with a nervous ailment. On account of nerves, my skin broke out in little pimples something like a rash.

The intern said: "Stop being so nervous and eventually it will go away."

But I was nervous only because they wouldn't sign me out. Sometimes they forgot. Sometimes they were missing something or other they needed. Sometimes someone who was supposed to be there didn't show up. And it was impossible to mark me off their books.

Then, finally, there was an invasion of sick women, and the whole staff was swept off its feet.

The intern says: "We're so overloaded, we just don't have time to sign patients out. Moreover, it's only eight days that you've been convalescing and already you're raising such a hullabaloo. Why, we have some convalescents who haven't gotten signed out for three weeks. Still, they wait patiently."

Soon, however, they signed me out, and I returned home.

My wife says: "You know, Pete, a week ago we thought you had departed for beyond the grave. We got an announcement from the hospital which said: 'On receiving this notice, appear at the appointed time for the body of your husband.'"

My wife, it seems, hurried to the hospital. There they apologized for a mistake somebody in the bookkeeping department had made. It was somebody else who had kicked the bucket, but they had gotten him mixed up with me. Even though by that time I was perfectly all right and had merely broken out in pimples on account of nerves.

In all, a feeling of unpleasantness lingered on account of this incident, and I wanted to run to the hospital in order to have it out with somebody. But as I recalled the kind of thing that went on there—well, you know, I just sort of changed my mind and didn't go.

And now when I get sick, it's at home.

Not long ago, I was eating in a restaurant and afterwards I looked into the billiard room. I wanted, as the saying goes, to see how the balls were clicking there.

No words—an interesting game. It's absorbing and distracts man from his sufferings. There are some who even find that the game of billiards develops manhood, sharp-sightedness, and aggressiveness. And doctors maintain that this game is a very useful corrective for touchy men.

I don't know. I don't think so. I once knew a touchy man who got so tanked up on beer while playing billiards that after the game he could scarcely slide home. So I doubt that it's much of a corrective for the nervous and distraught.

And whether it reinforces sharp-sightedness—how is one to tell? There was a fellow from our house—his partner was taking aim and banged him in the eye with the cue. Although he didn't go blind, he did slightly lose the sight of one eye. That much for the development of sharp-sightedness. And if they manage to get to his other eye, now, the man will be entirely deprived of sharp-sightedness.

So as far as usefulness is concerned, as the saying goes, it's an old wives' tale.

But, certainly, the game is entertaining. Especially when they play "for stakes"—it's quite diverting to watch.

Of course, they rarely play for money now. But they think up something original instead. Some arrange it so that the loser has to squat under the billiard table. Others arrange it so he has to treat, with a couple of beers. Or he has to pay for the game.

But when I entered the billiard room this time, I saw a very laughable picture.

One winner had ordered his mustachioed partner to crawl under the billiard table with all the billiard balls. He crammed the balls into his pockets, gave him a ball to hold in each hand, and, to top it all off, shoved one ball under his chin. And in this manner, the loser crawled under the billiard table amidst the laughter of all.

After another round the winner again loaded the mustachioed one with balls, and, to top it off, ordered him to take the cue in his teeth.

And that poor bastard had to crawl again, amidst the Homeric laughter of those assembled.

By the next round they didn't know what to think of next.

The mustachioed one says: "Make it something a little easier. You've exhausted me."

And his mustaches really were hanging down: that's how bushed he was.

The winner says: "Why, thanks to these punishments, you fool, I'm teaching you to play a splendid game of billiards."

The winner had a friend of his with him. This one says: "I've got it. If he loses, let's do it this way: let him crawl under the table, loaded with billiard balls, and we'll tie a cask of beer to his foot, to top it off. Let him crawl under like that."

The winner says, laughing: "Bravo! That's the way!"

The mustachioed one says in an offended tone: "If the cask is going to be full of beer, then I won't play. It'll be tough enough crawling with an empty cask."

In all, he lost again. And here, amidst general laughter, they loaded the mustachioed one up with billiard balls again, put the cue in his teeth, and tied a cask to his foot. To top it off, the winner's friend began to pull the mustachioed one by the cue so that he'd proceed more rapidly on his route of march under the table.

The winner was laughing so hard he collapsed on a chair and gasped from lack of breath.

The mustachioed one crawled out from under the table, no longer himself. He stared dully at all the assembled, and for some time he didn't even move. Then he unloaded the billiard balls from his pockets and began to untie the cask of beer from his feet, saying that he wasn't going to play any more.

The winner was laughing so hard, tears were rolling down his cheeks. He said: "Come on now, Egorov, *golubchik,* let's play another round. I've thought up another entertaining bit."

This one says: "Well, what did you think up now?"

Stifling with laughter, the winner says: "Come on, Egorov, let's play for your mustache. For a long time now I haven't gone for that fluff. If I win, I cut off your mustache. All right?"

The mustachioed one says: "No, for the mustache I won't play. Or else give me a forty-point lead."

In all, he lost again. And no one managed to remember how the winner seized a table knife and began to remove the fluffy mustache from his ill-fated partner.

In the room, they were dying of laughter.

Suddenly, one of those present goes up to the winner and says to him, like this: "It's likely your partner is a fool, agreeing to penalties like that. And you go and take advantage of this and mock a man in a public place."

A friend of the loser says: "What the hell business is it of yours? He agreed to it of his own free will."

The winner says to his partner in a sepulchral voice: "Egorov, come here. Answer to the group. Did you agree of your own free will to these penalties or did you not?"

His partner, hanging on to the half-cut mustache with his hand. says: "Of my own free will, it's well known, Ivan Borisovich."

The winner says, turning to the public: "Somebody else might let his chauffeur wait in the cold for three hours. But I deal humanely with people. This is our institution's chauffeur, and I always bring him in where it's warm. I don't treat him at all snootily—I play billiards with him in comradely fashion. I instruct him and punish him only a little. And now they're reproaching me—I really don't get it."

The chauffeur says: "Maybe there's a barber in the audience. If so, I'd appreciate it if he'd trim my mustache."

A man emerges from the crowd and says, taking a scissors out of his pocket: "I am sincerely delighted to trim your mustache. If you wish, I can fix it like Charlie Chaplin's."

While the barber was working on the chauffeur, I approached the winner and said to him: "I didn't know he was your chauffeur. I thought he was a friend of yours. I wouldn't have let you pull such tricks."

The winner, somewhat taken aback, says: "And what kind of a bird are you?"

I say: "I'm going to write an article about you."

The winner, getting scared, says: "I won't tell you my name."

I say: "I'll only describe the facts and add that this was a square-shaped reddish-haired man called Ivan Borisovich. Of course, you may get away with this little trick of yours, but if you do get away with it, at least let your rotten soul tremble before the printed lines."

The winner's friend, when he heard this business about the article, right away took to his heels and disappeared from the building.

The winner swaggered around for a long time and drank beer, shouting that he spat on everyone.

The chauffeur had his mustache trimmed and began to look a bit younger and handsomer. So I even decided to write a sketch of not too ferocious a character.

And when I got home, as you see, I wrote it. And now you are reading it, and it's likely you're surprised that such passionate gamblers exist and that one sometimes comes across such unappealing redheaded men.

This time, allow me to tell of a dramatic episode in the lives of people who are now dead.

And because this is all fact, we will not permit ourselves in our exposition to let too much laughter or too many jokes in, so as not to offend those still left among the living.

But inasmuch as this story is, to a certain degree, a comic one, and laughter, as the saying goes, may rise up of itself, we wish to beg the reader's pardon to begin with, for any involuntary tactlessness in regard to the living or the dead.

Of course, the fact in itself in its original sense has nothing of the comic about it. On the contrary, a man died, a certain unimportant worker, an individual not at all noteworthy in the brilliance of our days.

And, as often happens, after his death some intense conversations began: "You see, he perished at his post." "Ah, whom have we lost?" "There was a man for you." "What a pity we've been deprived of him."

Well it's completely and absolutely clear that during his lifetime no one said such unique things about him, and he himself, so to speak, had set out on the long journey without suspecting the image that would be made of him in the fantasy of his acquaintances.

Of course, if he hadn't died, it still wouldn't be known how this fantasy came about. Most likely these very same persons would have, as the saying goes, taken him for a toboggan ride.

But inasmuch as he had meekly died, they attributed him with something close to divinity.

On the one hand, friends, it's nice to die; on the other hand— *merci,* better not. We'll manage to get along somehow without your emotional gratitude.

Speaking briefly, a discussion took place in the hours after work in the institution where he had labored, and in this discussion various touching episodes from the life of the deceased were recalled.

Then the manager himself took up the word. And under the impetus of the oratorical art he worked himself up to such a frenzy that he easily burst into tears. And after bursting into tears, he praised the deceased beyond all measure.

At this point, passions become decisively overheated. And everyone competed in trying to show that he had lost a true friend, a son, a brother, a father, and a teacher.

From amidst the general hubbub, one shout broke through decisively, to the effect that they should arrange the most ardent possible funeral, so that other employees might also strive in this direction. And, seeing this, they might straighten themselves out a bit and try to earn for themselves a funeral like this one.

They all said: "That's right." And the manager added: "Let the union post it on the bulletin board—the funeral will be conducted at treasury expense."

Then someone else got up and said that such remarkable people, generally speaking, had to be buried to music, and not carried silently along empty streets.

At this point, tears rolling down his face, a relative of the deceased rises from his place, his blood nephew, a certain Kolesnikov. He speaks as follows: "My God, how many years was it I lived in the same apartment with my uncle! I won't say that we cursed each other out often, but anyway our life didn't always go smoothly since I didn't realize the kind of man my uncle was. But now, when you tell me about all this, your every word falls on my heart like white-hot metal. Ah, why didn't I make life comfortable for my uncle! Now this will torment me all the rest of my life.

"No, I won't be too lazy now to take off for a certain place I know, where there's a big band with six brasses and one drum. And we'll invite this band to play something special for my uncle."

They all said: "That's right, invite this band—this will in part make amends for your boorish behavior in regard to your uncle."

Speaking briefly, a funeral was arranged within two days. There were many wreaths and a mass of people. The musicians really played not at all badly and attracted the attention of passers-by who asked now and then: "Who's being buried?"

On the way, this uncle's nephew himself quietly approached the manager and said to him quietly, like this: "I invited this band, but they insisted on one condition—they be paid immediately after the funeral, since they have to leave right away for a guest performance in Staraya Russa. How are we going to manage to pay them without a special squeeze?"

The manager says: "But weren't *you* going to pay for the band?"

The nephew was surprised and even frightened. He says: "You said yourself that the funeral was at treasury expense. *I* just ran to ask the band!"

"Be that as it may, the band wasn't taken into account. Correctly speaking, the man who died was a small, insignificant person, and all of a sudden, willy-nilly, we've asked a band to play for him! No, I can't go along with it—the union would put me on the spot."

Those who were walking along beside the manager also said: "In the final analysis, an institution cannot pay for each of its deceased workers. You should be grateful that we paid for the hearse and all the funeral doings. As for the band, pay yourself, since it was your uncle."

The nephew says: "Are you nuts or something? Where am *I* going to get two hundred rubles from?"

The manager says: "Why don't you try getting together with your relatives, and then maybe you can get out of this jam somehow."

The nephew, beside himself, ran along the procession to the widow and informed her of what had occurred.

The widow wept still more, and refused to pay a thing.

Kolesnikov pushed his way through the crowd to the band and told them to stop blowing their horns, since the whole matter had gotten into a tangle and nobody knew now who would pay them.

In the ranks of the band, which was marching in formation, some confusion occurred. The leader said: "We won't stop playing, we will play to the end, and then we'll go to court to get the money from the man who gave us the commission."

And clashing his cymbals together, he put an end to the discussion.

Then Kolesnikov again pushed his way through to the manager, but the latter, anticipating unpleasantness, had sat down in an automobile and silently departed.

The hue and cry evoked surprise in the ranks of the procession. The manager's departure and the widow's loud moaning struck those present all the more. Discussions began, interrogations and whisperings; the more so, since someone had passed along a rumor that the manager had broached the problem of lowering wages.

In all, they arrived at the cemetery in complete disorder. The burial itself took place at an extremely rapid tempo and without speeches. And everyone dispersed, feeling little satisfied. And several insulted the deceased, recalling now one incident, now another, from his petty life.

The following day, the nephew of the deceased uncle pressed the manager so hard that the latter promised to discuss the matter with the union. But at the same time he expressed doubts that it would pass, since the union's task was to concern itself with the living and not to mess around with the dead.

One way or another, Kolesnikov, meanwhile, sold his overcoat in order to get out of the clutches of the band members who really would have stopped at nothing to get their "honorarium."

The nephew sold his coat for two hundred and sixty rubles. So that after he settled accounts with the bank, he still had some "fat" left over, sixty rubles worth. With this money, the nephew of this uncle made the third day's libations. And this circumstance informs us that the institution with the manager at its head was not at its full complement.

Having gotten thoroughly soused, the nephew of this uncle came to me and, wiping away the tears with his sleeve, told me about this whole petty unpleasantness of his, which was for him, of course, far from being the last.

For his uncle, however, this petty unpleasantness *was* the last. And that's just as well.

Here is what a certain worker of the city transport told me.

All in all, the little story he told is instructive not only for the transport. It is also important for all other participants in our life.

For this reason we decided to trouble the attention of our worthy readers with this little tale in the form of a short sketch.

So, once, in a certain administration, a certain rather large worker named Ch. was employed.

In the course of twenty years he occupied solid positions in the administration. Just think, at one time he was the head of the local committee. Then he was moved to the position of administrative director. Then he was made the boss of something else.

Briefly speaking, all twenty years saw him at the summit of his life. And everyone got used to this. And no one was surprised at it. And many thought: "That's the way things are."

Of course, Ch. was not an engineer or a technician. A specialist's education he did not have. And even in general, it seems, his education was rather on the weak side.

Anything special, he did not know how to do. He didn't even have a very good handwriting.

Nevertheless, everyone reckoned with him, respected him, wished him well, and so forth.

When meetings occurred, he was especially indispensable. Here, as the saying goes, he gave off steam as a god in the clouds. He molded various speeches, pronounced words, aphorisms, coined slogans. He opened every meeting with an introductory speech about this or that. And everyone thought that without him the world would revert back to the devil.

All his speeches, of course, were taken down in shorthand for posterity. And for his twentieth anniversary in office, he even thought up the idea of publishing his speeches as a separate brochure. But inasmuch as paper had recently been assigned to the increasing production of plates and cups for ice cream, there wasn't enough paper for his brochure. Otherwise, we would have read his original speeches with interest and expressed our surprise at the way people are.

One way or another, it was decided to make quite a celebration out of his twentieth anniversary. And a briefcase was even purchased with a metal plate on which were engraved the words: "You are this and that . . . twenty years . . . And so forth . . . We regard you . . . You are for us . . . *Merci* . . . And so forth . . . And et cetera."

Something along this line, all told.

However, this anniversary did not take place because an event occurred that notably lowered the significance of the proposed celebration.

This is what happened at the last meeting.

Our Ch. had just made a speech. He had made a burning and passionate speech: "The workers, that is . . . labor . . . they're working . . . alertness . . . solidarity . . ."

And exhausted by his speech, he took his seat beside the chairman amidst a thunder of applause, and he began to doodle distractedly on a sheet of paper.

And suddenly, just think, a certain worker gets up, one of the motormen. He's dressed exceptionally neatly in a gray jacket, with a forget-me-not in his buttonhole.

So he gets up and he talks like this: "Now that we've heard the convincing speech of Comrade Ch., I would like to ask him— well, what *is* it he wanted to say? We've been hearing his tenor voice for twenty years: 'Ah, workers, ah, labor, ah, et cetera . . .' But let us ask: What does this Ch. contribute to our work? What *is* he—a technician, an engineer, or an opera star sent here for our entertainment? Or is there something he knows how to do? The point is that he doesn't know how to do anything. He only makes empty speeches. But, just think, in twenty years we've outgrown this. Many of us have had an education in the seven-year school. And some of us have finished the ten-year school. And maybe they could even teach a thing or two to our respected Comrade Ch., since driving a trolley isn't what it used to be. In former times the driver only knew how to turn the lever for the motor, while at the present moment a driver is a specialist in his own way, one who can draw a diagram of the motor, or make a political speech, or give our orator Ch. a lesson in trigonometry."

Here a noise went up. Shouts. Exclamations.

The chairman got a little scared. He didn't know how he was supposed to react to all this.

But the exclamations go on: "Right!" "True, every word of it!" "Down with this Ch.!"

Then one worker gets up and says: "No, it isn't necessary to fire our famous orator, especially since he's been on his job for twenty years. But better let him sit in the local committee and lick stamps there, rather than always be making moral speeches at our production meetings."

At this point everyone shouted all over again: "Right!"

But one worker, inclined to extremes, got up and said: "It's likely this Ch. thought up a slogan with himself in mind: *'No free loaders.'* And for *this,* he found himself at our head."

Then the chairman interrupted the orator. He said: "It's not necessary to insult personalities."

At this point, everyone looked for an instant at this Ch. Everyone expected to see a storm of indignation on his face, discomfort, and the tension of emotions. But no such thing was seen.

Ch. got up, smiled, and, scratching the back of his head, said: "Properly speaking, what are you picking on me for? Because I'm here? But you put me here, and for my part I never ceased being amazed at it. Why, from the very beginning I told you I didn't know anything about your business. More than that, I began to boss you around, even though I've got little grammar. Why even now, I don't mind telling you, I make six mistakes every two lines."

At this point, everybody laughed. And Ch. himself laughed too.

He said: "Why, I'm really surprised at you myself. For twenty years I've been living in a kind of fairy tale."

Then a conductor gets up and says: "It's like in Pushkin . . . He traded a brick and didn't get away with it. He was left with a cracked trough."

The chairman, closing the meeting, said: "And this one was left with a cracked trough because he kept teaching for twenty years, and never learned anything himself."

Kochergà (THE POKER)

[In spite of his reluctance to scholasticize a joke, the translator must insert an explanation here. The word *kochergà*, which means "a poker," although common, is a strange one in Russian. It should be added also that the numerals two, three, four, in Russian, govern the genitive singular, whereas the numerals from five on govern the genitive plural. The abundant variety of diminutive forms in Russian is also a factor in this story.]

An amusing event took place this last winter in a certain institution.

One should say that this institution occupied a not very large separate house. At the same time, the house was of ancient construction. The usual vulgar stoves heated this building.

A special man—the stoker—looked after these stoves. He went his melancholy way carrying a *kochergà* (a "poker") from floor to floor, poked the wood, adjusted the drafts, closed the pipes, and so forth, all in this vein.

In the midst of contemporary technology, with hot water and steam heating, one can say that this picture had something almost unpleasant about it, an old-fashioned picture depicting the barbaric ways of our ancestors.

This year, in February, the stoker, while making his way along the staircase, inflicted a slight burn on a certain employee, Nadia R., with his poker. The employee herself was partly to blame. She was scurrying along the staircase and bumped into the stoker. In the process, she stretched out her hand and unfortunately happened to touch the poker, which was fairly warm, if not to say red-hot.

The girl gasped and shrieked. And the stoker also gasped. In all, this fussy girl's palm and fingers were slightly singed.

Of course, this is a trivial and empty incident, unworthy to be spread out in the pages of creative literature. Nevertheless, the unexpected consequences of this event were quite amusing. And they have provided us with this little story.

The manager of the institution called in the stoker and gave him a stern talking-to. He said: "So, you're going around with your poker diminishing the ranks of my employees. Better look out where you're going and not gawk around in all directions."

The stoker, sobbing brokenly, answered that he had only one poker for six stoves, and with this one poker he had to go hither and yon. Now if only there were a poker for every stove, then there might be something to carp about. But under such circumstances he simply couldn't guarantee the untouchability of the employees.

This simple idea—to have a *kochergà* for every stove—pleased the manager. And he, not being a red-tape bureaucrat, immediately began to dictate to his typist an order for supplies. Pacing the room, the manager dictated: ". . . Having only one *kochergà* to service six stoves, it is impossible to protect the employees from unfortunate accidents. For this reason, therefore, I request that you promptly issue to the bearer of this order five *k* . . ."

But at this point, the manager broke off. He ceased dictation and, scratching his head, said to the typist: "What the devil. I've forgotten how you write five *k* . . . Three *kochergi,* clear. Four *kochergi*—understood. But five? Five what? Five *kocher* . . ."

The young typist shrugged her shoulders and said that all in all she was hearing this word for the first time. In any case, she had never declined a word like that in school.

The manager called his secretary and, with a troubled smile, told him of his difficulty.

The secretary immediately began to decline this word: "Nominative—*kochergà* . . . Genitive—*kochergi* . . . Dative—*kochergà* . . ." But arriving at the plural, the secretary gulped and said that the plural number was spinning around in his head but he couldn't remember it now.

Then he asked two other employees but they too did not succeed in shedding any light on the matter.

The secretary said: "There is an excellent way out. Let us make two requests for supplies—one for three pokers, and one for two. That way we'll get five."

The manager found this awkward. He said that sending two separate request slips would demoralize bookkeeping. They'd find ways of reproaching him for this. Better, when it came to that, to call up the Academy of Sciences and ask them how you write five *koche* . . .

The secretary was about to call the Academy, but at the last moment the manager didn't permit him to do this. What if some smart-aleck scholar should chance to answer the phone, somebody who would write a sketch in the newspaper to the effect that the manager isn't too literate, to the effect that scientific institutions are being bothered with such nonsense. No, better proceed by one's own means. It might be a good idea to call the stoker again in order to hear the word from his lips. In any case, the man's been hanging around stoves all his life. Surely he ought to know how to say five *koche* . . .

They called the stoker right away and began to probe him with leading questions.

The stoker, assuming that they were going to chew him out again, answered all the questions in gloomy monosyllables. He muttered: "You see, we need five; then, you see, we can be more careful." Otherwise, if they wanted, they could take him to court.

Having lost patience, the manager asked the stoker directly what they wanted to know.

"You know yourselves," the stoker answered morosely.

But at this point, under pressure from the secretary and the manager, the stoker at last pronounced the sought-after word. On the stoker's lips, however, this word did not sound anything like what they had expected, but something like this—"five *kocheryzhek*."

Then the secretary hastened to the legal department and brought an employee from there who excelled in knowing how to draft papers so skillfully they could pass over any reefs.

They explained what was expected of him to this employee— he had to draft the necessary request in such a way that the word *kochergà* was not mentioned in the plural number while at the same time making sure that the institution would be supplied with five.

After chewing his pencil a bit, the employee sketched the following draft: "Until the present time our institution, while it has had six stoves, has had in all only one *kochergà*. In virtue of this, it is requested that five more be issued, so that each stove might have its own independent *kochergà*. Therefore, to be issued— five."

They were just about to send this paper off to the supply warehouse, when, at this point, the typist came up to the manager and said she had just called her mother, a senior typist with thirty years' experience. And *she* had assured her that one had to write —five *kocherëg*.

The secretary said: "I thought so, too. Only I blanked out for the moment!"

Right away the form was drafted and sent off to the supply warehouse.

The funniest thing about this story is that the request form was soon returned with a note from the warehouse manager: "Refused, no *kocherezhek* in stock."

By this time, spring has come. Soon it will be summer. It's a long way to winter. There's no point in thinking about the heating in the meantime. In the spring it is well to think of literacy, as it were, in connection with the spring tests in the middle schools. As far as the above-mentioned word is concerned, it really is a tricky one, worthy of the Academy of Sciences or a typist of thirty years' experience.

All in all, it is necessary to transfer as rapidly as possible to steam heat. So that people can already begin to forget these old-fashioned words connected with wood heating.

THE PHOTOGRAPH

This year I needed a photograph for my pass. I don't know how it is in other towns, but with us on the periphery, having a picture taken is not a simple, ordinary matter.

We have one artistic photographer's shop. But in addition to private citizens, this shop takes pictures of groups and enterprises. And perhaps that's why one has to spend such a long, long time waiting to have one's orders filled.

Since I was more a private person than a group or an enterprise, I took pains to get there early and had the picture taken two months before I needed it.

When they gave me my photographs, I was surprised at how unlike myself I seemed. Before me was a very old face of quite unattractive appearance.

I told the girl who had handed me the photographs: "Why do you snap people like that? Look, there are lines and wrinkles all through my face."

She says: "It was snapped as it usually is. Only it should be said that our retoucher is on sick leave. We didn't have anyone to touch up the defects of your unphotogenic appearance."

The photographer who had been behind the portiere says: "What's he griping about now? Not satisfied?"

I say: "You snapped it badly, honored sir. You disfigured me. Can it be I look like that?"

The photographer says: "I snap opera stars, and they never get insulted. And now a fellow like this turns up—he's got too many wrinkles . . . When the objective is focused too sharply, everything comes out in relief . . . You don't know the technique, and here you're setting yourself up as a critic!"

I say: "For what do I need to have my face in relief? Put yourself in my place. You should just snap me as I am," I say, "so one could look at it."

The photographer says: "Ah, he needs to look yet! We snapped his picture and he wants to look at it yet. Caprice, at a time like this. Defects, he sees . . . No, I'm sorry I snapped you so well.

Next time I'll snap you so you'll look at the photograph and groan."

No, I didn't stop to argue with him. It doesn't matter, I think, what kind of photograph I have for my pass. Everybody can see what I really look like.

And with these thoughts, I turn up at the department. The police sergeant began to fasten the photograph to my pass. Then he says: "In my opinion, that's not you on the photograph."

"What do you mean," I say, "not me? I assure you, it's me. Ask the photographer. He'll confirm it."

The sergeant says: "If I asked the photographer every time— what would come of it? No, on a photograph I want to see a given face, without having to call up the photographer. And here I can see, there's no resemblance. Looks like somebody sick with typhus. No meat at all around the cheekbones. Go take it over again."

I run to the photographer's shop. I say to the photographer: "You see what a lousy job you did. They won't even stamp your product."

The photographer says: "The product is quite a normal one. But, of course, you have to take into account that we weren't going to turn on full illumination just for you. We snapped the picture with one lamp. And that's why shadows fell across your face and darkened it. They didn't darken it completely, though. They didn't darken it so much that *nothing* could be seen. Just look how well your ears came out."

"Well, all right," I say—"the ears. But the cheeks," I say, "where are they? Cheeks, too," I say, "are part of the human face."

The photographer says: "I don't know. We didn't touch your cheeks. We have our own."

"Then," I say, "where are they? I," I say, "have spent two weeks in a house of rest. I gained ten pounds. And you here, with just one picture, God knows what you've made of me."

The photographer says: "Why, I suppose *I* removed your cheeks or something? Seems to me you were told quite clearly: a shadow fell on them. And that's why they didn't come out."

I say: "And how can it be, without cheeks?"

"Ah," he says, "as you wish. Snap it over again, I just won't. If I snapped them all over again I wouldn't fulfill my plan and

I'd lose all the premiums. And, to me, the plan is more dear than your unphotogenic face."

Customers say to me: "Don't get the photographer all worked up. Or he'll snap even *worse* pictures of people."

One of the customers says to me: "Honored sir, run down to the market. There's a photographer there snapping pictures with an old-fashioned camera."

I run down to the market. I find the photographer. He says: "No, I've got to have plates to snap a picture. Without plates, better not come to me; it's all the same, I just won't snap. But if you have a plate, I'll snap. And if you should happen to have a featherbed—then, too, I'll snap. My aunt just arrived from Barnaul and she hasn't got anything to sleep on."

I wanted to leave, but at this point I hear some kind of salesman is calling me over. He says: "Come along to my store. I have the finished product."

I look. He has spread out on a newspaper various kinds of ready-made photographs. About three hundred.

The salesman says: "Pick out the one you like best and do with it as you please. You can even paste it on your forehead. If you like, I'll pick one out for you myself. How would you like it, by size or by likeness?"

"By likeness," I say, "only," I say, "pick one that's got cheeks."

He says: "Can be done with cheeks. But they cost five rubles more . . . Now, take this photograph here . . . You won't find anything better than that. And cheeks, it has. And nobody could say that there isn't any resemblance at all."

I paid thirty rubles for two photographs and went to the department.

The police sergeant began to attach my photograph. Then he says: "Why, but this is an old woman."

"Where do you mean," I say, "an old woman? It's a man in a jacket."

"Where the devil is it a man if he's wearing a brooch on his chest? From this brooch I can tell—it's a woman."

I looked at the photograph, and I see it really is a woman. There's a marquisette blouse under the jacket. On her chest, a brooch with a landscape painted on. But a man's haircut. And *my* cheeks.

The sergeant says: "You come here with *real* photographs. But if you show me a woman's or a child's photograph again, I'll have you hauled off because I won't be able to avoid the suspicion that you're trying to conceal yourself under somebody else's face."

I spent a whole week as in a fog. I asked everyone where I might get a picture snapped. On the eighth day, while conversing with a photographer, I began to feel ill. Then they carried me out to the garden and stretched me out on the grass so that the fresh air might revive me. When I came to, I went to the department. I put my first photographs on the table—the ones without cheeks—and I said to the sergeant: "This is all I have, comrade chief. And I can see no way of getting anything better."

The sergeant looked at the pictures, and then at me. And he says: "There you are now, that's not bad. Likenesses."

I wanted to say that I hadn't snapped them over again at all. Then I looked at myself in the mirror—and, really, I see, there is a certain resemblance now. It came through.

The sergeant says: "Even though you look a little shabbier in the picture than in real life, still," he says, "I'd guess that in about a year it will equal out."

"It'll equal out before that, since I still have to get snapped for a travel document, for my party card, and for sending some snapshots to my relatives."

At this point the sergeant stamped my photograph and warmly congratulated me on my having received a pass.

THE ADVENTURES OF AN APE

In a certain city in the south, there was a zoo. It was a small zoo, in which there were one tiger, two crocodiles, three snakes, a zebra, an ostrich, and one ape, or in other words, a monkey. And, naturally, various minor items—birds, fish, frogs, and similar insignificant nonsense from the animal world.

At the beginning of the war, when the Fascists bombed the city, one bomb fell directly on the zoo. And it exploded there with a great shattering roar. To the surprise of all the beasts.

The three snakes were killed, all at the same time, not in itself a very sad fact perhaps. Unfortunately, the ostrich, too.

The other beasts did not suffer. As the saying goes, they only shook with fear.

Of all the beasts, the most frightened was the ape, the monkey. An explosion overturned his cage. The cage fell from its stand. One side was broken. And our ape fell out of the cage onto the path.

He fell out onto the path, but did not remain lying there immobile in the manner of people who are used to military activities. On the contrary. He immediately climbed up a tree. From there, he leaped on the wall. From the wall to the street. And, as though he were on fire, he ran.

He's running, and probably he's thinking: "Eh, if there are bombs falling around here, then I don't agree." And that means he's running like mad along the city streets.

He ran all the way through the city. He ran out on the highway. He runs along this highway till he leaves the city behind. Well, an ape. It's not a man. He doesn't understand the whys and wherefores. He doesn't see any sense in remaining in this city.

He ran and ran and tired himself out. He was all tired out. He climbed a tree. He ate a fly to recoup his strength. And then a couple of worms. And he fell asleep there on the branch where he was sitting.

At this time, a military vehicle came along the road. The driver saw the ape in the tree. He was surprised. Quietly he crept up to it. He flung his coat over it. And put it in his vehicle. He thought: "It's better I give him to some friend of mine rather than have him die of hunger, cold, and other hardships." So that means, on he went along with the ape.

He arrived in the city of Borisov. He went about his official business. But the monkey remained in the vehicle. He said to it: "Wait for me here, cutie. I'll be back soon."

But our monkey wouldn't wait. He climbed out of the vehicle through a broken window and went strolling along the streets.

And, so, he proceeds, the dear little thing, along the street, strolling, ambling along, tail up. The people, naturally, are surprised and want to catch him. But catching him isn't all that easy. He's lively and nimble, and runs quickly on all fours. So they didn't catch him, but only succeeded in tormenting the fugitive in vain.

Tormented, he wearied and, naturally, wanted to eat.

But in the city, where could he eat? There wasn't anything edible in the streets. With his tail, he could hardly get into a restaurant. Or a co-operative. All the more since he had no money. No discount. Ration coupons he does not have. It's awful.

Nevertheless, he got into a certain co-operative. Had a feeling that something was doing there. And they were distributing vegetables to the population: carrots, rutabagas, and cucumbers.

He scampered into this store. He sees: There's a long line. No, he did not take a place in this line. Nor did he start pushing people aside in order to shove his way through. He just leaped along the heads of the customers to where the goods were. He leaped on the counter. He didn't ask how much a kilo of carrots costs. And, as the saying goes, that's the kind he was. He ran out of the store, satisfied with his purchase. Well, an ape. Doesn't understand the whys and wherefores. Doesn't see the sense of remaining without rations.

Naturally there was commotion in the store, hubbub, confusion. The public began to yell. The salesgirl who was weighing rutabagas almost fainted from surprise. And, really, one could well be frightened, if instead of the usual, normal-type customer, a hairy creature with a tail hops up. And what's more, doesn't even pay.

The public pursued the ape into the street. And he runs and on the way he chews on a carrot. He's eating. He doesn't understand the whys and wherefores.

The little boys are running at the head of the crowd. Behind them, the grown-ups. And, bringing up the rear, the policeman is running and blowing on his whistle.

And from somewhere, Lord knows where, a dog leaped out into the melee. And also sets out after our little monkey. Not only is he yelping and yowling, but he's even trying to sink his teeth into the ape.

Our monkey picked up speed. He runs, and probably he's thinking to himself: "Och," he's thinking, "should never have left the zoo. Breathing was easier in the cage. First opportunity, I'm going to head right back there."

And, so, he runs as hard as he can, but the dog isn't giving up and still wants to grab him.

Then our ape hopped up onto some kind of fence. And when the dog leaped up to grab the monkey by the feet, as it were, the latter blipped him full force with a carrot on the nose. And he hit him so hard that the dog yelped and ran home, wounded nose and all. Probably he was thinking: "No, citizens, better I should lie quietly at home than go catching monkeys and experiencing such extreme unpleasantness."

Briefly speaking, the dog fled and our ape leaped into the yard.

In the yard at this time a teen-age boy was chopping wood, a certain Alesha Popov.

There he is, chopping wood, and suddenly he sees an ape. All his life he's dreamed of having an ape like that. And suddenly—there you are!

Alesha slipped off his jacket and with this jacket he caught the monkey who had run up the ladder in the corner.

The boy brought him home. Fed him. Gave him tea to drink. And the ape was quite content. But not entirely. Because Alesha's grandma took an instant dislike to him. She shouted at the monkey and even wanted to strike him across the paw. All this because, while they were drinking tea, grandma had put a piece of candy she had been chewing on a plate, and the ape had grabbed grandma's candy and tossed it into his own mouth. Well, an ape. It's not a man. A man, if he takes something, wouldn't do it right under grandma's nose. But this monkey—right in grandma's presence. And, naturally, it brought her almost to tears.

Grandma said: "All in all, it's extremely unpleasant having some kind of macaco with a tail living in the apartment. It will frighten me with its inhuman face. It will jump on me in the dark. It will eat my candy. No, I absolutely refuse to live in the same apartment with an ape. One of us is going to wind up in the zoo. Can it be that I should move straight over to the zoo? No, better let the monkey go there. And I will continue to live in my apartment."

Alesha said to his grandma: "No, grandma, you don't need to move over to the zoo. I guarantee that the monkey won't eat anything more of yours. I will train it like a person. I will teach it to eat with a teaspoon. And to drink tea out of a glass. As far as jumping is concerned, I cannot forbid it to swing from the lamp that hangs from the ceiling. From there, naturally, it could leap on your head. But the main thing is that you shouldn't be frightened if this happens. Because this is only an ape that means no harm, and in Africa it was used to leaping and swinging."

The next day Alesha left for school. And begged his grandma to look after the ape. But grandma did not begin to look after it. She thought: "What am I going to do yet, stand here looking after every monstrosity?" And with these thoughts, grandma went and fell asleep on purpose in her armchair.

And then our ape leaped out into the street through the open casement window. And walked along on the sunny side. It isn't known whether he maybe just wanted to go for a little stroll, or whether he wanted to go have another look at the store to see if there was anything he wanted to buy for himself. Not for money, but just so.

And along the street at this time a certain old man was making his way. The invalid Gavrilych. He was going to the bathhouse. And in his hands he carried a small basket in which there were some soap and a change of linen.

He saw the ape and at first he didn't even believe his eyes that it was an ape. He thought it only seemed that way to him because he had just drunk up a jug of beer.

So he looks with amazement at the ape. And it looks at him. Maybe it's thinking: "What kind of a scarecrow is this, with a basket in his hands?"

Finally, it dawned on Gavrilych that this was a real ape and not an imaginary one. And then he thought: "With luck, I'll catch it. Tomorrow I'll take it to the market and I'll sell it there for a hundred rubles. And with that kind of money I can drink ten jugs of beer in a row." And with these thoughts in mind Gavrilych set about catching the ape, murmuring: "P'st, p'st, p'st . . . here now."

No, he knew it wasn't a cat, but he wasn't sure what language to speak to it in. But then it struck him that this was, after all, the most highly developed creature of the animal world. And then he took a piece of sugar out of his pocket, showed it to the ape, and said, taking a bow: "Monkey, old friend, old beauty, wouldn't you like to eat a little piece of sugar?"

The latter replied: "Please, yes I would . . ." That is, actually, he didn't say anything because he didn't know how to talk. But he simply walked right up, grabbed this little lump of sugar, and started to eat it.

Gavrilych picked him up in his hands and put him in his basket. It was warm and snug in the basket. And our monkey didn't try to get out. Maybe he thought: "Let this old sot carry me in his basket. It's even rather pleasant."

At first Gavrilych thought of taking it home. But then he really didn't want to go home again. And he went to the bathhouse with the ape. He thought: "Better I should go to the bathhouse with it. There I can wash it up. It will be clean, pleasant to look at. I'll tie a ribbon around its neck. That way I'll get more for it at the market."

And so he arrived at the bathhouse with his monkey. And began to wash himself, and to wash it too.

And it was very warm in the bathhouse, boiling—just like Africa. And our monkey was quite pleased with this warm atmosphere. But not entirely. Because Gavrilych was washing him with soap and the soap got into his mouth. Naturally, it didn't taste good, but that was no reason to scream and kick around and refuse to be washed. Our monkey began to splash furiously, but at this point soap got into his eyes. And from this, the monkey really went out of his mind. He bit Gavrilych on the finger, tore himself loose, and leaped out of the bath as though he were on fire.

He leaped out into the room where people were getting dressed. And there, he frightened them all out of their wits. No one knew it was an ape. They see: something round, white, and foamy has leaped out. At first it leaped onto the couch. Then on the stove. From the stove onto the trunk. From the trunk onto somebody's head. And again up on the stove.

Several nervous-type customers cried out and started to run out of the bathhouse. And our ape ran out too. And went scampering down the stairs.

And there below was the ticket office, with a little window. The ape leaped through this little window, thinking it would be more peaceful there, and, most important, there wouldn't be such a fuss and commotion. But in the ticket office sat the fat woman who sold the tickets, and she sobbed and squealed. And ran out of the ticket office shouting: "Help! Emergency! Seems a bomb fell in my office. Quick, some iodine!"

Our monkey hated all this yelling. He leaped out of the office and ran along the street.

And there he is running along the street all wet and foamy with soap, and behind him, once again, people are running. The boys at the head. Behind them, the grown-ups. Behind the grown-ups, the policeman. And behind the policeman, our ancient Gavrilych, dressed harum-scarum, with his boots in his hands.

But at this point *that dog* leaped out again from some place or other, the very same one who'd been after the monkey the day before.

Having seen this, our monkey thought: "Well, now, citizens, I'm done for once and for all."

But this time the dog didn't go after him. The dog only looked at the fleeing ape, felt a sharp pain in its nose, and stopped running; even turned around. Probably thought: "They don't supply you with noses—running after apes." And although it turned around, it barked angrily: as much as to say, run where you will, I'm staying put.

At this very time our boy, Alesha Popov, returned home from school. He did not find his dear little ape at home. He was terribly roused up about it. And tears even came to his eyes. He thought that now he'd never see his glorious, divine little monkey again.

And so, from boredom and sorrow, he went out on the street. He walks along the street in a melancholy funk. And suddenly he sees—people are running. No, at first he didn't grasp that they were running after his ape. He thought they were running because of an air raid. But at this point he saw his ape—all soapy and wet. He flew toward it. He picked it up in his arms. He hugged it to himself, so as not to give it up.

Then all the people who had been running came and surrounded the boy.

At this point our ancient Gavrilych emerged from the crowd. And exhibiting his bitten finger for all to see, he said: "Citizens, don't let this fellow take my ape in his arms. I want to sell it on the market tomorrow. This is my very own ape, which bit me on the finger. Just look at this gored finger of mine. And that testifies that I'm telling the truth."

The boy, Alesha Popov, said: "No, this ape isn't his, it's my ape. Look how happily it came to my arms. And this testifies that I'm telling the truth."

But at this point yet another man emerges from the crowd— that very driver who had transported the ape in his vehicle. He says: "No, it's not your ape and it's not yours either. It's my monkey because I transported it. But I'm returning to my unit, so I'm going to give the ape to the one who keeps him kindly in his arms, and not to the one who'd sell him pitilessly on the market for the sake of a few driblets. The ape belongs to the boy."

And at this point the whole audience applauded. And Alesha Popov, beaming with happiness, hugged the ape still more tightly to himself. And triumphantly carried him home.

Gavrilych, with his bitten finger, went to the bathhouse to wash up.

And, so, from that time on, the ape came to live with the boy, Alesha Popov.

He's still living with him. Not long ago I took a trip to the city of Borisov. And I purposely went to Alesha's place to see how the ape was getting on. Oh, it was getting along very well indeed! It didn't run away anywhere. It had become very obedient. Wiped its nose with a handkerchief. Doesn't take candy from strangers. So that even grandma is satisfied now and doesn't get mad at it, and no longer wants to move to the zoo.

When I entered Alesha's room, the ape was sitting on the table. Sitting there with a sense of importance, like a ticket taker at the movies. And was eating some rice cereal with a teaspoon.

Alesha said to me: "I've educated him like a man, and now all children and even some grown-ups can take him as an example."

AN EXTRAORDINARY EVENT

This past summer I spent my vacation in a house of rest. The manager of our house of rest directed all his fatherly attentions to the diet of those who were resting, quite rightly assuming that a good table would make up for the many shortcomings of his institution.

He had hired an excellent cook who made splendid pirozhki, amazing salads, and cutlets that weren't bad at all. The dessert, prepared by the masterful hand of this cook, always evoked general approval.

For this reason, the vacationers were well disposed and more than once thanked the manager for his model enterprise.

Wishing to please the vacationers even more, the manager once told someone who had come to thank him: "With your permission," he said, "I will turn your excellency over to our cook, Ivan Fomich, who's working away there at the stove. This would undoubtedly encourage him. And that way we'd get even better results."

From the following day, the quality of the dinners really did improve even more. And then the manager, beaming with pleasure, said to the vacationers: "So, you see, the enthusiasm our cook is showing since he received your thanks. And that's just oral thanks —a bird in the sky. I sincerely advise you: compose a letter of praise to the cook. We'll post it on our bulletin board. And then we'll see what will happen."

The vacationers did just that. They posted a letter with five signatures on the bulletin board; in an ardent style they remarked on the outstanding culinary activity of the cook, Ivan Fomich.

At the same time a certain artist among the vacationers drew a handsome frame around the letter, decorated with scrolls, flowers, and laurel leaves.

The effect exceeded the manager's expectations.

The marvelous pirozhki prepared by our cook now literally melted in the mouth. The salads were now such that even a man who had eaten his fill went on eating more and more. But the dessert that day evoked general astonishment mingled with tumultuous enthusiasm.

But one of the vacationers demonstrated special enthusiasm—a young composer who sat at the table beside me. Accurately speaking, he bounced more than he sat. Some kind of released spring simply wouldn't permit his long thin body to sit still.

Behind our table were seated a doctor of philological science and his wife. The philologist was an unusually gaunt and silent person. But his wife more than made up for these defects.

So that, once, while dining, the young composer manifested exceptional enthusiasm, which even approached a kind of frenzy. Everything that was put on the table this time, he praised to an immoderate degree. But when they brought the dessert, he leaped up from his chair and exclaimed, turning to the philologist: "Taste this whipped-cream frosting right away! It's a miracle of the cooking art!"

The doctor of philological science, having tasted the whipped cream, said, "yes," and nodded his head in a sign of assent.

The philologist's wife began to explain to us that this whipped cream really was good and why frosting creams usually were of an inferior quality.

Without waiting to hear her through to the end, the composer once again exclaimed: "No, no, we have still not taken full measure of the great services of our cook! We are duty-bound, time and again, to keep encouraging this divine gift!"

The philologist's wife proposed that a certain sum of money be collected from among the vacationers in order to buy the cook a silver cigarette holder or a section of material for his uniform. The composer, however, exclaimed indignantly: "Och, that wouldn't do at all! Before us is an astonishing master of his craft —an artist! And we should honor him as we would an artist."

And with these words the composer began to applaud.

The diners looked at him with perplexity. And then the composer hastily ran around the tables and in low tones informed everyone that it had now been decided to greet the cook with applause, to arrange an ovation for him.

All agreed to this willingly. And, at a sign from the composer, the dining room broke into friendly applause.

The kitchen personnel did not instantly grasp the meaning of this noise. The scullery maid appeared on the dining-hall threshold. And from behind, the assistant cook, Fediushka, stuck out his head. Both were smiling, but they looked at the applauding people without understanding what was going on.

The office help ran in. The manager appeared. He immediately joined the crowd and cried out loudly: "Ivan Fomich! We want Ivan Fomich!"

The cook, Ivan Fomich, soon appeared. He was a massive man with a drooping gray mustache. His high chef's cap gave him a rather frightening appearance.

Well, naturally, the cook, Ivan Fomich, was already accustomed to recognition and success, but this ovation noticeably moved and even stunned him with its novelty. For some time he stood silently on the dining-hall threshold and, wiping his sweaty face with his apron, he looked askance at all those around who were standing up and applauding him.

The applause grew stronger. The composer ran over to the piano and played a flourish. And then the cook, Ivan Fomich, came out into the center of the dining room.

Now a complex mixture of emotions played across his face. Pride, agitation, enthusiasm, astonishment—that was what one could read on his features at one and the same time.

The manager raised a hand and, having obtained silence, turned to the cook with a short speech. This is what he said, without any notes: "Dear Ivan Fomich! For a long time your predecessors duped the public with their doubtful culinary doings. And only since you have taken charge has spiritual peace been obtained, an essential prerequisite for health. Allow me, in the name of all the vacationers, to congratulate you and congratulate you again for your high mastery, which, like the sun, has illuminated our modest house of rest!"

Here, amidst wild applause, the manager embraced the cook and kissed him three times on cheek and mustache.

Now it was proposed that the cook make a brief speech in reply. But Ivan Fomich did not seem to be a master of *that* complicated art. It could have been, however, that excitement had lost him his tongue. One way or another, Ivan Fomich dropped a few meager phrases, from which, however, one could gather the noble quality of his thoughts. Having removed his white cap, and hugging it to his heart, he said: "I tried . . . I managed . . . I promise to do my best from now on . . . I'm deeply grateful for this recognition . . . Thanks . . ."

Amidst stormy applause, music, and shouts of "bravo!" this

encounter between the vacationers and the cook came to an end. Having taken a modest bow, Ivan Fomich withdrew to the kitchen.

No, I was not a witness to the events which followed; but eye-witnesses have informed me with formal precision of what happened soon after.

At five o'clock, the cook, Ivan Fomich, accompanied by his nephew, Fediushka, made his way to the village to some fishermen friends. There, having drunk quite a bit, Ivan Fomich hired a boat with two rowers. He decorated this boat with carpets and shrubs. In the stern, he sat an accordion player who was an acquaintance of his. And in this boat, amidst the sound of music, they rowed along the lake and past the numerous rest homes and sanatoriums.

During this entire aqueous excursion the cook stood up in the boat with his hand on the shoulder of one of the rowers. During this entire excursion (according to eyewitnesses) Ivan Fomich stood like a monument between the carpets and the greenery. And when the accordion player was silent, the assistant cook, Fediushka, immediately began to plink away at his mandolin.

The considerable quantity of wine that the cook had downed, however, brought the expedition to an unexpected mishap. When the rowers turned the boat sharply for a second trip, Ivan Fomich didn't quite manage to keep his feet, and fell overboard. His portly body shook the frail craft, and, scooping up water, it overturned.

Fediushka and the rowers swam to shore. And fishermen fished out the cook and the accordion player and his instrument.

Ivan Fomich had swallowed a large amount of water, and for a long time he lay on the shore almost without moving. The inhabitants of the village wanted to give him artificial respiration, but he wouldn't let them. And along with his drenched nephew Fediushka, he hastened back to his own apartment.

And, there, in his own apartment (as people confirmed) Ivan Fomich drank, ate, and made an uproar until deep into the night.

This extraordinary event became known in our house of rest only the following day, when, instead of the usual excellent breakfast, people were served semolina with cranberry sauce.

At breakfast, the doctor of philological science said to us, smiling a little: "Well, I always said that people need unusual moral fiber to be able to stand up to ardent praise."

The philologist's wife began to expand on her husband's idea for us, and took it upon herself to explain in many, many words, that praising people was necessary, pedagogically it gave marvelous results; past a certain point, though, she said, sometimes strange and unexpected things happened—like the scandalous event involving our cook. From this it is demonstrable that excessive praise is dangerous for a weak spirit.

The young composer exclaimed with some inner agitation: "No, I do not agree with you! Even the most exalted praise couldn't damage the issue. And I am more than convinced that our cook, when he's recovered from his mishap, will more than exceed himself!"

That day we were fed a dinner obviously prepared by an unskilled hand. And for five days (by no means a short time for vacationers) the dinners were of quite doubtful quality. But toward the end of the week, the vacationers once again could not restrain themselves from demonstrative enthusiasm in the direction of our cook, Ivan Fomich.

And, then, the young composer, while eating his dessert after dinner, said excitedly to the philologist's wife: "Try these meringues! Ardent praise did not damage the issue in the least. Those honors that we showed the cook have only served to unfold his astonishing mastery!"

While praising the meringues, the philologist's wife stuck to her own opinion. She said that ardent praise was more dangerous for an inexperienced apprentice than for a first-class master. Inexperienced apprenticeship, after excessive praise, often remained stunted in its growth, considering that it didn't have any farther to go. Or spirits drooped with the first failure. And, then, there's the pursuit of forgetfulness in a glass of liquor.

The young composer leaped up from the table in order to give her some reply, but the philologist's wife continued without a pause: "And even for a first-class master," she said, "there's a certain danger here. Excessive praise often lulls conscience to sleep, rouses pride, and hinders a critical attitude to his own work. For this reason, even a first-class master—let's say an artist of the word—sometimes botches his mastery. He becomes a half-baked preacher, a bigot, an hysteric, and sometimes even an unstrung decadent."

The philologist's wife spoke long and volubly on this theme and concluded her speech with the following words: "Of course, such corruption can't befall our first-class cook. Ardent praise only upset his moral equilibrium for a short time. Judging by the meringues, it's all over and done with, to everybody's satisfaction. And now, apparently, our cook can be praised again without risking any more unpleasant surprises."

The doctor of philological science did not take part in this conversation, and, only at the very end, did he say to the composer in an elevated tone: "Moral fortitude, young man, is quite necessary in any profession, including the culinary business here, and especially music, which is so often accompanied by applause."

To this the young composer gave no reply, and with the unstrung pace of a man surfeited with honors and applause, he left the building.

The extensive dressing room is tastefully constructed and even not without beauty. There are carpet mattings on the floor. There are clean covers on the couches. At the entrance, there is a buffet with a centerpiece of flowers.

On the couch opposite me, there is a youngish father and his six-year-old son. While clumsily dressing the boy, the young father now and then proffers some instruction on the rules of behavior. In the tone of a stern teacher, he says to him: "Don't snuffle; take your handkerchief out of your pocket . . . Don't wiggle your foot in the air while papa's taking your pants off! . . ."

These scenes of an educational nature did not occupy my imagination too fully, and I began to look at the attendant whose appearance surprised me. He was a young fellow of blossoming appearance, no more than twenty-two years old. He wore sport shoes, striped trousers, and a white Russian blouse, belted with a bunched braid.

The work the fellow did was the very simplest. He takes back the zinc basin from those who have just finished washing, opens the linen closet with his key, and, waiting for the next customer, walks up and down the dressing room, looking wearily at the surface of the couches.

I felt like asking the young attendant how and why he had chosen such a career, so much more suitable for superannuated or exhausted lives. The following headlong events, however, prevented me from turning to the attendant with this question.

A short, solid man, who had just finished washing, entered the dressing room. His face was good-natured, almost gay. Through the gray stubble of a long unshaven face, flickered a soft hypertonic blush. His belly was enormous—it sagged with the weight of the no-less-than thirty tons of food it must have, in its time, taken in—and hung down heavily. On the belly, a surgical scar of ancient origin flashed whitely.

The old man, apparently, had been pawed more than once in the cruel embraces of life, but one sensed that he was still firmly attached to the world by the simple pleasure it offered.

Entering the dressing room with a zinc basin in his hands, the old man paused at the entrance, darting his eyes about in search of the young attendant. Streams of water flowed from his stout shoulders. A cloudlet of light steam hovered over the small bald spot on his gray head. The old man, apparently, had washed himself well, and now he was eager to get dressed as soon as possible.

Not finding the attendant, who was standing near the buffet, the old man called in a fluent tenor: "Hey, who opens the lockers around here?"

The young attendant moved hastily over to the old man and, having opened the necessary locker, stepped aside.

The old man did not linger around the open locker for long, and, having picked up his clothes, moved over to the couch in order to dress himself. But at this point, before reaching the couch, he tripped over the carpet matting and almost fell. The old man did not manage to hang on to his load and it slipped out of his arms to the floor.

In addition to the old man's linen, there lay a large package wrapped in newspaper. This package, which hit the floor hard, came undone, and all that it contained spilled out on the carpet matting. And what it contained was hundred-ruble notes, stoutly tied with bands from the bank, on each one of which was stamped the number—10,000.

There were no less than twenty such packets. In addition to this, there was one odd packet of hundred-ruble notes. Some of the notes from this packet were lifted by the draft and flew toward the couch across the room.

The young attendant, clasping his hands together, shouted in a frightened voice: "Money!"

Hastily collecting the dispersed packet, the old man said with displeasure to the attendant: "All right, money. What's there to blow about? Never seen any before?"

The young attendant, nervously gripping his white blouse, remained in wide-eyed astonishment.

"A heap like that I have never seen. Where did you get it all from, pop?"

"Well, you spend your life in such an out-of-the-way place," the old man answered, already with a certain irritation, having noticed that the bathhouse customers were watching his hurried activities from all sides.

"No, really, comrade, where did you get such a pile of money?"

the young father asked sternly. He had been moving in the direction of getting washed, with his naked son in tow, but had held back at the last moment and, to the child's annoyance, had sat down again on the couch.

The old man did not reply. Collecting the money in the torn newspaper, he was still crawling along the floor and was wetter now than he had been before.

A solid wall of customers formed around the old man. All were silent, not knowing what to say or how to behave in such an extraordinary instance.

But then, shoving people aside, a small thinnish man with a dark face and sharp spiny eyes under thick dark eyebrows arrived at the place of activity. He was still not quite dressed. His unbuttoned shirt revealed a narrow chickenlike chest. Lilac braces dangled from his scraggy rear-end.

They say that all the evil of the world comes from small thinnish men. It's possible that this is a slight exaggeration, but in the given instance the thinnish man in the next few moments displayed all the shadowy aspects of this type of person, of which he was a striking example.

Stepping forward, he said in a truculent tone to the old man: "Where's the money from? Just answer quickly, so you don't have time to think up a lie!"

Wiping himself with a bath towel, the old man replied caustically: "And you, peewee, who needs you here? Button up your shirt before you start talking to people. Could be I find it repulsive seeing you undressed."

These words did not divert the undersized customer. On the contrary, he came up closer to the old man and said in a hissing tone: "We'll see about that yet. We'll see who gets buttoned first, and who gets to go where when he's through here! Answer to the group—where'd you get this money?"

And, here, the thin man lifted his hand in a broad demagogic gesture as though gathering all of the bathhouse society around himself.

But even this classical gesture did not frighten the old man. Putting on his shirt, he shouted angrily at the thin man: "Get away from me! Or I'll pick you up by the pants and throw you out of the hall!"

This dreadful outburst took the wind out of the thin person's sails. Continuing to fuss, however, he said softly, turning to the bathhouse group: "People are not in the habit of taking such sums with them, either to the barbershop or to the bathhouse. And if he brought it with him—that means he wanted to hide this money from someone or destroy the traces of his illegal activities."

The young attendant exclaimed innocently: "It's likely he cornered loans at a cheap rate of interest and made hundreds of thousands on them!"

The thin man hissed through his teeth: "But it's not excluded that the money may be counterfeit . . . Where's the administration here?"

Swiftly flinging a black jacket around himself, the thin man moved toward the staircase, shouting back: "Don't let anyone out of the bathhouse!"

The owner of the money, seeing all the fuss, waved his hand with some indignation and even frowned.

The young father said sternly to his naked son, who had grown chilly and had begun to whimper: "Remember well, Icarus: people who steal or who deceive mama and papa are the most unworthy people on our planet. They slow down the progress of our time."

Icarus whimpered even more loudly and did not answer his father. The young attendant, who couldn't tear himself away, stared at the owner of the money, who was dressing himself without haste. Having probably come to the conclusion that the old man didn't look like a swindler, the attendant asked him once again: "No, really now, pop. Tell me, no kidding, where did you get all that money?"

Smiling, the old man answered the fellow: "This money, my friend, I earned by my own labor. I saved it up."

"Well, but how did you earn it? Doing what?" the attendant asked eagerly, and, sitting down beside the old man on the couch, he said in an intimate tone: "Take me, now, pop. I'm from the country. I've only had three years of school. I'm still not used to the city. I'd like to make a little money, but I don't know where to start. Tell me, pop! Explain to an orphan how you managed to bring this off in the city?"

The owner of the money laughed gaily till the tears came, and, then, wiping his eyes with the tail of his clean shirt, he said: "You'll hardly get rich in your post at the bathhouse. Where is there space for a falcon to spread his wings?"

Getting excited, the young attendant said: "That's just it, pop!

Where can I just stretch out a little bit? Here I am, walking around the dressing room as though I had the pox . . . So do me the favor, tell me how you made your fortune. With whom, for example, did you work?"

"I'm a locksmith by profession," the old man answered. "But once in a while I work as a mechanic. I worked at this job in the coal mines. After that I moved over to oil wells."

"And how much did they pay you for that?"

The old man answered without haste: "You've got to keep in mind, young man, where I was working. It was a long way from here. I was in the Far East and in Sakhalin—and I got time-and-a-half extra."

"What did this come to a month?"

"It was about three and a half in round figures. I spent a thousand, not allowing myself anything I didn't need, and two and a half went into my savings account. So, you see, in eight years I saved quite a bit."

The attendant moved his lips soundlessly, adding up the figures in his head. And having arrived at the sum, exclaimed loudly: "You saved two hundred and forty thousand!"

The crowd around the old man and the attendant diminished greatly. Many who had perceived that the case had evaporated left to wash and to dress. One of those who was leaving said with astonishment: "Such a sum the old devil saved up—a quarter million!"

The young attendant, whose stormy feelings had now reached their limit, leaped up from the couch and exclaimed to the old man: "But why did you give up a spot like that, pop? My God, I would have stayed a hundred years!"

Lacing up his boots, the old man replied without haste: "The doctors found I had high blood pressure. They ordered me back to Russia. So I arrived today by the Siberian express."

The bathhouse manager appeared in the doorway. This was a middle-aged woman in a dark cloth suit. On her jacket lapel hung a medal.

Hiding her eyes behind an unfolded newspaper so as not to disturb the undressed customers, the manager moved along the dressing room at a rapid pace. Directly behind her minced the thin man in the unbuttoned tunic.

Approaching the place where everything had happened, the

manager asked loudly: "Where is it? Who? Who has counterfeit money?"

The old man rose from the couch and, casting a fierce glance at the thin man, said to the manager: "I don't know what kind of money this midget has, but my money is issued by the state bank. Here is my bankbook, and in it you can clearly see how much was credited to my account and just when I drew out this sum with the exception of thirty-two kopecks."

Having looked through the old man's bankbook, the manager said: "Everything's in order. Only why in the world did you come to the bathhouse with money like that?"

The owner of the money replied: "I've been riding in the train for two weeks—I was covered with dust and desperate for a bath. From the train I went to the hotel, took a room, and put my things there. But, naturally, I took the money out of my trunk and took it along with me, so as not to leave it with no one watching."

"Understandable," said the manager. "But you shouldn't have taken the money out of your account. You should have had it accredited here."

"They told me about that in the bank," the old man acknowledged. "But I just didn't want to travel separately from my money."

"Understandable," said the manager once again and turned in order to make some comment to the undersized man who had so misinterpreted the event and who had been in such a hurry to see a crime where in fact there was none. But he had already whisked over to the couch and was dressing himself there hurriedly.

Once again hiding her eyes behind the newspaper, the manager withdrew. And then the young attendant hastily asked the old man: "Well, and how are you going to live now, pop, with all that money?"

Laughing, the old man answered: "And what the hell business is it of yours? No, my son, I have no intention of conversing with you on *this* delicate subject."

The elderly buffet attendant, coming out from behind his counter, said to the old man: "My nephew, Peter Egorkin, asked you a proper question. We're all extremely interested to know what you plan to do with your capital."

"What to do? Time will tell," the old man answered evasively, and frowned.

The buffet attendant, however, went on cross-examining undeterred: "But tell us anyway, honored sir, what kind of plans have you made for yourself?"

Wrapping his package of money up tightly in his dirty linen, the old man said without marked enthusiasm: "I haven't thought up any plans yet. In the next few days, however, there are some steps I want to take. Tomorrow morning, early, I'm going to go put my money in the bank, and then I'm going to go see if there's a job for me at the artel where I used to work as a locksmith before I left. But if, let's say, they won't take me, then I'll go look for a job in a factory somewhere. In my time I was a craftsman of the seventh grade."

The young attendant exclaimed: "With money like that, you want to go work in a factory?"

"What has money got to do with it?" the old man answered angrily. "Money is one thing. But without work, young man, there is little for me to do. I'm not used to lying in bed twenty-four hours a day."

The attendant laughed soundlessly and said through his laughter: "It turns out, pop, that you saved money for nothing . . ."

"What do you mean, nothing?" muttered the old man. "I'm planning to buy half a house outside the city if I can't find an apartment here."

The buffet attendant remarked: "They'll give you an apartment if you go to work in a factory. As for half a house—would that take much? Not more than thirty thousand. With your money, that's a drop in the bucket."

The old man got up from the couch, and, becoming more and more irritated, said: "Aye, well, money won't hurt me! I'll eat veal. I'll buy furniture. A phonograph. A piano."

The buffet attendant inhaled noisily and returned to his counter. The owner of the money, continuing to feel angry, put on his cap and picked up his wrapped package. The attendant, Peter Egorkin, unexpectedly even for himself, said to the old man in an elevated tone: "There are children among us here in the bathhouse! It would seem that with such a pile of money you could buy them a few candies."

The old man, who had been about to leave, waited. He said: "Children—that's another matter. I will never refuse to help a friend out of trouble and I will always have a little something for chilren. Where are the children here?"

The attendant turned to the couch where the young father and his son had been sitting, but it seemed that they had gone to wash. The attendant said with indignation: "The children have gone. They didn't wait."

"Well, if they didn't wait, I'm not going to run after them," muttered the old man and made his way to the exit. Then, all of a sudden he turned around and asked the attendant: "And you personally, young man, do you have children?"

Smiling, the young attendant replied: "I've got a daughter a-year-and-a-half old. Preschool age."

The old man went up to the counter and in his fluent tenor, he asked the buffet attendant: "And what do you have for children?"

"We don't stock anything for children except chocolate," the buffet attendant answered. "Here is 'Golden Anchor'—sixteen rubles a slab. We also have soybean chocolate at three rubles."

"Let's have the soybean at three rubles," said the old man.

At first, the young attendant refused the gift and even blushed, but the old man insisted, saying: "I'm not giving it to you, I'm giving it to your daughter. Only, look, don't eat it yourself. Give it right to your daughter."

"Why would I eat it?" answered the attendant. "I'll break off a small piece, naturally, just to taste. But the rest I'll give to my daughter. Clearly."

Giving him change from a ten-ruble note, the buffet attendant said to the old man: "You decided rightly to work in a factory, honored sir. When I didn't work for two months, I was in such a bad mood I didn't know what to do with myself. I couldn't even sleep. But when I went to work again, then I had good dreams."

"Yes, I don't get on well without work," muttered the old man, attentively counting his change.

This counting of change, for some reason, offended the buffet attendant very much. Smiling crookedly, he said to the old man: "My nephew, Peter Makarovich Egorkin, was absolutely right. You saved your capital for nothing. It suits you like a saddle on a cow. All you can do is take it to the bathhouse with you and entertain people."

Losing his temper, the old man asked: "Do you think I saved it up out of greediness, or what?"

Scratching a solid wart near his ear, the buffet attendant answered tactfully: "People put money away for different reasons. Naturally, there are some who save because they're greedy. Others —for their old age, or so they'll be able to buy various things they wanted. But then there are some who save because they respect capital."

I thought that an answer like that would further anger the old man, but this did not happen. Smiling broadly, he exclaimed: "You've gone over them all, master, but you haven't been able to discover my reason. I'll tell you. Since I was eight, I've dreamed of saving up a certain sum to free my parents from their constant need. My parents have been in the everlasting now for almost fifty years, but this childish little idea of saving money for some reason has stuck in my head. It has stuck like a splinter which sinks in more every time I try to pull it out. All my long life, I haven't succeeded. Now—I've saved up. Naturally, I'm glad, I don't conceal it. But I don't get any real satisfaction out of it. I don't have anyone to rejoice over it except myself."

This modest answer pleased the buffet attendant, and, while saying good-bye to him kindly, he said to him in a comforting way: "Generally speaking, money won't hurt you; there's nothing to be sad about."

The owner of the money nodded his head affirmatively and passed through the exit with his bloated package.

BEFORE THE SUN RISES

A NOVELLA

PREFACE

I thought of writing this book a very long time ago. Immediately after my *Youth Restored* saw the light.

I collected materials for this new book for almost ten years and waited for a peaceful year so I could sit down to write in the quiet of my study.

But this did not come about.

On the contrary. Twice, German bombs fell near my materials. The portfolio in which I kept my manuscripts was strewn with bricks and lime. Fire licked them. And I'm surprised, as things turned out, that they were preserved.

The collected material flew with me in an airplane over the German front, out of besieged Leningrad.

I took twenty heavy notebooks with me. In order to lessen their weight, I tore off the leather bindings. They still weighed close to eight kilograms, of the twelve kilograms of baggage allowed me for the flight. And there was a moment when I went into despair that I had taken this rubbish with me instead of warm underwear or an extra pair of boots.

Love of literature triumphed, however. I reconciled myself to my unhappy fate.

In a dark, torn portfolio I carried my manuscripts into central Asia, to the town of Alma-Ata, blessed from henceforth.

Here I was busy for a whole year writing various scenarios on themes that were needed in the days of the great Fatherland war.

I kept the material I had brought with me under the wooden couch on which I slept.

From time to time, I lifted them out of my couch. There, on the plywood bottom, rested twenty of my notebooks along with a sack of sweets which I had prepared according to my Leningrad custom.

I paged through these notebooks, regretting bitterly that there had been no time to take up this work, which seemed so unnecessary now, so far removed from the war, from the rumble of artillery and the whistling of bullets.

"It's nothing," I said to myself, "as soon as the war ends, I'll take up this work."

Once again, I packed away my notebooks in the bottom of my couch. And lying on them, the question flickered through my mind: When did I think the war would really be over? Not very soon, clearly. But *when*?—I could not really come to an answer.

"Well, then, why hasn't the time come for me to take up this work of mine?"—that's the way I was thinking. "But my materials have to do with the formation of the human intellect, of science, of the advance of consciousness. My work refutes the 'philosophy' of Fascism, which says that consciousness visits innumerable ills on people, that human happiness lies in a return to barbarism, to savagery, in a denial of civilization."

It might very well be more interesting to read about it now than at any time in the future.

In August 1942, I put my manuscripts on the table, and, without waiting for the war to end, I set to work.

1. PROLOGUE

Ten years ago I wrote the novella called *Youth Restored*.

It was an ordinary novella, one of those the majority of which are written by writers. But to it were added commentaries—notes of a physiological nature.

These notes explained the behavior of the novella's heroes and provided the reader with some information on the physiology and psychology of man.

I did not write *Youth Restored* for men of science. Nevertheless, they turned to my work with special interest. There were many disputes. There were quarrels. I heard many biting remarks. But some nice things were said, too.

It disturbed me that scholars took issue with me so seriously and so intensely. That doesn't mean (I thought) that I know a lot, but rather that science, it seems, has not sufficiently concerned itself with these problems which I, by virtue of my inexperience, had the boldness to touch on.

Be that as it may, the scholars discussed matters with me almost as with an equal. And I even began to receive summonses to the sessions of the "Brain Institute." And Ivan Petrovich Pavlov invited me to his "meetings."

But I, I repeat, hadn't composed my work for science. This had been a literary production, and the scientific material had been only a complementary part.

It always struck me: The painter, before he paints the human body is obliged of necessity to study anatomy. Only a knowledge of this science could deliver the painter from mistakes in drawing. But the writer, into whose compass more than man's body enters —his psyche, his consciousness—does not often strive to attain knowledge of a similar kind. I considered it my obligation to study something along this line. And, having studied, I shared the results with the reader.

That's the way *Youth Restored* came about.

Now that ten years have passed, I see very well the defects of my book: It was incomplete and one-sided. And probably I deserved to have been attacked more than I actually was.

In the fall of 1934, I got to know a remarkable physiologist.

When talk came around to my work, this physiologist said: "I prefer your usual stories. But I admit that what you write about *should* be written about. Studying consciousness isn't only a matter for the man of science. I suspect that it is as yet even more a matter for the writer than for the man of science. I am a physiologist, so I'm not afraid to say it."

I answered: "I think so too. The region of consciousness, the region of higher psychological activity, belongs more to us than to you. Man's behavior can and must be studied with the aid of dogs and lancets. But a man (and a dog, too) sometimes has fantasies which can in an extraordinary way change the momentum of his existence even in the course of one and the same stimulus. And in this sense it might sometimes be necessary to have a 'conversation with a dog' in order to analyze his dreams in all their complexity. And a 'conversation with a dog' —on the whole that's something in our province."

Smiling, the scientist said: "You're partly right. The correspondence between the intensity of the stimulus and the response is often disproportionate, especially in the field of sensation. But if you have pretensions in this province, you really must expect to run into us there."

After this conversation, some years passed. Having learned

that I was working on a new book, the physiologist asked me to tell him about this work.

I said: "In brief, it's a book about how I survived many unnecessary sorrows and became a happy man."

"Will this be a treatise or a novel?"

"It will be a literary work. Science will enter into it, as in other cases history enters into a novel."

"Will there be commentaries again?"

"No. This will be something integral. Like a gun and shell can be a single whole."

"Will this work be about yourself?"

"Half the book will be occupied with my person. I will not conceal from you the fact that this troubles me."

"You'll be telling about your life?"

"No. Worse than that. I will tell about things that it isn't entirely acceptable to talk about in novels. It comforts me that it will deal with the years of my youth. That's the same as talking about the dead."

"To what age will you go, in your book?"

"Roughly to thirty."

"Maybe it would be a good idea to add another fifteen years. Then the book would be fuller—about your whole life."

"No," I said. "From thirty on, I was quite a different man—no longer an appropriate subject for my work."

"How did such a change come about?"

"One can't even call it a change. It's an entirely different life, and it doesn't at all resemble the former one."

"But in what way? Was this psychoanalysis? Freud?"

"Not at all. It was Pavlov. I used his principle. It was his idea."

"But what did you do yourself?"

"Essentially, I did a very simple thing. I collected those things which disturbed me—incorrect conditioned reflexes, which had been mistakenly ingrained in my consciousness. I destroyed the false connection between them. I dissected the 'temporary connections,' as Pavlov called them."

"In what way?"

At that time I had not fully thought through my materials and therefore found it difficult to answer this question. But concerning the principle, I answered. True, I was very foggy.

Having pondered my reply, the man of science answered: "Go ahead and write. But don't promise people anything."

I said: "I'll be careful. I will promise only that which I've already achieved. And only to those people who have qualities close to mine."

Laughing, the scientist said: "That's not much. And it's right. Tolstoi's philosophy, for example, was useful only to him, and to nobody else."

I answered: "Tolstoi's philosophy was religion, not science. It was faith which helped him. I stand far from religion. I do not speak of faith or of a philosophical system. I speak of iron rules, confirmed by a great scholar. My part in this matter is a modest one: by the proof of a man's life I have verified these rules, and I have connected things which seemed not to have any connection."

I said good-bye to the scientist and I have not seen him since. He probably came to the conclusion that I gave up my book, never really coming to terms with it.

But I—as I have already explained—was only waiting for a year of peace and quiet.

This did not come to pass. It's too bad. I write badly to the sound of artillery. Beauty will undoubtedly be diminished. My agitation will make the style shaky. Alarms will stifle clear-sighted knowledge. Nervousness will be taken for haste. There will be seen in this a lack of caution with regard to science, a lack of respect for the world of scholarship . . .

Scholar!
Where you see my speech uncivil—
Root it out, I give permission.

May the enlightened reader forgive my trespasses.

II. I AM UNHAPPY—AND DON'T KNOW WHY

When I recall my early years, I am struck by the number of sorrows, false alarms, and fits of melancholy that I had.

The very best years of my youth were underlined in black.

When I was a child, I experienced nothing like that.

But my very first steps as a young man were overshadowed by this amazing melancholy which I do not know how to describe.

I strove toward people, life pleasured me, I sought friends, love, happy meetings . . . But I found no comfort for myself in any of this. It all turned to dust in my hands. Spleen pursued me at every step.

I was unhappy without knowing why.

But I was eighteen years old, and so I found an explanation. *"The world is terrible,"* I thought. "People are base. Their actions are comic. I'm not a ram from *that* flock."

Over my desk I hung a quatrain from Sophocles:

> The highest gift is never to be born,
> But if you've seen the light of day—
> The second best is a quick return
> To the native dark from which you made your way.

Naturally, I knew that there were other ways of looking at things—happy ones, sometimes even enthusiastic. But I did not respect people who were able to dance to the coarse and vulgar music of life. Such people seemed to me on a level with savages and animals.

Everything that I saw around me strengthened my point of view.

Poets wrote mournful verses and took pride in their melancholy.

My favorite philosophers also spoke of melancholy with respect. "Melancholics are possessed by a feeling of exaltation," wrote Kant. And Aristotle considered that "the melancholic frame of spirit assists profundity of thought and accompanies genius."

But poets and philosophers were not the only ones who were throwing wood on my pallid bonfire. It may seem surprising, but in my time sadness was considered the sign of a thinking person. In my milieu, broody melancholic types were respected and even those who were quite alienated from life.*

Briefly speaking, I came to consider that a pessimistic view of life was the only possible one for a man who was thoughtful, refined, and born into the gentry class, which was my origin.

That means, I thought, melancholy is my normal condition, and mournfulness and a certain disdain for life are the qualities of my mind. And apparently not only of *my* mind. Apparently—of any mind, any consciousness, that strives to be higher than that of an animal.

---

* Not long ago, paging through Bryusov's *Diary,* I found these lines: "Dear Iaroshenko. A sweet man. Strange to life . . ."

Very sad to be that way, but that's probably the way it is. In nature, coarse fibers win out. Coarse emotions, primitive ideas are victorious. Everything that has been delicately made goes to ruin.

So thought I, when I was eighteen. And I will not conceal from you that I still thought so even considerably later.

But I was mistaken. And now I am happy to inform you about this terrible mistake of mine.

At that time, this mistake almost cost me my life.

I wanted to die because I saw no other way out.

In the fall of 1914 the World War began, and I gave up the university and went off to the army so I could go to the front for the distinction of dying for my country, for my motherland.

In the war, however, I almost ceased to experience melancholy. It happened from time to time. But it soon passed. And in the war I felt myself almost happy, for the first time.

I thought: Why should this be? I arrived at the notion that it was because I had found excellent comrades here, and that was why I had ceased glooming. It was logical.

I served in the Mingrelsky Regiment of the Caucasian Grenadiers Division. We lived in a very friendly way. Both soldiers and officers. At least, that's the way it seemed to me then.

At the age of nineteen I was already a lieutenant.

At the age of twenty I had five medals and was recommended for promotion to captain.

But this didn't mean that I was a hero. It meant that for two years in a row I was in the front lines.

I took part in many battles, was wounded, poisoned by gas. My heart went bad. Nevertheless, my happy mood was almost constant.

At the beginning of the Revolution I returned to Petrograd.

I had no regrets for the past. On the contrary, I wanted to see a new Russia, not like the mournful country I had known. I wanted there to be around me healthy, blossoming people, not such as myself—inclined to spleen, melancholy, and sorrow.

I didn't go through any of the so-called "social divergences." Nevertheless, I began to experience melancholy as before.

I tried to change towns and professions. I wanted to escape from that terrible melancholy of mine. I felt it was destroying me.

I went to Archangel. Then, on the frozen sea to Mezen. Then, I returned to Petrograd. I went to Novgorod, to Pskov. Then, to

Smolensk province, to the town of Krasny. Once again I returned to Petrograd . . .

Spleen followed at my heels.

In three years I changed towns twelve times and professions ten times.

I was a policeman, a bookkeeper, a shoemaker, an instructor in poultry husbandry, a telephone operator for the border guard, a detective, the secretary of a court, a clerk-expediter.

This wasn't on account of hard times, this was on account of confusion. For half a year I went to the front again in the Red Army—at Narva and Yamburg.

But I had a bad heart from poison gas and I was obliged to think of a new profession.

In 1921 I started to write stories.

From the time that I became a writer, my life changed very much. But spleen remained as before. Moreover, it attacked me more frequently.

Then I had recourse to doctors. In addition to spleen, I had something wrong with my heart, something with my stomach, something with my liver.

The doctors went at me, energetically.

They began to treat me for three of my illnesses with pills and water. For the most part with water—inside and out.

It was decided to drive off the spleen with a combined blow—at once from all four sides: flanks, rear, and front—by trips, sea-bathing, Charcot sprays, and the amusements so necessary to my tender years.

I began to go to sanatoriums twice a year—to Yalta, Kislovodsk, Sochi, and other blessed places.

In Sochi I got to know a certain man whose melancholy was significantly greater than mine. Twice a year at the minimum he was extracted from the noose into which he had shoved his head because an unmotivated melancholy tormented him.

With a feeling of the greatest respect, I began to converse with this man. I assumed I would see wisdom, intellect, an over-abundance of knowledge, the scornful smile of genius which is forced to drag along on our transient earth.

I saw nothing of the kind.

This was a narrow-minded man, uneducated, without even the shadow of enlightenment. He had read no more than two books in his entire life. And he wasn't interested in anything except money, food, and women.

Before me was the most commonplace man, with vulgar thoughts and vacuous desires.

I didn't even grasp immediately that that's the way it was. At first it seemed to me that the room was smoky, or that the barometer had fallen and a storm was brewing. Because something didn't seem quite right when I was talking to him. Then I look—it's just that he's a fool. Simply a dunderhead with whom it was impossible to talk for more than three minutes.

My philosophical system gave a shudder. I grasped the fact that it was not exclusively a matter of a high degree of consciousness. But *what,* then? I did not know.

With the greatest humility I gave myself up into the hand of the doctors.

In two years I consumed half a ton of powders and pills.

I drank every nauseating mess.

I allowed myself to be cut, x-rayed, and imprisoned in baths.

But cure did not follow. And things went even so far that my friends no longer recognized me on the street. I got terribly thin. I was like a skeleton with a little skin stretched over it. I became terribly stiff. My hands trembled, and even the doctors were astonished at the yellowness of my skin. They had begun to suspect that I had hypochondria to such a degree as to render their methods useless. What I needed was hypnosis and a clinic.

One of the doctors succeeded in hypnotizing me. He began to suggest to me, once I was hypnotized, that I languished and mourned in vain, that everything was well in the world and there was no reason for such grief.

For two days I felt a considerable lift, then I became considerably worse than I had been before.

I almost ceased to emerge from my house. Every new day found me in the dumps.

I ceased to go to sanatoriums. Closer to the truth, I went and languished there for two or three days, and then went home again in a more fearful melancholy than when I had arrived.

Then I turned to books. I was a young writer. Only twenty-seven years old. It was natural that I should turn to my great comrades—writers, composers . . . I wanted to know if they had gone through anything similar. If they had not experienced a melancholy similar to mine. And if they had, what reasons, what motivations they assigned to it. And what they did to get rid of it.

And then I began to note down everything that related to spleen. I took these notes without any special system or plan. I did, however, try to select that which was characteristic for a given man, that which turned up often in his life, that which did not seem accidental, a moment's fancy, an outburst.

These notes engaged my imagination for several years.

[There follows a number of melancholy quotations from Chopin, Gogol, Nekrasov, Poe, Flaubert, Saltykov-Shchedrin, De Maupassant, Bryusov, and Tolstoi.]

I filled a whole notebook with similar notes. They struck me, even shook me. But I had deliberately not selected people whose lives had been particularly touched by a particular sorrow, misfortune or death. I chose a condition that repeated itself. I chose those people of whom many said themselves that they didn't understand where this mood came from.

I was struck, bemused. What kind of suffering was this to which people were subject? And how to come to grips with it, by what means?

Maybe this suffering is the result of a disharmony in the life around us, of social griefs, world problems? Maybe *this* is the basis for such melancholy?

Yes, it is so. But at this point I recalled the words of Chernyshevski: "It isn't because of world problems that people drown themselves, shoot themselves, and go out of their minds."

These words disturbed me even more.

I could find no solution. I did not understand.

Could it be, after all (I thought once again), this is a scorn for the world to which great men are subjected by virtue of their higher degree of consciousness?

No! Along with these great men whom I listed, I saw no fewer great men who experienced no such melancholy, although their consciousness was on as high a level. And sometimes it was even significantly higher.

During an evening dedicated to Chopin, they played his second concerto for piano and orchestra.

I sat in the last rows, exhausted, tormented.

But the second concerto drove off my melancholy. The powerful, masculine sounds filled the hall.

Joy, struggle, extraordinary force, and even triumph resounded in the concerto's third part.

Where did this weak man get this immense force—this composer of genius whose sad life I knew so well by now? Where did he get such joy, such enthusiasm? Does it mean that all this was in him? Only constrained? By what?

At this point I thought of my own stories, which made people laugh. I thought of laughter, which was in my books but not in my heart.

I will not conceal it from you: I was frightened. Then suddenly the idea came to me that I had to find the reason—why my forces were constrained, and why I found life so unhappy; and why there are people like myself in the world, inclined to brooding and unmotivated melancholy.

In the fall of 1926 I braced myself to go to Yalta. And I braced myself to stay there for four weeks.

For ten days I lay in my hotel room. Then I went out for a stroll. I walked into the mountains. And sometimes I sat for hours at the seashore, rejoicing that I was better, that I was almost well.

For a month I improved a lot. My spirit grew calm, even gay.

In order to strengthen my health still further, I decided to continue my rest. I bought a boat ticket for Batum. From Batum I wanted to go to Moscow by direct train.

I took a separate cabin. And in a marvelous mood, I left Yalta.

The sea was calm, without a murmur. And I sat on the deck all day admiring the Crimean shore and the sea, which I loved so much and for the sake of which I usually went to Yalta.

In the morning, still scarcely light, I was on deck again.

A wonderful dawn broke.

I sat in the chaise longue, relishing my excellent mood. My thoughts were the happiest, they were gay. I thought of my trip, of Moscow, of friends I would meet there. Of the fact that my melancholy was now behind me. And let it remain a riddle, as long as it bothered me no more.

It was early morning. Thoughtfully, I gazed out at the light ripple of the water, at the patches of sunlight, at the sea gulls who sat on the water with a loathsome squawking.

And suddenly, in a single moment, I felt bad. This wasn't simply melancholy. It was agitation, quivering, almost terror. I could scarcely get up from the chaise longue. I barely reached my cabin. And for two hours I lay on my bunk without moving. And, once again, melancholy arose, of an intensity that I had not yet experienced.

I tried to struggle with it. I went out on deck. I started listening to people's conversations. I wanted to cast it off. But I did not succeed.

It seemed as though I should not and could not continue the journey any farther.

I could hardly wait for the stop at Tuapse. I went ashore with the intention of continuing on my way after a few days.

A nervous fever shook me.

I took a trolley to a hotel. And there I lay down.

It was only after a week that I recovered my will and began to prepare myself for the road.

The road diverted me. I began to feel better. The terrible melancholy disappeared.

It was a long way, and I began to think of my unfortunate illness, which could vanish so swiftly and reappear in the same way. Why? What were the reasons?

It was as if there weren't any reasons. Must be simply "weak nerves," an excess of "feeling." Must be. It happens all the time and sends me swinging like a pendulum.

I started to think: Was I born that weak and emotional, or did something happen in my life that undermined my nerves, corrupted them, and turned me into an unfortunate flake of dust, driven and shaken by every wind?

And suddenly it struck me that I could not have been born so unhappy, so defenseless. I might have been born weak, fragile, I might have been born with one arm, one eye, without an ear. But to have been born to brood and to brood without reason—just because the world seems base! But I'm no Martian. I'm a child of my own planet. I must, like any animal, feel some joy in existence. Experience happiness, if all goes well. And struggle, if it goes badly. But to brood?! When even an insect that has only four hours to live rejoices in the sun! No, I could not have been born such a monster.

And suddenly I understood clearly that the reason for my misfortunes must be contained in my life. No doubt—something happened, something took place that acted on me in this oppressive way.

But what? And when did it happen? And how to find this unfortunate event? How to find this reason for my melancholy?

Then I thought: I have to recall my life. And feverishly I began to recall. But immediately I grasped that nothing would come of this if I did not introduce some kind of system into my reminiscences.

There is no need to recall everything, I thought. Only to recall the most powerful, the most striking things. It should be sufficient to recall those things which I associate with my spiritual distress. That was the only way I could solve the riddle.

And then I began to recall the most striking pictures that had remained in my memory. And I noticed that my memory had preserved them with unusual precision. Trifles had been preserved, details, colors, even smells.

Spiritual distress, like a magnesium flare, illuminated all that had occurred. These were candid photographs which remained in my mind.

With unusual agitation I began to study these photographs. I noted that they agitated me even more than the desire to find the reason for my misfortunes.

III. FALLEN LEAVES

1912-15

I'M BUSY

The yard. I'm playing football. I'm bored playing, but I still play, furtively glancing up at a second-floor window. My heart contracts from melancholy.

Tata T. lives there. She's grown up. She's twenty-three years old. She has an old husband. He's forty. We high-school kids are always teasing him when he comes home from work, a little stooped.

And so the window opens. Tata T. adjusts her hairdo, stretching and yawning.

Seeing me, she smiles.

Ah, she's very fine. She's like a young tigress from the zoo— such striking, flashing, blinding colors. I almost can't bear to look at her.

Smiling, Tata T. says to me: "Mishenka, come on up here for a minute."

My heart gives a happy leap, but, without lifting my eyes, I answer: "You can see, I'm busy. I'm playing football."

"Then hold out your hat. I'll throw you something."

I hold out my school hat. And Tata T. throws a small package into it, wrapped in ribbon. It's chocolate.

I toss the chocolate into my pocket and I go on playing.

At home, I eat the chocolate. And the ribbon—after touching it to my cheek for a moment, I toss it on the table.

AN AUTHENTIC COPY

Getting out of school, I meet the realist Serezha K. He is a tall, blond, despondent youth.

Nervously smacking his lips, he says to me: "Yesterday, I broke off with Valka P. once and for all. And just think, she asked me to return all her letters."

"Then you should return them," I say.

"Naturally, I'll give her letters back," says Serezha. "But I want to keep a copy . . . What's more, I'd like to ask a favor of you. I need you to confirm these copies . . ."

"What for?" I ask.

"Well, just in case," says Serezha, "she might say she never loved me at all . . . But if there are confirmed copies . . ."

We approach Serezha's house. Serezha is the son of the fire-chief. Therefore, his place has a certain attraction for me.

Serezha puts three letters on the table and the three copies he has already made.

I do not feel like signing the copies, but Serezha insists. He says: "We're not kids any more. Our childhood's past . . . I beg you to sign."

Without reading them, I write on each sheet: "An authentic copy." I sign my name.

As a token of his appreciation, Serezha takes me into the yard; and, there, he shows me the emergency ladder and the fire hoses, which are drying in the sun.

EASTER NIGHT

I'm hurrying for matins. I'm standing in front of the mirror dressed in my school uniform. In my left hand I'm holding a pair of white kid gloves. With my right hand I'm adjusting the astonishing parting of my hair.

I am not especially pleased with my appearance. Very young.

At sixteen, I should look older.

Carelessly flinging a cloak around my shoulders I go out to the stairs.

Tata T. is climbing up the stairs.

She looks surprisingly well today, in her short wool jacket, with a muff in her hands.

"Aren't you going to church?" I ask.

"No, we're entertaining at home," she says, smiling. And coming up closer, she adds: "Christ is arisen! . . . Mishenka . . ."

"It isn't midnight yet," I mutter.

Throwing her arms around my neck, Tata T. kisses me.

This was not three Easter kisses. This was one long kiss that lasted a minute. I begin to grasp that this is not a Christian kiss.

At first, I have a feeling of joy, then surprise, then—I laugh.

"Why do you laugh?" she asks.

"I didn't know people kissed like that."

"*People* don't, you idiot," she says. "Men and women do!"

Her hand caresses my face and she kisses my eyes. Then, hearing someone knocking at the door by her apartment, she rushes up the stairs—beautiful and mysterious, really such as I would always wish to love.

IN THE UNIVERSITY

At the gate there's a police officer. Since I don't have a ticket, he asks me to show my student registration. I show my documents.

"Go on in," he says.

In the yard there are armed soldiers and police.

Today is the anniversary of Tolstoi's death.

I walk along the university corridor. Here, there is noise, fuss, animation.

Prutchenko, the warden of the school district, is walking slowly along the corridor. He is tall, broadly built, red-faced. On the white shirt front under his uniform there are small diamond buttons.

Around the warden there is a living wall of students. These are students from the academic corporation, "white linings." Hand in hand, they formed a chain around the warden; they are protecting him from possible excesses. A long-faced pimply student in uniform, with a sword at his side, takes command and fusses more than anyone.

Hellish noise all around. Someone shouts: "They led an elephant along the street." Jokes. Laughter.

The warden slowly moves forward. The living wall respectfully moves along with him.

A student appears. He's short. Not handsome. But his face looks surprisingly intelligent, energetic.

Approaching the wall, he comes to a stop. Involuntarily, the wall with the warden inside comes to a stop, too.

Raising his hand, the student asks for silence.

When it gets quieter, the student shouts, emphasizing every word: "We have two misfortunes in Russia: the power of darkness below; and, above, the darkness of power."

An outburst of applause. Laughter.

The long-faced student grasps the hilt of his sword for effect. The warden mutters wearily: "It's not necessary, stop . . ."

The student with the sword says to someone: "Find out what that boor's name is . . ."

A PROPOSAL

I'm walking along past the freight cars. In my hands I have a railroad-ticket punch.

My ticket punch has been working for half a month.

It's the chic branch line, Kislovodsk–Mineral Waters, served in the summer by students. And that's why I'm here in the Caucasus. I came here to earn a little money.

Kislovodsk. I go out on the platform. At the entrance to the station there's an immense gendarme with medals on his chest. He is massive, like a monument.

Bowing politely and smiling, the ticket seller approaches me.

"Colleague," he says to me (although he is not a student), "a word with you . . . Next time don't punch the tickets with your punch, but return them to me . . ."

He pronounces these words calmly, as though he were talking about the weather.

Perplexed, I mutter: "What for? . . . So you can . . . sell them again? . . .

"Well, yes . . . I have an understanding with almost all your friends . . . Half and half."

"Scoundrel! . . . You lie!" I mutter. "With all?"

The ticket seller shrugs his shoulders.

"Well, not with all," he says, "but with a lot . . . And what surprises you so? Everybody does it . . . Why, I could hardly live on my thirty-six rubles a month . . . I don't even consider it a crime. They egg us on to this . . ."

I turn sharply and leave. The ticket seller runs after me.

"Colleague," he says, "if you don't want to, you don't have to, I don't insist . . . only don't *think* of telling anybody about it. In the first place, no one will believe you. In the second place, it's impossible to prove. In the third place, you'll pass for a liar, a troublemaker . . ."

Slowly, I mutter my way home . . . It's raining . . .

I am more surprised than at any time in my life.

ELVIRA

The station stop Minutka. I have a quiet room with windows on the park.

My peace and quiet do not last long. In the neighboring room there enters, just having arrived from Penza, the circus performer Elvira. On her passport she is called Nastia Gorokhova.

This robust person is almost illiterate.

In Penza she had a brief romance with a general. The general had gone off with his wife to the "sour waters" [Kislovodsk] Elvira arrived after him—it isn't known what she was counting on.

All Elvira's thoughts from morning to night are oriented in the direction of the unfortunate general.

Showing her arms, which under the circus tent had supported three men, Elvira says to me: "Generally speaking, I could kill him without blinking an eye. And I wouldn't get more than eight years for it either . . . What do you think?"

"But really, what is it you want from him?" I ask her.

"What do you mean *what?*" says Elvira. "I came here entirely for his sake. I'm living here for almost a month, and like a fool I'm crying my eyes out. I want he should be decent enough to pay my train fare both ways. I want to write him a letter about this."

Because of Elvira's illiteracy, I write this letter. I'm inspired. The hope guides my hand that Elvira, once she's received the money, will leave for Penza.

I don't remember what I wrote. I only remember that when I read this letter to Elvira, she said: "Yes! That's the outcry of a woman's soul . . . And I'll kill him immediately if he doesn't send me anything after this."

My letter turned the general inside out. And he sent Elvira an enclosure of fifty rubles. That was an immense and even a grandiose sum in those days.

Elvira was stunned.

"With money like that," she said, "it would just be dumb to leave Kislovodsk."

She remained. And she remained with the notion that I was the sole reason for her wealth.

She almost never left my room.

It was just as well that the World War began soon after that. I left.

1915-17

NERVES

Two soldiers are butchering a pig. The pig is squealing so, one cannot bear it. I come up closer.

One soldier is sitting on the pig. The hand of the other, armed with a knife, skillfully rips open the belly. The white lard of that unbounded fatness spills out on both sides.

The squealing is such, one has to stop one's ears.

"You might stun her with something, brothers," I say. "Why shred her up like that?"

"Impossible, your excellency," says the first soldier, sitting on the pig. "It wouldn't have the same taste."

Seeing my silver sword and the emblem on my shoulder straps, the soldier jumps up. The pig breaks loose.

"Sit, sit," I say, "just finish up as quick as you can."

"Quick isn't good either," says the soldier with the knife. "If you're too quick, you spoil the fat."

After looking at me with compassion, the first soldier says: "Your excellency, it's war! People are suffering. And *you* feel sorry for a pig."

The second soldier says, after having made a final gesture with the knife: "Nerves, their excellencies have."

The conversation is assuming an overly familiar tone. This won't do. I want to leave, but I don't.

The first soldier says: "In the Avgustovsky forests, I had a bone shattered in this hand. To the operating table, right away. Half a glass of liquor. They cut. But I'm eating sausage while they do."

"And weren't you sick?"

"How not sick? Damn sick . . . I ate the sausage. I say, 'Give me some cheese.' I'd just eaten the cheese, and the surgeon says, 'Finished, let's sew it up.' 'Please,' I say . . . What would you have done, your excellency? You wouldn't have been able to stand that."

"Weak nerves, their excellencies have," the second soldier says once more.

I leave.

REGIMENT IN A BOX

The regiment, stretched along the highway. The soldiers are worn out, exhausted. For the second day, almost without resting, we are plodding along the fields of Galicia.

We are retreating. We don't have any ammunition.

The regimental commander orders us to sing songs.

The machine gunners, on their prancing horses, are singing: "Along the ocean's blue waves."

On all sides we hear shooting, explosions. One has the impression that we are in a box.

We pass through a village. The soldiers run to the huts. We have an order to destroy everything on the highway.

It's a dead village. No point in feeling sorry. There isn't a soul here. There aren't even any dogs. There isn't even one of those chickens that usually scratch around deserted villages.

The grenadiers run up to the small huts and set fire to their straw roofs. Smoke lifts upward to the sky.

And, suddenly, in a moment, the dead village comes to life. Women are running, children. Men appear. Cows bellow. Horses neigh. We hear outcries, weeping, and squealing.

I see how one soldier, who has just set fire to a roof, confusedly snuffs it out with his cap.

I turn aside. We go on.

We go on till evening. And then we go on by night. All around, the glow of fires. Shots. Explosions.

Toward morning, the regimental commander says: "Now I can say it. For two days our regiment has been in a box. Tonight we got out of it."

We drop down on the grass, and, immediately, we are asleep.

MADE IT FOR NOTHING

As a courier, I approach the high gate. This is division staff headquarters.

I'm nervous and alarmed. The collar of my field jacket is undone. My cap is on the back of my head.

Dismounting from my horse, I walk through the gate.

The staff officer, Lieutenant Zadlovsky, approaches me head-long. He speaks through set teeth: "That's no way . . . Button up that collar."

I button my collar and straighten my cap.

Staff officers are standing near the saddled horses.

I see the division commander among them, General Gabaev, and the chief of staff, Colonel Shaposhnikov.

I report.

"I know," the general says irritably.

"What message shall I take back to my commander, your excellency?"

"Take this . . ."

I feel some insult is on the tip of the general's tongue, but he restrains himself.

The officers glance around. The chief of staff is almost laughing.

"Take *this* back . . . Well, what *can* I send back to a man who has lost his regiment? . . . You made it here for nothing . . ."

I leave, embarrassed.

Again, I go galloping off on my horse. And suddenly I see the commander of my regiment. He is tall and thin. He's holding his cap in his hands. The wind stirs his side whiskers. He stands in the field and tries to restrain the soldiers who are making off. These soldiers are not from our regiment. The commander runs up to each one with a shout and a prayer.

The soldiers walk submissively to the edge of the forest. I see our reserve battalion there, and a train of carts.

I approach the officers. The regimental commander is approaching them too. He mutters: "My glorious Mingrelsky Regiment has been destroyed."

Hurling his cap to the ground, the commander stamps his foot in anger.

We comfort him. We say that we have five hundred men left. That's not just a few. We'll have a regiment again.

COME BACK TOMORROW

At the entrance I meet Tata T. She is so beautiful and so dazzling that I turn my eyes away from her as from the sun.

Seeing me, she laughs. She examines my figure with curiosity and touches the silver hilt of my sword. Then she says that I'm quite grown up now and that it isn't even nice for us to be seen together like this. Right away there would be gossip.

We climb the stairs.

Tata adjusts her hair in the mirror. I come up to her and embrace her. She laughs. She is surprised that I've become so bold. She embraces me as she once did on the staircase.

We kiss. Compared to this, the whole world strikes me as worthless. She, too, is oblivious to what is going on around us.

Then she looks at her watch and gives a little screech of terror. She says: "My husband's coming any minute."

And, at that moment, the door opens and her husband enters. Tata scarcely manages to adjust her hairdo.

The husband sits down in an armchair and looks at us silently.

Without losing her presence of mind, Tata says: "Nicholas, just look at him, how he's grown. Why he just this moment arrived from the front."

Smiling sourly, the husband looks at me.

The conversation gets nowhere. So, bowing ceremoniously, I take my leave. Tata accompanies me.

Opening the door to the staircase, she whispers to me: "Come back tomorrow at noon. He leaves at eleven."

I nod my head silently.

Her husband's face and his sour smile do not leave my mind that whole day.

In the morning I send Tata a note that I'm leaving right away for the front.

In the evening I leave for Moscow. I spend a few days there, and return to my regiment.

THE TWENTIETH OF JULY

I'm standing in the trenches and looking curiously at the ruins around me. This is Smorgon. The right wing of our regiment rests against the kitchen gardens of Smorgon.

This little place is not without renown. It was from here that Napoleon took flight, turning over his command to Murat.

It's getting dark. I return to my hut.

A stifling July night. Removing my field jacket, I write letters.

It's already close to one. I need to get some sleep. I want to call my orderly. But, suddenly, I hear some kind of noise. The noise grows. I hear footfalls. And the clinking of pots. But no outcries. And no shooting.

I run out of my hut. And, suddenly, a sweet, stifling wave engulfs me. I cry out: "Gas! . . . Masks! . . ." And I fling myself back into the hut. My gas mask is hanging there on a nail.

The candle had gone out when I had rushed headlong out of the hut. I groped for the gas mask with my hand and began to put it on. I forgot to open the lower stopper. I'm suffocating. Once having opened the stopper, I run out into the trenches.

Around me, soldiers are running, bandaging up their faces with masks of gauze.

Having fumbled up some matches from my pocket, I light the brushwood which is lying in front of the trenches. This brushwood has been prepared earlier. In case of gas attack.

Now the fire illuminates our positions. I see that all the grenadiers have gotten out of the trenches and are lying beside the bushes. I am also lying near a bush. I don't feel well. My head is spinning. I swallowed a lot of gas when I shouted: "Masks!"

Near the bush, things go a little more easily. Even quite well. The fire drives the gas upward, and it passes away without immersing us. I take off my mask.

We lie there four hours.

It begins to grow light. Now it is apparent how the gas is proceeding. It is not a solid wall. It is a cloud of smoke about ten yards wide. Slowly it moves upon us, driven by a gentle breeze.

We could go off to the right or to the left, and then the gas would move on past without touching us.

Now it is not terrifying. From somewhere I already hear jokes and laughter. It is the grenadiers pushing one another into puffs of gas. A racket. Laughter.

I look at the German side through my binoculars. Now I see how they're letting the gas out of cylinders. It's a repulsive spectacle. Anger flares up in me when I see how methodically and cold-bloodedly they are doing it.

I order my men to open fire on those scoundrels. I order them to fire all machine guns and small arms, though I understand well enough that we can do little harm at this distance of about fifteen hundred yards.

There is a weak burst. The grenadiers fire a few shots. And suddenly I see that many soldiers are lying dead. And they are the majority. Others are groaning and are unable to lift themselves from out of the brush fire.

I hear the sounds of a bugle in the German trenches. The poisoners are blowing retreat. The gas attack is over.

Leaning on a stick, I make my way to the hospital. There's blood on my handkerchief from a terrifying fit of retching.

I walk along the road. I see the yellowed grass and a hundred dead sparrows that have fallen on the road.

1920-26

RUBBISH

The editorial offices of the literary journal *Sovremennik*.

I had given this journal five of my best small stories. And I had come for an answer.

Before me is one of the editors—the poet, M. Kuzmin. He is polite to the point of courtliness. Even beyond the call of duty. But I see by his face that he intends to communicate something unpleasant.

He hesitates. I come to his aid.

"Probably my stories don't quite fit in with the journal's plan?" I say.

He says: "You understand, this is a literary journal . . . But your stories . . . No, they are very funny, amusing . . . But they are written . . . But this . . ."

"Rubbish? Is that what you want to say," I ask. And I see in my mind's eye the comment a teacher had once written on a high-school composition of mine: "Rubbish."

Kuzmin makes an open gesture with his hands.

"God forbid. I didn't want to say that at all. On the contrary. Your stories show a great deal of talent . . . But you'll agree yourself—they lean a bit to caricature."

"No. Not caricature," I say.

"Well, take the language you use, for example . . ."

"The language isn't a caricature. That's the syntax of the street . . . of the people . . . I heightened it, maybe, just a little, so it would be satiric, so it would criticize . . ."

"Let's not argue," says he softly. "Give us one of your conventional novelle or stories . . . And, rest assured, we think very highly of your work."

I leave the office. I do not have the same feelings I had in high school. I am not even indignant.

"God help them," I think. "I'll make out without literary journals. They need something 'conventional.' They need something that looks like a classic. That imposes itself on them. It would be easy enough to do. But I'm not about to write for readers who don't exist. The people have a different view of literature."

I am not grieved. I know I am right.

MYSELF TO BLAME

Evening. I'm walking along the Nevsky with K.

I got to know her in Kislovodsk.

She is pretty, gay, she has wit. She has that joy in living which I lack. And perhaps this attracts me to her more than anything else.

We walk tenderly arm in arm. We go out along the Neva. We walk along the dark path of the shore.

K. is saying something that has no end. But I don't pay much attention to what she is saying. I hear her words as music.

But then I hear something I don't quite like in this music. I listen more closely.

"This is the second week I've been walking the streets with you," she says. "We've been all over these stupid shores and parks. I'd just like to sit down with you in a parlor somehow, and chatter and drink tea."

"Let's go to a *café*," I say.

"No. We'd be seen there."

Ah, yes, I'd quite forgotten. She leads a complicated life. A jealous husband, a very jealous lover. Many enemies who would report they had seen us together.

We remain on the shore. We embrace one another. We kiss. She mutters: "Och, how dumb it is that this is a street."

We walk a little and kiss again. She puts her hand over her eyes. These endless kisses are making her head spin.

We come to the gate of some house. K. mutters: "I've got to go in here, to the dressmaker. You wait for me here. I'm only going to have a dress measured, and I'll be right back."

I walk around near the house. I walk for ten minutes, fifteen, finally she appears. She's gay. She's laughing.

"Everything's all right," she says. "I'm getting a very nice dress. It's very modest, without pretensions."

She takes me by the hand and I accompany her home. I meet her again five days later. She says: "If you wish, we can be alone together in a house today. It belongs to a friend of mine."

We approach some house. I recognize this house. It was here

at the gate that I waited for her for twenty minutes. This is the house where her dressmaker lives.

We go up to the fourth floor. She opens the apartment with her key. We enter a room. It's a very well laid-out room. It's unlikely that this room belongs to a dressmaker.

From professional habit, I page through a book I find on the night table. On the first page I see a name that's known to me. It's the name of K.'s lover.

She laughs.

"Yes, we're in his room," she says. "But don't worry. He's gone to Kronstadt for two days."

"Ugh!" I say, "I'm worried about something else. That means you were with him then?"

"When?" she asks.

"When I was waiting for you at the gate for twenty minutes."

She laughs. She closes my mouth with a kiss. She says: "You had only yourself to blame."

THE TRAIN WAS LATE

Alia came to me all out of breath. She said: "He almost wouldn't let me go . . . I say, 'Oh, come on, Nicholas, I've got to see my best friend off. She's leaving for Moscow and God knows when she'll return . . .' "

I asked Alia: "When does the train leave with that friend of yours?"

She laughed and clapped her hands.

"So you see," she said, "you believed it, too . . . No one is leaving. I thought it up so I could come to you."

"The Moscow train leaves at ten-thirty," I said. "That means you've got to be home around eleven."

By the time she looked at her watch, it was already twelve. She gave a little cry. She ran to the telephone without even putting on her slippers.

Taking off the phone, she sat down in an armchair. She was trembling from the cold and from agitation.

I tossed her a small rug. She covered her feet with it.

"Why are you calling?" I told her. "Better get dressed as quick as you can and go."

She waved her hand at me indignantly.

"Nick, dear," she said into the phone. "Just think, the train was late and didn't leave till now. I'll be home in ten minutes."

I don't know what her husband said to her, but she answered: "I told you in plain Russian—the train was late. I'll be home right away."

Must have been, the husband said, it's twelve o'clock.

"Is it really?" she said. "Well, I don't know, by your watch, but here at the station . . ."

She turned her head upward and gazed at my ceiling.

"Here at the station," she said, "it's about eleven."

She squinted her eyes as though she were looking at a distant clock in the railway station.

"Yes," she said, "about eleven, maybe a couple minutes past. You've got an archaic watch . . ."

Hanging up the phone, she started to laugh.

At that time this sawdust-stuffed little doll might well have been one of my most welcome guests. But at that particular moment I was angry with her. I said: "Why do you lie so shamelessly. He'll check his watch and see you're lying."

"But he really believed that I'm at the railroad station," she said, applying some lipstick to her lips.

Having finished with the lipstick, she added: "And what kind of talk is this anyway. I don't like to hear it at all. I know how to go about it myself. He runs around with a revolver, threatens to kill my friends and me with them . . . What's more, he doesn't even take into account that you're a writer . . . I'm convinced he'd shoot you splendidly."

I growled something in reply.

When she was dressed, she said: "What's the matter, angry? Maybe you don't want me to come any more?"

"As you like," I answered.

"Yes, I won't come to you any more," she said. "I can see that you don't really love me at all."

She left, giving me a haughty toss of the head. She did this splendidly for her nineteen years.

My God, how I'd weep now! But then I was satisfied. Moreover, within a month she came back.

THE READING

I consented to give readings in several cities. That was an unlucky day in my life.

The first reading was in Kharkov, then one in Rostov.

I was taken aback. They greeted me with storms of applause;

but when I was through, they hardly clapped. That means, somehow I don't please the audience, I'm cheating it somehow. How?

It's true, I don't read like an actor, but rather monotonously, sometimes sluggishly. But don't they, after all, come to my performance merely to hear a "humorist" perform? That's it! Maybe they think: If actors read so amusingly, what will the author himself kick up with now.

Every evening I was stretched on the rack.

It's hard for me to go out on the stage. The awareness that I'm "cheating the public again" spoils my composure more and more. I open the book and I mutter the title of a story.

Someone shouts from the gallery: "Read 'Vania' . . . 'The Aristocrat' . . . What rubbish you read!"

"My God!" I think. "Why did I ever agree to these performances?"

I take a melancholy look at my watch.

They're sending slips of paper up to the stage. That's a breather for me. I close the book.

I turn over the first slip. I read it aloud: "If you're the author of these stories, why are you reading them?"

I'm annoyed. I cry out in response: "But if you're a reader of these stories, why in the hobgoblin do you listen to them?"

Laughter in the audience, applause.

I unfold another slip: "Why do you read us what we all know, tell us something funnier, how you managed to get here, for instance."

In a furious voice, I shout: "I sat in the train. My family wept and begged me not to go. They said: 'They'll torture you with idiotic questions.' "

An outburst of applause. Laughter.

Ah, if I'd only walk across the stage on my hands now, or roll across on a single wheel—it would be a dandy performance.

My manager whispers something to me from backstage: "Tell something about yourself. The audience likes that."

Submissively, I begin to recount my autobiography.

The slips of paper come flying up to the stage again: "Are you married? . . . How many children do you have? . . . Do you know Esenin? . . ."

It's quarter to eleven. Possible to quit.

Sighing morosely, I leave the stage amidst applause.

I console myself with the thought that these are spectacle

seekers who would show up with the same enthusiasm for the performance of any comedian or juggler.

Without having fulfilled all the terms of my contract, I return to Leningrad.

MADNESS

A man enters my room. He sits down in an armchair.

For a moment he sits in silence, listening. Then he gets up and shuts the door tight.

He goes up to the wall, and, putting his ear to it, he listens.

I begin to grasp that he's a madman.

Having listened at the wall, he sits down in the armchair again and hides his face with both his hands. I see that he is in a state of desperation.

"What's wrong?" I ask.

"They're after me," he says. "I was riding in the trolley just now and I clearly heard voices: 'There he is . . . get him . . . grab him . . .' "

He covers his face with his hands again. Then he says calmly: "You're the only one who can save me . . ."

"How?"

"We will change names. You will be Gorshkov, and I will be the poet Zoshchenko." (That is just what he said: "poet.")

"All right. I agree," I say.

He flings himself toward me and shakes my hand.

"And *who* is after you?" I ask.

"That I can't say."

"But from now on I've got to know, since I bear your name."

Wringing his hands, he says: "That's just it—I don't know myself. I only hear their voices. And at night I see their hands. They reach out for me from all sides. I know they will seize me and strangle me."

His nervous chill communicates itself to me. I don't feel well. I'm dizzy. There are spots in front of my eyes. If he doesn't leave right away, I will probably pass out. He influences me murderously.

Pulling myself together with all my strength, I mutter: "Go. You've got my name now. You can rest easy."

He leaves with his face alight.

I lie down in my bed and I feel a terrifying melancholy possess me.

IV. CONCLUSION

[Re-examining these "candid photographs," of which in the original there are sixty-three, Zoshchenko comes to the conclusion that, although he has had a hard life, these incidents, either in themselves or in their totality, do not really account for his extreme melancholia. He begins to feel that the solution to his problem lies in pushing his memories farther back, to the years of his childhood. Childhood scenes begin to obsess him.]

From 5 to 15 Years

> It is only in myth that the prodigal
> son returns to his father's house.

GOLDFISH

There is a bowl of goldfish on the window sill.

Two fishies are swimming around in the bowl.

I throw them a little piece of sugar. Let them eat. But the fish swim past indifferently.

Must be they feel ill, that they don't eat. Maybe it's all the days they spend in water. Now, if they'd only lie on the window sill for a bit. Then, maybe, they'd have an appetite.

Dipping my hand in the bowl, I haul out the fishies and put them on the window sill. No, they don't care for it there, either. They thrash about. And still refuse to eat.

I throw the fishies back into the water again.

But in the water things are even worse for them. Look, now they're swimming belly up. Must be they're asking out; out of the fish bowl.

I haul the fishies out again and put them in a cigarette box.

In half an hour, I open the box. The fish have died.

Mama says angrily: "What did you do that for?"

I say: "I wanted them to be better off."

Mother says: "Don't be an idiot. Fish are made to live in water."

I weep bitterly, humiliated. I know myself that fish are made to live in water. I only wanted to rescue them from this misfortune.

228

GO TO SLEEP, NOW

It's dark in the room. Only a small lamp is burning. Near our beds, our nurse sits and tells a story.

Rocking on her chair, the nurse speaks monotonously: "The good fairy dipped her hand under the pillow, and there was a serpent. She dipped her hand under the mattress, and there were two serpents and a viper. The fairy looked under the bed, and there were four serpents, three vipers, and a hedgehog.

"At this the good fairy said not a word, but dipped her feet in her slippers; but in each slipper, two toads are sitting. The fairy tore her coat from the hook, to dress herself and leave that place. She looks, and in each coat sleeve there are six vipers and four toads.

"The fairy gathered all this filth together, and she says: 'I'll tell you what. I shall wish you no harm, but don't you hinder me from leaving this place.'

"Then all this filth spoke and answered the good fairy like this: 'We will do you no harm, good fairy. We thank you that you have not killed us for this.'

"But at this point a thunderclap was heard. And before the good fairy stood the wicked fairy.

" 'I'm the one,' she says, 'who loosed all this filth on you. But you,' she says, 'made friends with them, and that surprises me. Thanks to this, I am going to enchant you into an ordinary cow.' At this point a thunderclap was heard again. We look and, instead of the good fairy, an ordinary cow is grazing there . . ."

The nurse falls silent. We tremble in terror. My sister Julia says: "But what happened to the filth?"

The nurse says: "About that, I don't know. Probably the wicked fairy scattered them about her place, just as they were."

"Is that *under the mattress and under the pillow?*" I ask, sitting up from my pillow.

Nurse rises from her chair and says as she goes out: "Well, enough talk. Go to sleep, now."

We lie in our beds, afraid to move. Lelia whispers on purpose in a terribly hoarse voice: "H-o-o-o."

Julia and I give a little shriek of terror. We beg Lelia not to frighten us. But she is already asleep.

I sit up in bed for a long time, unwilling to risk lying down on my pillow.

In the morning I refuse to drink milk, because it comes from the enchanted fairy.

I AM NOT TO BLAME

We are sitting at the table eating *bliny*.

Suddenly, my father takes my plate and begins to eat my *bliny*. I bellow.

My father is wearing glasses. He looks serious. Has a beard. Nevertheless, he laughs. He says: "Look how greedy he is. He begrudges his father a single *blin*."

I say: "One *blin*—if you like; eat. I thought you were going to eat them all."

The soup is brought in.

I say: "Papa, would you like my soup?"

Papa says: "No, I will wait until dessert. Then, if you let me have your dessert—you really *are* a good boy."

Thinking we were going to have cranberry sauce with milk for dessert, I say: "If you like. You may eat my dessert."

Suddenly they bring in whipped cream, to which I am by no means indifferent.

Pushing my plate of whipped cream over toward my father, I say: "If you like, eat it; if you are so greedy."

My father frowns and leaves the table.

My mother says: "Go to your father and excuse yourself."

I say: "I won't go. I am not to blame."

I leave the table without having touched my dessert.

In the evening, when I'm lying in my bed, my father comes up to me. He is holding my plate of whipped cream in his hands.

My father says: "Well, why didn't you eat your whipped cream?"

I say: "Papa, let's go halves. Why should we quarrel about it?"

My father kisses me and feeds me the whipped cream with a spoon.

IN THE STUDIO

[In a number of previous sketches not included here Zoshchenko already indicated something of the complex relationship between his mother and his handsome artist-father, much loved by women.]

Papa has not been with us for a long time. My mother is dressing me, and we are going to see my father in his studio.

Mama walks hurriedly. She pulls me by the hand and I can hardly keep up.

We climb to the seventh floor. We knock. Papa opens the door.

Seeing us, he frowns at first. Then, taking me in his arms, he throws me up in the air, almost to the ceiling. He laughs and kisses me.

Mama smiles. She sits down with papa beside her, on the divan. And they start up some sort of mysterious conversation. I walk around the studio. There are paintings on the easels. On the walls there are also paintings. Immense windows. Disorder.

I look at the boxes of paints. Brushes. All kinds of little bottles.

I've seen it all already, but my parents are still talking. It's very pleasant that they are talking so quietly, without shouting. They are not quarreling.

I do not disturb them. I walk around the boxes and the pictures a second time.

At last my father says to my mother: "Well, I'm very glad. All is well."

When we say good-bye, he kisses mama. And mama kisses him. And they even embrace.

Dressed in our coats again, we leave.

On the way, mama suddenly begins to scold me. She says: "Ah, why are you strapped on to me? . . ."

I found this rather strange. I wasn't strapped to her at all. She herself had dragged me to the studio. And now she was displeased.

Mama says: "Ah, how sorry I am I brought you with me. Without you, we would have made up for good."

I whimper. But I whimper because I don't understand what I've done wrong. I had behaved quietly. I hadn't even run around the studio. And now such injustice.

My mother says: "No, I will not take you with me any more."

I wanted to ask her what it was, what had happened. But I keep silent. I would grow up and then everything would become clear. It would become clear why people were blamed for things when they had done absolutely nothing wrong.

[Zoshchenko concludes that, although he was a difficult child, and a number of sad and even tragic things occurred to him, these by no means serve to account for his melancholy, and his childhood was not at all unusual. He decides that the trouble must lie farther back, in the murky period "before the sun rises," his early childhood between the ages of two and five. Here he has only very fragmentary glimpses of himself, surrounded by darkness. But as he thinks of these, he feels his excitement growing, and concludes that he must be approaching "the wound." One of these glimpses is given below.]

V. BEFORE THE SUN RISES

OPEN YOUR MOUTH

On the blanket—an empty box of matches. The matches are in my mouth.

Someone yells: "Open your mouth!"

I open my mouth. I spit out the matches.

Some fingers fish around in my mouth. They pull out a few matches still there.

Someone is crying. I am crying louder, and for this reason: because the matches tasted bitter, and because they were taken out of my mouth.

[These fragmentary memories fail to disclose, however, what Zoshchenko was looking for. He concludes that he must push even farther back, to the period before two years, to the preconscious stage. But here words and memory fail. As a way to a solution, Zoshchenko begins to read works on the physiological aspect of the psyche, especially Pavlov. There follows a lucid but rather elementary digression on Pavlov, an exposition of what is meant by "conditioned reflexes," "temporary associations," etc., and a description of some of Pavlov's experiments with dogs and monkeys. What follows is a classic example of Freudian self-analysis, in spite of the Pavlovian conclusions. Whatever its interest or lack of interest as a contribution to science, it is translated below as a vivid, partly sardonic, partly heroic, self-portrait of the author and his troubles.]

6

This great discovery, this law of conditioned reflexes, this law of temporary nervous associations—I wanted to apply it to my own life.

I wanted to see this law in action, in concrete examples from my early life.

It seemed to me that my unhappiness could have arisen from the fact that early in my life "untrue" conditioned associations had been established in my brain, which haunted me in terror through my later development. It seemed to me that *spray* terrified me, and that by this means the poison must at some time have been spread.

I wanted to destroy these erroneous mechanisms that had been established in my brain.

But once again there was an obstacle before me. I could remember nothing of my early life.

If I could only remember even one scene, a single event, I might press on farther. No, it was all wrapped in a cloudy oblivion.

But someone told me that if I wanted to remember something forgotten, it would help to go back to the place where it had occurred, and that then what was forgotten might be more easily recalled.

I asked my relatives where we had lived when I was a child. And my relatives told me where I had lived during the first years of my life.

There had been three houses. But one had burned down. In another I had lived when I was two. In the third I had spent no less than five years, from the age of four.

And there was still another house. This house was in the country where my parents went every summer.

I wrote down the addresses, and with unusual agitation I went to have a look at these old houses.

I looked for a long time at the house in which I had lived as a three-year-old. But I could remember absolutely nothing.

And then I went to the house in which I had lived for five years.

My heart fell when I approached the gates of this house.

My God! How familiar everything seemed here. I recognized the stairway, the little garden, the yard, the gates.

I recognized almost everything. And yet, how unlike it was my memories of it.

At one time the house had seemed like an immense hulk, a skyscraper. Before me now stood a smallish, rather shabby three-story dwelling.

At one time the garden had seemed fabulous, mysterious. Now I saw a pitiful little patch.

It had seemed that a massive, high iron fence had girdled this little garden. Now I touched pitiful iron bars no higher than my waist.

How different the eyes were, then and now!

I climbed up to the third floor and found the door to our apartment.

My heart contracted from some obscure pain. I felt badly. Convulsively, I grasped the banister, without understanding what was wrong or what disturbed me so.

I ran down the stairs and sat for a long time on the pedestal by the gate. I sat until the gatekeeper approached. Eyeing me suspiciously, he ordered me to leave.

7

I returned home quite sick, exhausted, disturbed without knowing by what.

In a terrible melancholy, I returned home. And now this melancholy did not leave me day or night.

By day I lumbered about my room—I could neither lie down nor sit. By night terrible dreams tormented me.

Formerly, I had not had any dreams. Or, rather, I had them but forgot. They were brief and incomprehensible. I usually had them toward morning.

Now they appeared as soon as I shut my eyes.

They were not even dreams. They were nightmares, terrible scenes, from which I awoke in terror.

I began to take bromides to stifle these nightmares, to be more at peace. But the bromides didn't help.

Then I called a certain doctor and begged him to give me something against these nightmares.

When he learned that I was taking bromides, the doctor said: "What are you doing?! On the contrary, you *need* to see these dreams. You have them because you are thinking about your childhood. These dreams are the key to your illness. Only in your dreams will you see those scenes from infancy that you are looking for. Only through the dream can you penetrate that long forgotten world."

Then I told the doctor my latest dream, and he began to analyze it. But he analyzed it in such a way that I was disturbed and did not trust him.

I said I had seen tigers in my dream and some kind of hand emerging from the wall.

The doctor said: "It's more than clear. Your parents took you to the zoo too young. There you saw an elephant. Its trunk frightened you. The hand—that's a trunk. The trunk—that's a phallus. You have a sexual trauma."

I did not trust this doctor and I was disturbed. Having taken some offense, he answered me: "I analyzed your dream according to Freud. I'm a disciple of his. There is no truer science that can help you."

Then I called several more doctors. Some laughed, saying that the analysis of dreams was nonsense. Others, on the contrary, attributed the greatest significance to dreams.

Among these latter, there was one very clever doctor. He explained a lot to me and told me a lot. And I listened very attentively to him. I even wanted to become a disciple of his. But then I rejected this notion. It seemed to me that he wasn't right. I did not believe in his therapy.

He was a frightful opponent of Pavlov. Except for experiments of a zoological nature, he saw nothing in the latter's work. He was an orthodox Freudian. In every act of child or adult, he saw the sexual. He analyzed every dream in terms of erotomania.

This method did not concur with what I considered infallible; it did not concur with Pavlov's method, with the principle of conditioned reflexes.

8

Nevertheless, the method of this therapy struck me.

There is something absurd in the discussion of dreams. It had seemed to me that such preoccupations had sprung to life from the minds of old women and people of a mystical bent.

It had seemed to me that this was incompatible with science. I was very surprised when I learned that all of medicine had arisen, essentially, from a single source, from a single cult—from the science of dreams.

All of ancient, so-called "temple," medicine had developed and had been cultivated on a single basis—the analysis of dreams. This was the significance of the cult of Aesculapius, the son of Apollo, the god of healing among the Greeks.

[There follows a brief digression on Greek medicine. Zoshchenko then returns to modern works on the physiology of dreams.]

9

What is a dream from the point of view of contemporary science?

First of all, it is a certain physiological condition from which all the external manifestations of consciousness are absent. Or, better—all the higher psychic functions are excluded, and the lower ones released.

Pavlov considered that at night a man was "disconnected" from the external world, and during sleep inhibited forces came to life, suppressed emotions, repressed desires.

This occurs because while there is some inhibition operative during sleep, it is only partial: it does not cover the whole of our brain; it does not cover all points of those great hemispheres.

Our brain, in the opinion of physiologists, has, as it were, two levels. The higher level is the cortex. This is the center of control, logic, the critical faculties, the centers of acquired reflexes, life experience. And the lower level is the source of inherited reflexes, the source of animal drives, animal powers.

These two levels are joined together by means of the associations or connections of nerves, which we have already mentioned.

At night the higher level sinks into sleep. Therefore, consciousness is absent. Control, the critical faculties, acquired habits, these are all absent.

The lower level continues to keep its watch. The absence of control, however, permits it to some degree to declare itself to the town.

Let us suppose that logic or intellect has hindered or stifled the terror that rose up at one time in the child. In the absence of control, the terror may rise up again. But when it rises up again, it assumes new shapes.

Therefore, the new shape is a continuation of the man's psychic activity in the absence of control.

And, therefore, the new shape may serve as a clue to the nature of the forces that inhibit the man, that terrify him, and that are capable of snuffing the light of logic, the light of consciousness.*

It becomes comprehensible why ancient medicine attributed such significance to dreams.

10

And so, our brain has two levels—a higher and a lower.
Life experience, acquired habits, keep house with inherited

---

* Further developments have shown that the dream is not the only means by which one can get at the reason for pathological inhibition.

experience, with the habits of our ancestors, with the habits of animals.

As though there were two worlds enclosed in the complex apparatus of our brain—the civilized world and the world of the animal.

These two worlds are often in conflict. The higher forces struggle with the lower. They conquer them and push them lower down, but rarely do they entirely banish them.

This struggle would seem to be the source of many a nervous ailment.

But this is not at all the source of trouble.

I do not wish to run too far ahead of myself, but I will linger on this briefly. Even if one admits that this conflict of the higher with the lower is the cause of nervous ailments, it is by no means all-embracing; it is only a partial reason, by no means the most important, and by no means basic.

This conflict of the higher with the lower could (let us assume) lead to certain sexual psychoneuroses. But if science saw in this conflict, in this struggle, the only cause—it could go no farther than the revelation of sexual inhibitions.

This struggle, however, is a kind of norm. It is not a pathology.

It seems to me that on precisely this point, Freud's system goes astray.

This mistake was an easy one to make since the mechanisms revealed by Pavlov were not taken into account.

Inaccuracy in his basic assumptions, lack of clear focus in his formulation of the struggle between the higher and the lower forces, led Freud to an inaccurate conclusion, led him to one side, to the side of the sexual drives. But this did not encompass the matter. This was only part of a whole.

11

In the conflict of the higher with the lower, in the collision of atavistic drives with the emotion of modern, civilized man, Freud saw the source of nervous ailments. Freud wrote: "Forbidden entry into civilized life and driven into the depths of the subconscious, these drives exist and make themselves felt, erupting into our consciousness in a distorted manner . . ." Therefore, the victory of intellect over animal instincts is seen as a cause for tragedy. In other words—the lofty intellect is subjected to doubt.

There are many occasions in the history of human thought in

which troubles were ascribed to the intellect, in which assaults were made on the notion of a high state of consciousness, and therefore people sometimes saw the tragedy of human life as residing in a high state of consciousness, in the conflict between the higher and the lower forces. It seemed to them that the victory of consciousness over the lower instincts bore a terrible burden, the burden of disease, nervous ailments, weakness of spirit, psychoneuroses.

This seemed a tragedy from which there was only one way out —a return to the past, a return to nature, leaving civilization behind. It seemed that the ways of the human intellect were mistaken, artificial, unnecessary.

I do not consider this philosophy as the equivalent of the philosophy of fascism. Fascism has other roots, a different nature; but as far as its attitude toward the intellect is concerned, Fascism did draw something from this philosophy, distorting it, simplifying, lowering it to the level of the dull of wit.

A return to barbarism—this is not simply a formula invented by the Fascists for the needs of war. This is one of the basic principles of Fascism, its basic draft of the future image of man.

Better barbarism, savagery, the instincts of an animal, than the further progress of consciousness.

Stupidity!

People, artificially returned to barbarism, would in no way escape the nervous ailments that alarm them. Scoundrels would populate the world, from whom all responsibility for their vileness had been removed. But these would still be scoundrels who had not escaped their former ailments. These would be suffering scoundrels, even more unhealthy than they had been before.

The return to harmonious barbarism, concerning which people had fantasies, would not have been possible even a thousand years ago. But even if it had been possible—the source of sufferings would have remained. For the mechanisms of the brain would have remained. We are unable to destroy them. We can only study and adjust them. And we must study them with an art that is worthy of high consciousness.

These mechanisms revealed by Pavlov, we must study them until we have reached a full understanding. The capacity to come to terms with them will free us from those immense sufferings which people tolerate with barbaric resignation.

The tragedy of the human intellect proceeds not from the height of consciousness, but from its insufficiency.

12

And so, having pondered all this, I understood that I could now attempt to penetrate into the closed-off world of infancy. The keys were in my hands.

At night the doors of the lower level open. The sentinels of my consciousness sleep. And then, the shadows of the past, languishing underground, appear in their transfigurations.

I wanted to meet these shadows immediately, to see them, in order finally to understand the tragedy or error that had been performed in the light of day, before the sun rose.

I wanted to bring back to mind one of those dreams of not long ago, of which I had seen so many. But I could not recall a single dream in full. I had forgotten.

Then I began to think about the dreams I had most often, about what I saw in them.

And at this point I recalled that I most often saw tigers that entered my room, beggars who stood at my doors, and the sea in which I swam.

VI. DARK WATERS

1

Accidentally, I visited the village where I had spent my childhood.

I had been thinking of going there for some time. And then, strolling along the riverbank, I saw a steamer at a wharf. Almost mechanically, I got aboard this steamer, sat down, and went to the village.

The village was called Peski ("Sands"). It was on the Neva River, not far from Schlüsselburg.

I had not been in those parts for more than twenty years.

The steamer did not stop at the village Peski. There was no wharf there. I crossed the Neva in a rowboat.

Ah, with what agitation I got out on the shore. I instantly recognized the small round chapel. It was intact. I instantly remembered the huts opposite, the village street, and the winding ascent from the shore, where there had at that time been a wharf.

All this now seemed a sorry miniature, compared to the grandiose world that had remained in my memory.

I walked along the street, and everything there was so familiar it hurt. Except the people. I could not recognize a single one of the people I met.

Then I entered the yard of the house where we had once lived.

In the yard stood a woman no longer young. In her hands was an oar. She had just chased a calf out of the yard. And now she was standing there angry and flushed.

She did not want to talk with me. But I mentioned the names of several villagers whom I remembered.

No, all these names belonged to people already dead.

Then I mentioned my own family name. And the woman smiled. She said she had been a very young girl then, but she remembered my dead parents very well. Then she began to mention the names of our relatives who had lived here, the names of acquaintances. No, all the names mentioned also belonged to the dead.

Sadly I returned to my boat.

Sadly I walked along the village street. Only the street and the houses were the same. The people who lived in them were different. Those from the past had lived here as guests and gone away, disappeared. They would never return. They had died.

It seemed to me that I understood that day what life was, and death, and how one had to live.

2

With heightened sorrow, I returned home. And at home I did not even begin to think of my searchings, of my childhood. I was indifferent to everything that had happened to me.

It all seemed trash and nonsense compared to the image of brief life I had seen today.

Is it worth while thinking, struggling, searching, defending oneself? Is it worth while trying to master a life that flashes past headlong at such offensive, such absurd speed?

Wouldn't it be better just to live along without grumbling, and then give up one's sorry place to other fugitives of the earth?

Someone laughed in the next room, just as I was thinking about these things. And it seemed strange and savage to me that people could laugh, joke, or even talk, when everything was so stupid, so senseless, so offensive.

It seemed to me easier and simpler to die than to wait stubbornly and dimly for that fate which awaits everyone. In this decision I unexpectedly saw manliness. How amazed I would have been if someone had said to me then what I now know, that this was not manliness at all, but rather an extreme degree of infantilism. It was produced by the terror I had felt as an infant confronted now by that which I wanted to find. It was resistance. It was flight.

I decided to put an end to my searchings. And with this decision I fell asleep.

During the night I awoke in terror from a frightening dream. My terror was so strong that I continued to tremble even after I woke up.

I turned on a light and wrote my dream down so I could think about it in the morning, if only out of curiosity.

But I could not get to sleep, and I began to think about this dream.

In substance, the dream was an extremely stupid one. A dark, stormy river. Murky, almost black waters. Something white floats on the water—a piece of paper or a rag. I am on the shore. That is, I'm running hard as I can away from the shore. I'm running along a field. The field for some reason is sky blue. And someone is pursuing me. And he's catching up and wants to grab me by the shoulder. This man's hand is already reaching out for me. Flinging myself forward, I escape.

I began to ponder this dream, but understood it not at all.

And then I began to think that here again I had seen water in a dream. This dark, black water . . . And suddenly I recalled Blok's poem:

> An old, old dream . . . Out of the shadows
> The street lights run—but where?
> Only black waters there,
> Only oblivion forever.

That dream was very like mine.

I was running from the black waters, from "oblivion forever."

3

I began to remember dreams connected with water. Now I am swimming in a stormy sea. I'm struggling with the waves. Now I'm wandering off somewhere, water up to my knees. Or I'm sitting on the shore, and the water breaks at my feet. Or I'm walking along the very edge of the shore. And suddenly the water begins to rise higher and higher. Terror seizes me. I run away.

I remembered yet another dream. I'm sitting in my room. Suddenly, from all the chinks, the floor is flooded with water. Another minute and the room will be full of water.

I usually woke from such dreams, weary, sick, and dispirited. My melancholy usually waxed stronger after such dreams.

Perhaps the frequent floods in Leningrad had influenced my psyche? Perhaps there was something else connected with water?

No doubt water was connected with some powerful sensation. But which?

Perhaps I was afraid of water in general? No. On the contrary. I'm very fond of water. I can admire the sea for hours. I usually travel only where the sea is, or a river. I have always tried to find a room with windows on the water. I have always liked to imagine living somewhere on the shore: very close to the water, so that the waves would reach almost to the porch of my house.

Often the sea or a river had returned me to peace and calm, when I was in the grips of that melancholy which visited me so often.

What if this were not a love for water, but terror?

What if, behind this exaggerated love, a deferential terror were concealed?

Perhaps I do not like water, but put up with it? Perhaps I like it when it is calm, when it does not threaten to drown me?

Perhaps I put up with it from the shore, from the window of my room? Perhaps I go closer to it in order to be more secure, to make sure that it won't take me by surprise?

Perhaps it is that kind of terror that does not reach consciousness, that imbeds itself in the lower level of the psyche, imprisoned there by logic, by the control of intellect?

I laughed. It seemed at the same time so absurd and so right.

No doubt remained. A terror of the water existed in my mind. But it was deformed. It did not have the shape by which we generally recognize it.

4

Then it seemed to me that I understood my dream. It undoubtedly related to the days of my infancy. In order to understand it, it was necessary to abstract the usual forms, it was necessary to think in the images of an infant, to see it with an infant's eyes.

Of course, not entirely with his eyes—undoubtedly they were too inadequate. They changed with his development. But their symbolism, evidently, remained as before.

The murky, stormy river—that was a bath or a tub of water. The blue shore—a blanket. The white rag—a diaper that remained in the tub. The child has been taken out of the water in which he had been bathed. The child was "saved." But the threat remained.

I laughed again. This was absurd, but believable. It was naïve, but not more naïve than it should have been.

But how could this come to pass? All infants are bathed. All children are immersed in water. Terror does not remain with them. Why was I terrified? It means that water was not the prime reason, I thought. It means that there are some other objects of terror, associated with water.

At this point I remembered the principle of conditioned reflexes.

A single stimulus could evoke two centers of alarm, for between them a conditional nervous association must have been established.

The water in which I had been immersed could hardly in itself have aroused the agitation I felt. That means the water must have been conditionally associated with something else. That means it was not concerning the water I felt terror, but that the water evoked terror, for nervous associations connected it with yet some other threat. In this connection lay the solution to the problem, and that was the reason water had the power to terrify.

But with what was water associated? What kind of "poison" did it contain? What does the second unfortunate stimulant consist of, "igniting" in combination such a stormy response?

I still had not begun to guess at the second stimulus, the second center of alarm, with which the nervous associations were so clearly connected.

However, this stimulus was already in part apparent from the dream itself. The world of infancy is a meager one, objects are very limited in their number. Stimuli are by no means numerous. But my inexperience did not permit me to discover this second stimulus instantly.

The riddle was not solved, but the keys were in my hands.

Further events showed that I was basically not mistaken. I was mistaken only in the number of centers of alarm. They turned out to be not two, but several. And they were interlaced with each other by a complex network of conditioned associations.

5

The principle of conditioned reflexes states that nervous associations have a temporary character. A repetition of experience is required before they become confirmed. Without such experiences, they die down or disappear altogether.

Well, so. Water in the given instance was an excellent and frequent stimulus in an infant's life. Repetition, there undoubtedly was. I still did not know the nature of the second stimulus, but it seemed understandable to me that its conditional association with water could be confirmed.

With the child's development, however, this association should have disappeared. For the repetition could not recur perpetually. For it was not an infant and not an adolescent, but, finally, now, a mature man whom this false association could tear apart. But it *was* false, mistaken—that was obvious.

One's intellectual development really does struggle with untrue, false, illogical images. The child, while developing, however, could meet with other, more logical indications of the danger of that which he fears.

Once again, I began to examine my memories associated with water.

Indications of the danger of water were at every hand.

People drown in water. I can drown. Water floods the city. Suicides fling themselves into water.

These are weighty indications of the danger of water.

No doubt—it could terrify a child, prove to him that the infantile images he had formed had been correct.

This kind of "false" proof might have accompanied me all my life. Undoubtedly, that's the way it had been. Water preserved the elements of fear, nourished my infantile terror. The temporary associations formed in connection with water might not have disappeared; they might have been more and more powerfully confirmed.

That means that a man's intellectual development does not destroy the temporary conditional associations, it merely transforms them, lifts these false indications to its own level of development. And perhaps it seeks out these indications obsequiously, not testing them too hard, for even without verification they may well establish neighborly relations with a logic that grows on sickly soil.

These false indications are often intermeshed with authentic indications. Water really *is* dangerous. But the neurotic does not accept this danger in its true measure, and his reaction to this danger is also not in the measure of the normal.

But if this were so, if water was one of the elements of my fear, one of the stimuli of my neurotic complex, then how sad and pitiful was the picture that opened before my gaze.

For they had been treating me with water. With water they had been trying to rescue me from my melancholy.

They had been prescribing water both inside and out. They sat me in baths, rolled me in wet sheets, sprayed me with showers. They sent me to the sea—to travel and to swim.

My God! From this therapy alone my melancholy might easily have arisen.

This therapy could intensify the conflict, could create an impasse.

And yet water was only part of the trouble, perhaps even an insignificant part.

The therapy, however, did not create an impasse. It was possible to avoid this therapy. And so I did. I ceased taking the cure.

In order to cure myself, I invented a by-no-means-stupid theory that for fullness of health a man must be always at work, without interruption. I stopped going to sanatoriums; it was a superfluous luxury.

In this way, I liberated myself from the therapy.

But I could not liberate myself from constant confrontations with that which frightened me. The terror continued to exist.

This terror was unconscious. It was sequestered in the lower level of my psyche. The sentinels of my intellect did not allow it freedom. It had the right to emerge only at night, when my consciousness was not in control.

This terror lived a nocturnal life, in transfigurations. But by day, in confrontation with the object of fear, it declared itself only by indirection—by mysterious symptoms which could escape the diagnosis of any doctor.

We know what terror is, we know its action on the work of our body. We know its defensive reflexes. Basically, they are attempts to escape danger.

The symptoms of terror are various. They depend on the force of the terror. They express themselves in the form of nosebleeds, spasms of coughing, muscular cramps, increased speed of heartbeat, and so forth. An extreme degree of terror brings on partial or full paralysis.

These were precisely the symptoms that my *unconscious* terror created. To some degree they were expressed in heart attacks, shortness of breath, spasms, and muscular cramps.

These were, above all, the symptoms of terror. Its chronic presence violated the normal functioning of my body, created constant inhibitions, led to chronic incapacities.

At the basis of these symptoms was a certain "expediency"— they blocked my way to "danger"; they prepared flight.

The animal who cannot escape danger plays dead.

Now I was playing dead, sick, weak, whenever it was impossible to get away from "danger."

All this was a response to a stimulus received from outside. It was a complex response, for the conditioned nervous associations, as we shall see farther on, were quite complicated.

7

I struggled with this malady, defended myself from this unconscious ill. And the nature of my defense always corresponded to the stage of my development.

In my childish years, my behavior usually reduced itself to flight, but to some extent it rose to a desire to master water, to make it "my own." I tried to learn how to swim. But I did not learn. Terror held me firmly in its grip.

I learned to swim only as an adolescent, fighting this terror.

This was my first victory, and, if you like, my only one. I remember how proud I was.

In later years, too, my consciousness did not lead me away from this struggle. On the contrary, my consciousness forced me to it. I always tried to come to grips with my formidable opponent as quickly as I could, to measure forces with him once again.

Actually, there was a conflict here which disguised my terror.

I did not avoid steamers, rowboats, I did not avoid being on the sea. Against my terror, as it were, I went constantly into single combat. My consciousness did not want to admit defeat, or even lack of spirit.

I recall an incident at the front. I was leading my battalion to a position. Before us was a river. I hesitated for a moment. The crossing was not a difficult one; nevertheless, I sent scouts to right and left to find an easier crossing. I sent them in the secret hope of finding some dry way across the river.

It was the beginning of summer and such a path was unthinkable.

I was troubled only for a moment. I called the scouts back and led the battalion across the river.

I remember my agitation when we entered the water. I remember the pounding of my heart which I could scarcely control.

It seemed that I had acted correctly. Crossings were always the same. And I was happy that I had not hesitated, that I had acted decisively.

That means, I was not a blind instrument in the grip of my terror. My behavior was always the product of duty, conscience, consciousness. But the symptoms of a malady were all too obvious. I knew nothing of their origin. Doctors defined them roughly as a neurosis produced by exhaustion.

Sensing an inequality in the opposing forces, nevertheless I continued to wage a struggle against my unconscious terror. But how strangely this struggle went. What strange paths were found to a dubious victory.

8

The thirty-year-old man tried to liberate himself from his terror by a systematic study of water. The struggle proceeded along the line of knowledge, of science.

All my journals and notebooks began to fill up with information about water.

These journals are now before me. I go through them with a smile. Here are notes concerning the most violent storms and floods in the world. Here are the most detailed figures—the depth of seas and oceans. Here is information about the stormier waters. About rocky shores, which boats dare not approach. About waterfalls.

Here is information about people who have been drowned. About artificial respiration and first aid.

Here is a note underlined in red pencil: "71 per cent of the earth's surface is under water, and only 29 per cent is dry."

A tragic note! Written in red pencil: "Three-fourths of the globe—water!"

Here are other tragic notes, concerning the percentage of water in the bodies of people, animals, and plants: "Fish—70-80 per cent; jellyfish—96 per cent; potato—75 per cent; bones—50 per cent . . ."

What enormous labor! How senseless.

Here is a whole notebook full of information about winds. It's understandable—the cause of floods, storms, tempests.

Excerpts from my notes: "3 meters a second—stirs the leaves; 10 meters a second—rocks large branches; 20 meters a second—strong wind; 30 meters a second—storm; 35 meters a second—storm, on the verge of a hurricane; 40 meters a second—hurricane, destroys houses."

Under this, a supplement: " 'ty-,' extreme; 'phoon,' wind; typhoon in 1892 (island of Mauritius)—54 meters a second!"

Here is still another notebook on Leningrad floods.

Paging through these notebooks of mine, I smiled at first. Then the smile changed to a frown. What a tragic struggle. What an "intellectual" and, at the same time, what a barbaric path my consciousness had found to subdue the opponent, to destroy terror, to maintain a victory.

What a tragic path was found. It corresponded to my intellectual development.

This path found a reflection in my writing.

But at this point I should make some reservations. I do not at all wish to say that this path—terror and the wish to overcome it—predetermined my life, my footsteps, my behavior, my melancholy, my literary intentions.

Not at all. My conduct remained exactly as it would have if the terror had never existed. But the terror complicated my footsteps, reinforced my incapacity, and heightened my melancholy, which might have existed even without it for reasons and circumstances which all people share.

Terror did not predetermine the way, but it was one element in a complex of forces.

It would be a mistake not to take this element into account. But it would be an even cruder mistake to take this element for the totality, as the only force acting on a man.

Only in a complex account can the problem be solved.

We have seen this complexity in my conduct. The prime mover was not terror but other forces—duty, intellect, conscience.

My conduct was basically intelligent. Terror did not lead me by the hand, like a blind man. But it lived in me, violated the healthy functioning of my body, and prompted me to flee "dangers" when higher feelings or obligations were not present.

It pressed down on me and influenced my physical condition.

My consciousness was determined to root it out. Intellectual development discovered the way of knowledge. The professional habits of a writer also took part in this struggle. Among many themes which absorbed me was a theme connected with water. To this, I had a special inclination.

For half a year I studied materials dealing with the wreck of the "Black Prince."

I diligently studied everything that related to it. I made myself familiar with diving operations and with the work of reclamation. I gathered literature on all inventions in this area.

Having finished my book, *The Black Prince,* I immediately began to collect materials on the wreck of the "Submarine 55." I never finished that book. The theme ceased to absorb me, for about this time I discovered a more intelligent way to pursue the struggle.

And so, by the systematic study of water in all its properties, I wished to free myself from my misfortune, from my unconscious terror. This terror was not even related to water. But water evoked the terror, for it was conditionally connected with the other object of my fear.

What a tragic struggle. What grief and suffering it inflicted on me.

But how can one speak of the malady of a high state of consciousness?

One can only speak of an intellect that lacks knowledge. One can only speak of the small, unfortunate savage who makes his way along a narrow cliffside path, barely touched by the first rays of the morning sun.

10

And so, convinced of my strength, I proceeded farther in pursuit of the unhappy incident that had provoked my malady.

To Be Continued

[Alas, it was not to be. Presumably, Zoshchenko had completed his self-analysis, and it had been accepted for publication, when he and the editors of the journal in which the above appeared were viciously attacked by party officials. The editors apologized abjectly. The rest of Zoshchenko's "autobiography" has never appeared.]

Selected Ann Arbor Paperbacks
Works of enduring merit

For a complete list of Ann Arbor Paperback titles write:

THE UNIVERSITY OF MICHIGAN PRESS ANN ARBOR